Profiting in America's Multicultural Marketplace

How to Do Business Across Cultural Lines

Sondra Thiederman, Ph.D.

Lexington Books

An Imprint of Macmillan, Inc.
NEW YORK

Maxwell Macmillan Canada
TORONTO

Maxwell Macmillan International
NEW YORK · OXFORD · SINGAPORE · SYDNEY

HF
5718
.T457
1991
159159
may/1993

Library of Congress Cataloging-in-Publication Data

Thiederman, Sondra B.
Profiting in America's multicultural marketplace: how to do business across
cultural lines / by Sondra Thiederman.

p.   cm.

Includes bibliographical references and index.
ISBN 0-669-21929-0 (alk. paper)
1. Business communication. 2. Intercultural communication.
I. Title.

HF5718.T457   1991   303.48'2—dc20   91-10833
                                                                        CIP

Lexington Books
An Imprint of Macmillan, Inc.
866 Third Avenue, New York, N.Y. 10022

Maxwell Macmillan Canada, Inc.
1200 Eglinton Avenue East
Suite 200
Don Mills, Ontario M3C 3N1

Macmillan, Inc. is part of the Maxwell Communication
Group of Companies.

Printed in the United States of America

printing number

1 2 3 4 5 6 7 8 9 10

For my daughter Shea—to our friendship,
our love, and our growing up together

Contents

Preface and Acknowledgments

Scrawled on a partition in a large international airport was the sentiment, "Immigration—the sincerest form of flattery." These words ought to make the United States proud and probably even a bit swell-headed, especially if we recall that a Haitian founded Chicago, an Arab invented the ice-cream cone, an Irishman designed the White House, a Pole discovered vitamins, and a Russian stuffed the first teddy bear.

Ever since the native Americans first witnessed the arrival of European explorers, the United States has participated in the process that one early writer described as "a constant reflex action whereby the native modifies the foreign as much as the foreign modifies the native."[1] This is not to say that everyone has always been enthusiastic about the arrival of new Americans. Benjamin Franklin, for one, lamented the settling of Pennsylvania by Germans. He feared that they would "herd together" and "establish their language and manners to the exclusion of ours." Even George Washington was less than pleased with the idea of immigration. In a letter to John Adams, he expressed the view that "with respect to emigration . . . except for particular descriptions of men . . . there is no need of encouragement."

Fortunately, these early opinions did not prevail. We are a nation of immigrants and descendants of immigrants. At my alma mater, Hollywood High School, 87 percent of the students are foreign born with fifty-seven languages spoken and ninety countries represented.

The purpose of this book is to give you the tools to form profitable, harmonious relationships with these new Americans and their descendants, who retain the cultures and sometimes languages of their forebears. The information and techniques presented here will enable you to bridge cultural and language barriers to effective customer service, sales, management, and negotiations. By helping you do business in a diverse society, I hope to perpetuate in some small ways the tradition of national prosperity that has been the direct result of the effort and ingenuity of millions of immigrants.

Some Words of Caution

The greatest challenge in writing this book has been to present the material fairly and in such a way that no one would be offended. When dealing with such a subject, there is the constant danger of inadvertently displeasing someone because of an irresponsible generality, unintended misstatement of fact, or accidental misunderstanding.

I assumed that having spent more than ten years as a speaker and trainer on the topic of cultural diversity, I would have no difficulty avoiding these pitfalls. I naively thought that I would produce a work of unparalleled accuracy and impartiality by simply setting down on paper the words and ideas that have been a part of my presentations for so many years.

Only pages into the manuscript, however, I began to feel uneasy. I realized that there is something frightening in committing thoughts about so delicate a subject as cultural diversity to the printed page. In front of a live audience, I have the luxury of explaining sensitive issues in detail, of reading the audience's reaction, and of responding on the spot to criticism and disagreement. The printed word deprives us of that opportunity for dialogue.

Every attempt has been made to avoid reckless generalities and to present accurate and timely information. Nevertheless, it is possible that some comments will be inconsistent with your own personal experience, will appear to be applied too broadly, or will in some way offend or upset you. Please accept my apologies for this. Much of the fascination in the study of cultural diversity lies in its constant flux. Behaviors and attitudes found among some members of a culture will be absent in others; cultural characteristics that at first appear to be deeply rooted will change according to time and circumstance and be subject to the vagaries of human nature and individual psychology. As professionals, we all must keep a vigilant watch for the exception to every statement that gives working in a culturally diverse environment its peculiar fascination.

Acknowledgments

Foremost among the sources used for this book are the hundreds of participants who contributed so much to dozens of cultural-awareness workshops. These individuals, from diverse industries and cultural backgrounds, supplied the core of material around which this book is structured. Were it not for their generous sharing of firsthand experiences and current knowledge of what it means to work in a multicultural environment, this book would never have come about.

Special mention needs to be made of those whose expertise in language diversity contributed to the information found in the appendix: Elizabeth Mariscal and Krystyna Srutwa of SpeechCraft, Paco Sevilla, Elizabeth Estes, and, my friend and colleague, Susan Montepio. Susan's insights into Filipino culture were also indispensable. My dear friend Molly Drummond contributed the magical combination of boundless emotional support and extraordinary proofreading skills, both of which relieved a great deal of useless anxiety.

In the sense that culture is transmitted from generation to generation, this book is about family and the continuity that family brings to culture. One of the many blessings in my life has been a seemingly inexhaustible supply of loving and supportive families. Although they passed away long before this project began, my mother and father were instrumental in shaping the emotional and intellectual roots from which it has grown. Mother's compassion, fascination with world events, and curiosity about human nature furnished me with a compulsion to learn and explore that will never end. My father's unconventional career choices left me with the need to find my own unique niche in the, then unusual, field of cultural-diversity training. It was from him, too, that I inherited a passion for the "big project" and a sometimes irksome attention to detail. My parents' willingness to reward every effort and their obvious pride in even my most modest accomplishments support me always. My only regret is that neither of them are here to see what their influence has wrought.

We each have had a teacher somewhere in our school days who made a real difference in our lives. I am fortunate to have had two; both showed me that learning was fun and persuaded me that I was capable of just about anything. The first of these was the sometimes winning, sometimes losing football coach and history teacher at Hollywood High School in Los Angeles; Lou Birnbaum had a way of passing his love of learning onto those around him. After high school came the years at UCLA, where I was blessed to encounter Professor Wayland Hand who soon became my teacher, mentor, and friend. It was an honor and a privilege to have known and worked with one of the university's finest scholars and most charming gentlemen.

It was Mom Thiederman's love and faith that saw me through some very difficult years and that continue to nurture today. She has my admiration, love, and undying gratitude. The enthusiasm and patience that Jane and Åke, the third family to enter my life, continually show is a source of amazement to me. To have as superb a scholar as Dr. Åke Sandler and as compassionate a woman as Jane Sandler on my side is a blessing indeed. My sister, Susan, has stood by me through more long projects than either of us would care to remember. She, along with many friends, too numerous to mention, have no doubt long since wearied of the constant talk of "the book"—my thanks to them for their patience.

I also thank my stepdaughter Krista. Her genuine enthusiasm and her patient understanding of the barricaded office door and requests for the muted stereo were more appreciated than she will ever know. My dear husband Tom preserved his sense of humor and thereby my sense of perspective while washing untold dishes and never losing faith in me or in the value of the project. He makes it all worthwhile.

Finally, this book is dedicated to my daughter, Shea. From the days when she sat on my lap while I ground out the doctoral dissertation to her enthusiasm for this latest effort, I am awfully glad she was there and immensely proud of the fine human being she has become.

Sondra Thiederman, Ph.D.
San Diego, California

What This Book Can Do for You

It is not the intellectual . . . that survives, but the one that is able to adapt best to the changing environment.
—*Charles Darwin*

One of every four Americans is ethnic or foreign born. Add to this the large number of internationally owned corporations now operating within the United States and it becomes clear that learning how to do business across cultural and language barriers is a necessity. No matter what your role in your business, from owner to most junior frontline employee or sales representative, only a firm grasp of the principles of cross-cultural communication will enable you to prosper in this increasingly diverse environment.

Cultural and ethnic diversity is changing the way we do business. No longer do all customers want to be called by their first names or to buy a product just because it is "the latest thing." Clients and business colleagues will not necessarily be impressed with your ability to get "straight to the point," and workers cannot be counted on to be thrilled at the prospect of being honored as "Worker of the Month."

The rules have changed. The strategies you have cultivated no longer apply in every situation or to every person. There are many times, of course, when it is still good form to supply reams of hard data when making a sale, to offer a worker his or her picture in the company newsletter, or to push for a close when negotiations get bogged down. The difference is that it is no longer safe to assume that these approaches are always the best.

My purpose is to help you adapt to this increasingly diverse business environment while continuing to build on the knowledge and professional strengths that you already possess.

Who Will Benefit from This Book?

This book is intended for the reader who has professional contact with people whose cultural background and, in some cases, language is different from his or her own. Specifically, it is intended for:

1. The business owner who needs to serve, negotiate with, sell to, or manage culturally different people

2. The customer-service representative or frontline employee who wishes to communicate with and meet the needs of immigrant and ethnic customers and international visitors

3. The sales professional whose prospects are of diverse ethnic and cultural backgrounds

4. The manager who requires the skills to interview, motivate, and retain immigrant and ethnic workers

5. The interested reader who realizes that the ability to communicate with and understand people of diverse backgrounds is necessary in all our personal and professional relationships

If you fall into one or more of these categories, this book will help you acquire a good working knowledge of the essentials of cross-cultural communication, which will give you a competitive advantage in the multicultural marketplace.

How Will This Information Make Your Job Easier?

Right about now you are probably not terribly thrilled at being told that after all these years you have still more to learn about relating to customers, clients, and workers. Do not despair; what I am asking you to learn will make your jobs easier, not harder. You are not being told to become an anthropologist, nor to give up your own culture or to be anything that you are not. You are only being asked to explore a fascinating subject, one that will take the anxiety and uncertainty out of your cross-cultural business dealings.

This book will enable you to achieve:

• Better two-way communication despite accent and language barriers

- Increased client and customer satisfaction through an understanding of cultural variations in needs, values, and tastes

- More success in cross-cultural sales and negotiations

- A more productive, efficient, and harmonious multicultural workplace

It will enable you to minimize:

- Customer or client alienation that can result from errors in assessing client needs, etiquette, and values

- Delayed or failed business transactions that can result from ignorance of cultural variations in negotiation strategies

- Unnecessary employee terminations and costly discrimination suits that result from communication breakdowns and misinterpretations of employee behavior

This does not mean that this book will render flawless cross-cultural business dealings. You will still make mistakes from time to time—you will misinterpret the behavior of a Hispanic worker, tousle the hair of an immigrant Asian's child, or push too hard to make a sale with a Mexican-born entrepreneur—but this is all right. An error in etiquette, a mispronounced name, a poorly designed strategy, all of these will be easily forgiven if it is obvious that you cared enough to try.

Who Is This Book About?

This book is about consumers, colleagues, and workers who possess a culture and/or language that is different from that of mainstream American society. These individuals may be immigrants or members of an ethnic population that has held on to its cultural roots and native language. They might also be international visitors or businesspersons who are in the United States temporarily.

As a general rule, individuals of a particular ethnic background are referred to by that name alone—*Mexican, Hispanic, Asian,* etc. For the sake of brevity, I will not make a distinction between those persons of a given ancestry who were born in the United States (*Asian-American,* for example, is not used) and those who have come here from other countries.

Although many of the principles outlined here apply to conducting business abroad, the specific focus of this book is cultural diversity as it is found within the boundaries of the United States. A number of cultural groups are discussed throughout, with greatest emphasis on the Asian, Hispanic, Middle Eastern, and European cultures. These are the largest immigrant and ethnic populations found in the United States today and also represent those groups most likely to travel here for vacation or for business purposes.

This does not mean, of course, that the information in this book applies only to these groups. Many of the techniques for effective communication, such as looking at the nonnative English speaker's lips in order to understand him or her better or correctly pronouncing the names of foreign-born and ethnic clients no matter how unusual those names might seem, apply to any cross-cultural relationship and are just as valuable when doing business with a Nigerian as with a Frenchman.

A caution is in order here: The final criterion for whether a customer, colleague, or worker is *culturally different* is if he or she identifies himself or herself in those terms. A client, customer, or worker may, for example, have emigrated to the United States from Cuba some years ago and have chosen to completely adapt to mainstream American culture and to the ways of doing business in the United States. Such a person will consider him- or herself, not *ethnic* or *culturally different*, but simply *American*. To instantly assume a cultural difference is to deny who that person is and how he or she wants to be treated. Do not make any assumptions about how ethnic or culturally different a person is, those labels are for them, not you, to assign.

Obviously, if this book is about clients, customers, and workers, it is also about the professionals doing business with them. You will notice that throughout the book, there are frequent references to *mainstream Americans, mainstream American culture,* or to an all-encompassing *us* or *we*. These labels in no way imply that those who will benefit from this book were all born and raised in the United States, nor that they are of white, Anglo-Saxon extraction. What it does imply, however, is that the businessperson who needs this material was either raised in the values and perspective of mainstream American culture or has become largely assimilated into that culture. This also applies to any references to the *mainstream American,* or *American* customer, client, or worker.

Many of you are either ethnic or foreign born, but have adopted the methods of American business and the culture of mainstream American society. You, as well as the native-born businessperson, will benefit from learning about other cultures and about the techniques necessary to communicate across cultural and language barriers.

How Can We Get Around the Problem of Generalities?

When dealing with the issue of cultural diversity, there is always the danger of making irresponsible generalizations. Having said this, the most casual of readers will notice that these pages are filled with general statements like "Filipino customers are not likely to complain" or "Mexican business owners prefer to build trust slowly."

While there is really no excuse for such generalizations, it would be extremely cumbersome to stop at every statement to reiterate that it is a generality and does not pertain to all members of the group in question. Every statement in this book is intended only as a guideline. To apply any cultural characteristic to all individuals within a particular population would be unwise and disrespectful to the uniqueness of that human being.

Generalizations become still more dangerous when large populations like Asians, Hispanics, or Middle Easterners are lumped together. "Hispanic women tend to have more decision-making powers than it first appears" is a good example of this sort of thing. Certainly members of these groups share common cultural characteristics, but there is also considerable diversity. Koreans, for example, are very different from the Japanese as are Cubans from Mexicans and Iraqis from most other Middle Eastern cultures.

I have made every effort to focus only on those characteristics common to the larger group. The importance of "face," for example, is widespread throughout Asia, although manifested somewhat differently in Japan than in China.

To take the problem of generalities one step further, sometimes I ascribe a characteristic or attitude to foreign-born or ethnic people in general. At first glance, this may appear to be a gross grouping of people very different from each other in culture and outlook. I have, however, tried to ascribe to these large and diverse groups only the characteristics they might reasonably be expected to share. A desire for formality, for instance, is valued by most immigrant populations and distinguishes them from many native-born or highly assimilated Americans who are generally more comfortable with a more casual attitude even in a business setting.

Finally, the issues I discuss are the ones most likely to surface within the United States. It is impossible, however, to be certain how often an individual will encounter a particular behavior or attitude. I caution you not to assume that you will find it in a person just because he or she happens to have been born in another country or to have an ethnic background. Being alert and aware is one thing, but imagining a cultural difference when it does not exist is quite another.

How Can You Get What You Need from This Book?

I have arranged this material to make it easy for you to find and apply the information you need to do a better job in a multicultural environment. A number of features have been included that will simplify this task. Here are six suggestions on how to use these features most effectively:

1. *Before beginning to read, take a moment to do the exercise entitled "Defining Your Goals."* This exercise is designed to clarify your thinking about what you want to gain from your reading so that you will be better able to watch for, and benefit from, the material of greatest concern to you.

2. *Take the "Cultural-Diversity Quiz."* Not only is this quiz fun, it will help you find out how expert you already are in the area of cultural diversity. It also will enable you to focus further on those issues you need to keep an eye out for in your reading. When you are finished, do not forget to check your "Cultural I.Q." score.

3. *Use the table of contents and the index to locate specific information.* I do not mean to discourage you from reading the book in its entirety. Using the book only as a reference tool, looking up isolated pieces of information as you need them, risks the constant danger of taking delicate points out of context and missing key issues. If you really are unable to read the whole book, I strongly advise that you read at least Chapter 1, which provides the basics of cultural diversity, without which much of the rest of the material could be easily misunderstood.

4. *Do the exercises, including the section called "Solidifying Your Learning" at the close of each chapter.* Scattered throughout the text are exercises intended to promote awareness of your previous behaviors, attitudes, or knowledge or to facilitate a knowledge of your own culture or of stereotypes that might be interfering with the accurate perception of other cultures. I suggest that you do these exercises; they are an important part of the learning process. All can be completed in a matter of moments. In particular, the "Solidifying Your Learning" exercises found at the end of each chapter, encourage you to identify what you have learned so far and to put it into words so that you will be more apt to remember and apply it.

5. *Take advantage of the features provided to help you review the material.* At the close of each chapter is a "Summary" and at the end of the book is the section entitled "A Recap of What You've Learned". These features are *not* intended as substitutes for reading the body of the book; the material is presented without elaboration and can easily be misunderstood when taken out of its proper context.

6. *Utilize the supplementary material found in the appendix.* The appendix supports the suggestion made in Chapter 2 to learn a few words of the languages you encounter most often. It includes phonetically rendered phrases in several languages.

As you read, watch for the central themes that are repeated throughout the book. The importance of saving face, for example, is discussed under values, etiquette, customer service, sales, and management. These common threads are the meat of the material. If a point keeps coming up in the text, that means that it also appears with considerable regularity in the culturally diverse business world.

Honor the small bits of specific information as much as the more general principles. The general themes of cross-cultural communication —the importance of avoiding stereotypes and the value of communicating respect, for example—apply to all instances of cross-cultural interaction. These general principles are, however, only part of the picture. A tiny piece of information, for example, knowing when to praise an employee or whom to look at while speaking, can be just as important. It is often these seemingly inconsequential choices that can communicate the respect necessary to cement a good working relationship.

Why Is Cultural Diversity a Gift to Us All?

Cultural diversity is challenging, no one who has ever married into another culture, sojourned abroad, or even moved into an ethnic neighborhood would deny that. But like any other challenge in life, once it is understood, it begins to feel more like an opportunity. In this case, it is an opportunity to be exposed to new ways of thinking, new perspectives, and new ideas about how problems can be solved.

This book will help bring about that shift in attitude. Even if you never step outside the borders of the United States again, cultural diversity will be part of your life for many years to come. If you get confused and a bit impatient, if you begin to long for the days when everyone was just like you, stop and remember your Italian grandfather and his tales of Ellis Island, your African-American great-grandmother and her long trek north, or that landless Scotsman who brought your ancestors here so many years ago. We are all part of the immigrant experience and without each and every one of us, there would be no America and no American dream to build together.

Defining Your Goals

Here is a list of some of the goals of this book. By ranking each statement according to its importance to you, you will focus your thoughts and be better able to spot the issues that will help the most as you do business across cultural lines.[1]

By Reading This Book, I Hope to Learn:

_____ To feel more comfortable and confident in a multicultural business environment

_____ Negotiation, customer service, and sales strategies that are effective across cultural boundaries

_____ To manage and motivate ethnic and immigrant workers

_____ How to assess the culturally specific needs of diverse customers, clients, and employees

_____ Tips for communicating more effectively with those whose native language is not English

_____ Techniques for assessing if my message has been understood in the face of language differences

_____ To understand clients, colleagues, and workers despite the presence of heavy foreign accents

_____ How to avoid offending those immigrant and ethnic people whose values and etiquette might differ from my own

_____ To interpret correctly the behaviors of those who were born and raised in a culture different from my own

_____ More about my own culture so as to avoid projecting it onto others

_____ How to avoid applying stereotypes that can distort my perception of individual members of a group

_____ To read and accurately interpret nonverbal language

Add Some Goals of Your Own:

Cultural-Diversity Quiz: How's Your "Cultural I.Q."?

This quiz will give you an idea of how much you already know about cultural diversity. In some cases, there is more than one correct response to each question. On page xxvii, you will find the answers along with an evaluation of your "Cultural I.Q." The contents of each question are discussed in greater detail throughout the book. GOOD LUCK!

1. On average, how long do native-born Americans maintain eye contact?

   a. 1 second
   b. 15 seconds
   c. 30 seconds

2. *True or false:* One of the few universal ways to motivate workers, regardless of cultural background, is through the prospect of a promotion.

3. Learning to speak a few words of the language of immigrant clients, customers, and workers is:

   a. Generally a good idea as the effort communicates respect for the other person
   b. Generally not a good idea because they might feel patronized
   c. Generally not a good idea because they might be offended if a mistake is made in vocabulary or pronunciation

4. *True or false:* American culture has no unique characteristics; it is composed only of individual features brought here from other countries.

5. When communicating across language barriers, using the written word:

   a. Should be avoided; it can insult the immigrant or international visitor's intelligence
   b. Can be helpful; it is usually easier to read English than to hear it
   c. Can be confusing; it is usually easier to hear English than to read it

6. *True or false:* Behaving formally around immigrant colleagues, clients, and workers—that is, using last names, observing strict rules of etiquette—is generally not a good idea as it gives the impression of coldness and superiority.

7. In times of crisis, the immigrant's ability to speak English:

   a. Diminishes because of stress
   b. Stays the same
   c. Improves because of the necessity of coping with the crisis
   d. Completely disappears

8. The number of languages spoken in the U.S. today is:

   a. 0–10
   b. 10–50
   c. 50–100
   d. 100+

9. *True or false:* Immigrant families in the United States largely make decisions as individuals and have generally abandoned the practice of making decisions as a group.

10. When you have difficulty understanding someone with a foreign accent:

    a. It probably means that he or she cannot understand you either
    b. It probably means that he or she is recently arrived in this country
    c. It is helpful if you listen to all that he or she has to say before interrupting, the meaning might become clear in the context of the conversation
    d. It is helpful for you to try to guess what the speaker is saying and to speak for him or her so as to minimize the risk of embarrassment

11. When an Asian client begins to give you vague answers before closing a deal, saying things like "It will take time to decide," or "We'll see," the best thing to do is:

    a. Back off a bit, he or she may be trying to say "no" without offending you
    b. Supply more information and data about your service or product, especially in writing
    c. Push for a "close," his or her vagueness is probably a manipulative tactic
    d. State clearly and strongly that you are dissatisfied with his or her reaction so as to avoid any misunderstanding

12. Apparent rudeness and abruptness in immigrants is often due to:

    a. Lack of English-language facility
    b. A difference in cultural style
    c. Differing tone of voice

13. *True or false:* Many immigrant and ethnic cultures place greater importance on how something is said (body language and tone of voice) than on the words themselves.

14. The avoidance of public embarrassment (loss of face) is of central concern to which of the following cultures?

    a. Hispanic
    b. Mainstream American

c. Asian

d. Middle Eastern

15. *True or false:* One of the few universals in etiquette is that everyone likes to be complimented in front of others.

16. In a customer-service situation, when communicating to a decision maker through a child who is functioning as interpreter, it is best to:

    a. Look at the child as you speak so that he or she will be certain to understand you

    b. Look at the decision maker

    c. Look back and forth between the two

17. Which of the following statements is (are) true?

    a. Most Asian workers like it when the boss rolls up his or her sleeves to work beside employees.

    b. Taking independent initiative on tasks is valued in most workplaces throughout the world.

    c. Many immigrant workers are reluctant to complain to the boss as they feel it is a sign of disrespect.

    d. Asians are quick to praise superiors to their face in an attempt to show respect.

18. *True or false:* The "V" for victory sign is a universal gesture of good will and triumph.

19. Which of the following statements is (are) true?

    a. It is inappropriate to touch Asians on the hand.

    b. Middle Easterner men stand very close as a means of dominating the conversation.

    c. Mexican men will hold another man's lapel during conversation as a sign of good communication.

20. Building relationships slowly when doing business with Hispanics is:

    a. A bad idea; if you don't move things along, they will go elsewhere

    b. A bad idea; they expect native-born professionals to move quickly so will be disoriented if you do not

    c. A good idea; it may take longer, but the trust you build will be well worth the effort

Answers
1. a
2. False
3. a
4. False
5. b
6. False
7. a
8. d
9. False
10. c
11. a
12. a, b, and c
13. True
14. a, c, and d
15. False
16. b
17. c
18. False
19. c
20. c

Determining Your Cultural I.Q.

Number Correct	*Evaluation*
16–20	Congratulations! You are a "cultural-diversity genius" and are no doubt doing very well in the multicultural business world.
11–15	You are culturally aware and are probably very receptive to learning more about cultural differences.
6–10	Oops! You have a ways to go, but are obviously

interested in the subject and see the need to learn more. That's an important first step.

0–5   Do not be discouraged. The knowledge reflected in this quiz is new to most professionals in the United States. By reading the following chapters, you will quickly reach the status of "cultural-diversity genius."

1

Making Diversity Work

A Look at the Basics

Immigration . . . the sincerest form of flattery.

—*Anonymous*

Have you ever eaten Thai food prepared by a Mexican cook or dined in a Cuban cafe that boasted a Korean chief? Maybe you have seen customized license plates in Chinese or graffiti in Farsi or possibly your children attend schools at which algebra is taught in Assyrian and Cantonese.

Are you aware that the United States is attracting nurses from the Philippines, economists from India, entrepreneurs from Korea, and engineers from Japan? Did you know that Albanians own apartment buildings in New York, East Indians run motels in California, and Middle Easterners are the proprietors of scores of small groceries and liquor stores? Do you realize that 11 percent of the population speaks a language other than English in the home and that by the turn of the century, almost one-third of the work force will be ethnic or foreign born?

What does this cultural and ethnic diversity mean for your business and professional life? It means a growing client and customer base with unique needs, negotiation styles, and expectations—a client base, by the way, with a purchasing power that exceeds the gross national product of Canada. This diversity also means that corporations and small businesses are employing a creative, hard-working, and culturally diverse work force that requires employers and managers to possess special knowledge of their needs, values, and communication skills.

Cultural diversity is here to stay. Whether you are a business owner, executive, salesperson, customer service professional, front-line employee, or manager, your success will increasingly depend on your ability to function in a culturally diverse marketplace.

What Is Culture?

What do you think of when you see the word *culture?* What comes to your mind when the concept of *cultural diversity* is mentioned? Take a moment to think about it before reading further . . .

Perhaps an image of ethnic food or *Cinco de Mayo* popped into your mind, or maybe you thought of your Asian employees or the Hispanic families to whom you sell so much of your product. Whatever culture means to you, if you look at it closely, you will see that what distinguishes one culture from another is a set of shared ideas about how to live and how to get along with people. Culture is an agreed-upon set of rules that consists of components ranging from seemingly inconsequential edicts about how to shake hands or dress on a date to more cosmic ideas about the existence of God or the nature of man. Some of the components of culture are:

- General style of behaving
- Etiquette
- Values
- Language
- Tastes and preferences
- Traditions and customs
- Food, dress, and musical tastes
- Belief systems and world views

As you read further, you will learn that these categories tend to overlap and influence each other. The Hispanic cultural style of emotional expressiveness, for example, is reflected in the value of building well-rounded personal relationships with professional colleagues and contacts. The value many immigrant and ethnic groups place on respect for authority is directly responsible for the preferred etiquette of addressing superiors and new acquaintances by their last names. The Arab belief in the will of God is closely tied to the high value placed on fatalism and, in turn, to the etiquette of not aggressively seeking promotions in the workplace and a preference for not making purchases that require excessive planning for the future.

TIP: Culture is strongest in the home and in social situations. For those of you who deal with the public and especially those who enter private homes, be aware that cultural differences in etiquette, style, and values will be far more pronounced under these circumstances.

Just as culture tells us how to behave, it also colors our interpretation of the behavior of others. Because mainstream Americans associate a hearty handshake with strength and purpose, they are likely to assume incorrectly that the more gentle grasp of the Asian is a sign of weakness or indecisiveness. Such ethnocentrism can create harmful misunderstandings in the multicultural business environment.

What Is the Purpose of Culture?

Culture simplifies the everyday decisions of living. It tells us what to wear and how to behave. It also helps us with the greater challenges of maintaining harmony in society, achieving spiritual peace, and structuring our governments.

Although cultural rules are only informally agreed upon, they have an amazing ability to dictate ideas and behavior. Without culture, society would be in disarray. Have you ever wondered, for example, who decided that it is "polite" to say "thank you" after an exchange? Some cultures consider it rude to say "thank you" because it ends what ought to be an infinite flow of give and take. Why do we think it intrusive when a stranger sits next to us in an empty subway car? In many other countries, it would be regarded as an insult if the person sat elsewhere.

This is not to say that every tenet of every culture is strictly adhered to. Some cultural precepts might be regarded as more ideal than real. Mainstream American culture, for example, theoretically places great value on equality between its citizens. Although this idea is treasured by the majority of society, it is not consistently practiced. Other examples of the dichotomy between that which is held up as ideal and that which is actually practiced are found throughout the world and is one reason that learning about other cultures can be so complex.

What Kinds of Cultures Are There?

The focus of this book is on national and ethnic cultures. There are, however, other kinds of cultures to be found in the multicultural business environment. Cultures differ, for example, between regions within the United States. Who would deny that the Northeast is different from the South and, certainly, from the West Coast?

Similarly corporations, occupations, vocations, sexes, and age groups all have unique values and styles that qualify them as true cultures. We are all part of at least one of these subcultures, and for this reason each of us is exceptionally experienced in conducting ourselves properly in cross-cultural relationships.

You have, for instance, probably had to adjust to the values of a new company after a job change. Maybe you had to get used to a more casual, egalitarian style or, alternatively, adjust your expectations when it became obvious that your new corporate culture called for adherence to strict rules and respect for a firm hierarchy of leadership.

Perhaps you took up a new hobby and had to learn the etiquette of the ski slopes, the jargon of golf, or the dress code of the tennis courts. Or maybe you have had the wrenching experience of moving from a small town to a big city where you discovered it was no longer proper to look everyone in the eye and say "good morning" to strangers but where you suddenly found new acquaintances calling you by your first name.

If you have ever been through any of these experiences, you are already initiated into the world of cultural diversity. Each is an example of cultural adaptation and requires the ability to observe another way of acting and make the adjustments necessary to function in the new situation.

How Can You Tell the Difference between Culture and Personality?

How can professionals tell when a colleague, client, or worker's behavior or attitude is a reflection of cultural differences or simply a function of the individual's personality?

There is no easy answer to this dilemma, but sometimes one technique can help: observation. Observe the attitudes and behaviors of others who share the ethnic background of the person in question. If the behavior at issue is found among other clients, customers, or workers of the same group, it is fairly safe to assume that it is rooted in cultural differences. If, for example, women seem to make the purchasing decisions in the Mexican families with whom you do business, you can probably assume that this is the result of cultural style and preference and not just the nature of one particular Hispanic family. If several of your Asian workers seem reluctant to tell you about problems on the job, it is likely to be a cultural sanction rather than simply the shyness of a particular employee.

The accurate interpretation of anyone's actions is the first step toward the kind of understanding that results in successful business relationships, satisfied customers, and productive employees. An approach based on an individual's personality is likely to be very different from one based on a culturally rooted behavior.

How Can You Diagnose and Cure Your Own Culture Shock?

Diagnosing Culture Shock

Culture shock is a state of mind that occurs when people find themselves immersed in a strange culture. It is a phenomenon that we usually associated with travel overseas or with attempting to set up a new life in a foreign country.

Because of the diversity in the United States today, many professionals are suffering from culture shock right here at home. The fact that you picked up this book tells me that you are at least somewhat befuddled by the cultural diversity around you. That befuddlement is the root cause of culture shock—an emotion that is amplified because it is unexpected. When going to another country, you at least anticipate some confusion, but when the cultural differences are encountered at home, the feelings of shock and disorientation are greatly intensified.

The questions in exercise 1–1 are designed to diagnose culture shock. Respond to each question candidly and quickly. Resist the temptation to think about or analyze your answers before writing them down.

Exercise 1–1. Have You Experienced Culture Shock?

1. When a customer does not accept my final decision regarding a matter but insists on speaking with my superior, I feel . . .

2. When a worker gives me a gift and there is no special occasion, I feel . . .

3. When I compliment a colleague in front of other people and he or she vigorously denies the compliment and seems upset, I feel . . .

4. When potential clients say that a business transaction "might" work out and that they will call me in a few days, but I later find out that the deal was off all along, I feel . . .

5. When I offer a qualified worker a desirable promotion only to have it turned down, I feel . . .

There are as many ways to complete these statements as there are emotions. To number 1 you might have answered: angry, insulted, confused, or even embarrassed. When faced with an inappropriate gift, embarrassment and possibly confusion ("What are my obligations to this person?") are likely. Embarrassment and confusion are the usual responses to failed efforts to please as in number 3. In number 4, you probably feel angry and disoriented when you think you are being told one thing that turns out to be another. Situations such as that in number 5 can make us feel inadequate, confused, and disappointed.

These are the emotions of culture shock. You are apt to confront each of these situations in the multicultural business world. If you examine these examples carefully, you will see that each falls into one or more of the following categories. Either they involve:

1. An unexpected behavior on the part of the other person
2. An unexpected response to your behavior along with the message that the cultural "rules of the game" have changed and you no longer know what is appropriate
3. The absence of expected and appropriate credit for your effort, gesture, or achievement

You are apt to become "culturally shocked" when a customer who is unaccustomed to the American tradition of standing in line moves to the front of a crowd. You become aware that the rules have changed when your efforts to be casual and friendly with Asian prospects by patting them on the back and using first names are met with coolness. Finally, it can be very upsetting to prepare a lengthy report filled with hard data only to discover that the foreign-born client or colleague is far more interested in getting to know you and your company than in being apprised of every detail.

Curing Culture Shock

If you have experienced any of these responses, you have suffered culture shock. Culture shock can make you feel irritable, aggressive, frustrated, inadequate, sensitive, and fatigued. The problem with it is that, because it makes us feel so bad, it can cause us to want to avoid people of different cultural backgrounds. You might be tempted to cure the disease by hiring fewer immigrant and ethnic workers, cultivating only mainstream clients, and seeking out and marketing to only native-born or assimilated customers. This approach is not just bad business; it also doesn't work. The following three approaches are far more effective and will also immunize you against a recurrence of the symptoms:

1. Expose yourself to as much cultural diversity as possible. The more diversity you experience, the more comfortable and less "shockable" you will become.
2. Learn as much as possible about the groups with whom you interact. Read and ask questions. Ask your diverse contacts about their cultures. As long as your interest is honest and respectful, your questions will be appreciated and answered with enthusiasm.
3. Bring culture shock out into the open. Admit that it exists and talk about it. Negative emotions always lose their punch once they are explained and understood. By realizing what culture shock is, why it happens, and how it affects us, the "shock" quickly loses some of its intensity.

Culture shock can attack anyone—your immigrant workers, an international businessperson in the United States on temporary assignment, or you. If you take the steps outlined here and have faith that the more you know, the better you will feel, you will be surprised how quickly the symptoms pass and how comfortable you will become doing business with people of very different backgrounds.

Is It All Right to Notice the Differences between Cultures?

The person who said, "We do not have to be twins to be brothers" must have been well versed in the science of cultural diversity. This wise observer understood that it is all right, and even desirable, to notice the differences among peoples. It might have been the same philosopher who commented, "Just because we are equal does not mean we are the same."

It is permissible—and it is *not* racist—to acknowledge the differences among peoples and cultures. The problem is that some of us have difficulty recognizing cultural differences. People afflicted with this culture blindness believe that besides speaking different languages human beings are all alike.

If the culture blind of the world are correct and language is the only thing that separates us—if there are no true cultural differences among people—then why is it that there is such a shock when the assertive New Yorker moves to the genteel South or the unwary American inadvertently offends a staid English colleague? Clearly there is a lot more to differences among peoples than just language.

Why Are We Reluctant to Notice Differences?

What is it about acknowledging cultural differences that makes people uncomfortable? Why do so many say that there is no cultural diversity in the world of business even though that world is populated by employees, clients, and colleagues from so many ethnic or cultural backgrounds?

The first reason for this is the delusion that if we notice the differences among peoples, we are racist. The opposite is true. Ask yourself this question: If all cultures are alike, what culture represents the norm to which they all conform?

The answer is easy. If all cultures are alike, they must be just like the culture of the observer—the culture-blind American. This amounts to a negation of the unique characteristics, strengths, and weaknesses of other groups. It is a way of saying that other cultures do not really exist.

We will look in a moment at the negative ramifications of this type of thinking. For now, let us just say that this attitude is disrespectful of people who are culturally different because it denies who they are and ignores their most cherished values and ways of doing things. Remember that very few of us ever pretend that all our friends are exactly alike. Some enjoy the beach, and others are fond of football, or antique auctions, or social gatherings. If we ignore these differences, not only are we in danger of treating each friend inappropriately but we also fail to get the most out of the relationship. The same applies to the cultural diversity. Acknowledging and learning about the differences among cultures can only enhance our relationships with those whose background is different from our own.

The second reason that people are reluctant to notice differences is the fear that if we look at how cultures differ, we will fail to see how they are alike. The reassuring fact is that human beings are more alike than different. We all have the same basic needs for dignity, survival, and social contact. What is different between groups is how these needs are satisfied. The mainstream American might satisfy his or her social needs through having many friends, whereas the Asian might make his or her extended family the primary source of warmth and camaraderie.

Another reason for this reluctance to see the difference among cultures is the concern that if we examine the ways in which people are different, we will automatically perpetuate stereotypes. This fear too is unfounded. Acknowledging that Germans are more formal, or that Middle Easterners feel it wrong to plan inordinately for the future are simple statements that no more perpetuate stereotypes than if we were to acknowledge that southern Californians tend to be health conscious, sales representatives outgoing, or that many Southerners value hospitality.

Obviously these statements do not apply to every southern Californian, sales representative, or Southerner; they are merely guidelines. But just because they are not universally true is no reason to discard them. There are ways to distinguish between informative guidelines about cultural groups and confining stereotypes that interfere with understanding.

Simple denial is the fourth reason that so many of us do not want to notice differences. Life seems easier if we assume that everyone is alike. This way of thinking eliminates all fear of making a mistake, all need to learn new ways, and all necessity to make uncomfortable adjustments. To notice differences is to open up a world of complexity and uncertainty. Many people would prefer to avoid facing these challenges.

Finally, when we have the courage to notice the differences among people, we are forced to face the fact that our own culture does not have a monopoly on truth. For some that raises the exciting prospect of learning from other cultures, that our way may not be the only way. To others it is a threat that makes the acknowledgment of cultural differences intimidating.

Why Is It Important to Notice Differences?

If it is true, as Ralph Waldo Emerson said, that "fear springs from ignorance," then ignoring the differences among cultures can only perpetuate the discomfort found in the multicultural environment.

The more we know about something, the more control we feel and the less disorientation or culture shock we experience. By noticing and learning about other cultures, we become more comfortable with diversity and therefore more willing to seek out diverse clients and customers and more willing to hire culturally different workers.

Acknowledging difference also communicates respect for the other person. The importance of communicating respect cannot be overemphasized. It is one of the basic principles of successful cross-cultural communication. When we disregard the unique characteristics of someone's culture, we deny an important part of that person's identity. Mexicans and Mexican-Americans, for example, place great value on the development of well-rounded relationships. Once the professional realizes this, he or she can communicate respect for that value and, in turn, for the Mexican, by taking time to learn more about that individual. Small gestures like this can have far-reaching effects in terms of mutual respect and increased cooperation.

Finally, only by noticing the unique values, expectations, and desires of diverse peoples, will professionals be able to function successfully in a multicultural business environment. In the workplace it is only by noticing the unique values, expectations, and desires of immigrant and ethnic workers that managers will be able to motivate and communicate effectively. For example, in mainstream American culture rolling up one's sleeves and working beside subordinates is a sign of an egalitarian attitude that fosters teamwork. Many Asians, however, interpret this behavior as an accusation that the employee's work is lacking. In extreme cases, such an insult, and the accompanying loss of face, could result in the Asian's resignation. Worse, the worker might lose respect for a manager who did not remain aloof. Numerous other examples of the importance of acknowledging cultural differences will be found throughout the book.

Where Do Stereotypes Fit In?

Have you ever noticed that when you do not know very much about a category of things, everything within that category looks alike? Take sailboats as an example. There are many different kinds of sailboats, each with a unique design and function and each with different strengths and weaknesses. When most of us look out into a harbor, however, all we see are dozens of boats floating on the water, they all look alike.

For a true sailor, on the other hand, or even the dedicated hobbyist, no two sailboats are exactly alike. Some are faster, some sturdier, some meant for long journeys across the sea, and others for hugging the coast. The difference between the casual observer and the devoted sailor is knowledge. As we learn more about sailboats, each vessel begins to look different, and the stereotype that "all sailboats are just pretty white things that float on the water" begins to fade. The same applies to cultures. The more we know about a particular group, the less likely we are to see all members of that group as exactly alike.

When we say *stereotype,* what are we talking about? The term *stereotype* is a bit of jargon that originated in the world of printing. A stereotype was an inflexible mold used to print the same image over and over again. For our purposes, a stereotype is a set of inflexible statements about a category of people, statements usually based more on ignorance than evidence. Journalist Walter Lippman put it well when he said, "For the most part, we do not see first and then define, we define first and then see."

A stereotype is not the same as information about another culture. It is possible to say, for example, that Middle Eastern men tend to maintain direct eye contact or that Greeks generally place great value on personal honor, without being guilty of stereotyping.

The distinction is that stereotypical statements are inflexible. Stereotypes allow no room for individual differences. On the other hand, general facts about a group, like those presented in this book, are merely guidelines or starting points. To say, for example, that Laotians tend to be good at repetitive tasks or that Asians on the whole value education is merely to present guidelines—bits of information that certainly do not apply to everyone.

Stereotypes can be positive as well as negative, but both types are equally distorting and destructive. Two stereotypes, for example, that have been responsible for a great deal of injustice in the United States are that African-Americans are musical and athletic. These are wonderful talents, but to apply them to every member of the group serves only to confine all African-Americans to these categories of achievement.

Why Do We Stereotype?

The primary reason that people stereotype is to relieve anxiety. It is human nature to feel anxious when in ambiguous or unpredictable situations. By stereotyping, by constructing categories and boxes into which human beings can be placed, this anxiety is relieved, and we regain a sense of control and predictability.

Although stereotypical thinking is certainly not confined to the United States, it is a practice that fits well with the nature of mainstream

American culture. Americans tend to be linear in their thinking, rational, and attuned to consistent cause-and-effect relationships. Situations and behaviors that are hard to "pigeonhole" are difficult for many Americans to tolerate.

Everyone has what psychologists call a "confirmation bias"—a desire to fit new information into old categories. What this means is that if our culturally diverse workers, colleagues, and customers do not fit our stereotypes, we will distort our perception of the external reality to fit our expectations.

Look at the case of Martha, a human-resource director at a large hotel in California. Martha had a sales position to fill and needed someone who was very outgoing, talkative, and assertive. One of the applicants for the job was a young Japanese woman named Katsumi.

During the interview, Katsumi was extremely gregarious and outgoing; she did not fit the usual stereotype of Japanese women as shy, unassertive, and retiring. Because Martha had internalized this stereotype of the soft-spoken Japanese woman, she could not accept that Katsumi was really suited to the sales position. In order to reconcile her previous idea of Japanese women with the extroverted applicant in her office, Martha assumed that Katsumi was merely trying to make a good impression and was not ordinarily so talkative.

Martha's refusal to trust her own eyes, to abandon her stereotypical thinking, caused her to make a serious mistake. Rather than place Katsumi in the sales position for which she was obviously highly qualified, Martha applied another stereotype and assumed that "all Asian women are good at math." She placed Katsumi in the accounting department, where she proceeded to do very poorly.

Before long, reports filtered up to Martha's office that although Katsumi was not very good with numbers, she certainly had a lovely, outgoing personality and was particularly charming on the telephone. Fortunately, Martha had the courage and wisdom to admit her mistake and promptly transferred the young woman to sales.

Certainly there are times when individuals do fit a stereotype. After all, these ideas originated somewhere. The problem is that when our stereotypes are confirmed, we take this as evidence that we can apply them to anyone. On the other hand, when someone does not fit our previous ideas, as in the case of Katsumi, we find a way to rationalize this "exception to the rule."

Why Are Stereotypes Often Inaccurate?

Individual members of a culture differ for a variety of reasons. Any one individual might have unique characteristics because of one, several, or all of the following variables.

SOCIOECONOMIC STATUS. Socioeconomic status can account for considerable diversity within a given culture. In fact, variation in education level, social class, and financial status account for most of the differences among members of a group. Some Vietnamese, for example, are highly educated, having spoken English and French and received advanced degrees long before being forced to flee to the United States. Others are illiterate in their own language and have had very little formal education.

GEOGRAPHIC DIFFERENCES. Individuals from various regions within one nation may vary as dramatically as midwesterners from Californians. Filipinos from Manila speak a different dialect and have a culture that varies significantly from that of Filipinos from the outlying islands.

There are dozens of different Hispanic cultures, which can have very practical ramifications for the businessperson. Some real estate agents, for example, have noticed that Cubans and Mexicans are more likely to purchase homes than Puerto Ricans largely, it appears, because some Puerto Ricans have the expectation of someday returning to the homeland. Further, rural Mexicans are very different from those from Mexico City.

TIP: Take special care not to lump groups together when speaking within earshot of the immigrants themselves; this can be very offensive. Cambodians, Vietnamese, and Laotians, for example, are often grouped together when, in fact, they have a very strong sense of individual identity. Similarly, Iraquis have a culture that differs in many ways from other Arab nations.

AGE AND GENDER. Older members of a group might adhere to their native culture more closely than do more youthful immigrants, and men are likely to manifest a culture differently from women. Hispanic and

Middle Eastern males, for example, are generally more assertive and direct than their female counterparts.

TIME AND ASSIMILATION. The validity of any generality is compromised by the amount of time that the individual has been in the United States and the degree of assimilation that has taken place. After an immigrant has been in the United States for some time, it becomes very difficult to predict just how much of his or her original culture is still being adhered to. Be particularly careful of this one, do not assume that a person thinks of him- or herself as ethnic just because he or she happens to have been born in another country or have an ethnic appearance or name. Some immigrants disassociate themselves from their national heritage and would prefer to be referred to, and treated, as mainstream Americans.

HISTORICAL EXPERIENCES. The historical experiences of individuals can also make it difficult to generalize about cultural features. The reasons for migration to the United States, for example, can vary and can have a tremendous impact on each person's perspective and values. The Vietnamese, Cuban, or Iranian who has come here as a matter of survival may have a very different attitude from the Korean who has come, in the old tradition, to seek the American dream. Likewise the Iranian student who came to study and stayed may have a different attitude from the immigrant who fled the Shah.

INDIVIDUAL PSYCHOLOGY. We all know native-born Americans who appear to conform to the culture. When we get to know them better, however, it becomes obvious that their outlook is far more consistent with the culture of Great Britain, Japan, or Scandinavia. Their personality just does not fit with mainstream American values, and, to treat them as if it does, is a grave error in judgment. The same applies to people from other cultures. Some individuals do not fit, in terms of style or temperament, into the culture of which they are believed to be a part.

VARIATIONS OVER TIME. Finally, and much to the dismay of the already confused businessperson or manager, it is impossible to predict the behavior of one person over time. Just as members of a cultural group are not all alike, each individual can change under different circumstances. No matter how well a person may fit into a national or ethnic stereotype, outside events can cause his or her behavior to vary. In times of crises, for example, or when under pressure, even the most assimilated immigrant may suddenly revert to his or her culturally specific way of dealing with the situation. This happens because the process of assimilation usually takes place from the outside in—behaviors change first, with the attitudes that underlie those behaviors changing last.

When a crisis strikes, as in times of extreme stress, these underlying attitudes can emerge. Immigrants may even surprise themselves when, in times of crisis, they begin to call upon long-forgotten, culturally specific coping mechanisms. The Laotian who goes to the ethnic community for help, the Japanese who leaves a position because of loss of face, or the Mexican who turns to the group leader for representation are all examples of how cultural roots can affect behavior years after the process of assimilation is apparently complete.

Why Are Stereotypes Dangerous?

All Mexicans are family loving; all Japanese are technically skilled; all French are good cooks; all Germans are efficient. Each of these is a "positive" stereotype and yet each is just as destructive and dangerous as the vilest racial slur. The reason is that positive stereotypes limit our definition of a person.

Stereotypes result in cases of mistaken identity, interfere with our ability to see people for who they really are, negate the individual, and minimize the likelihood that people will be valued for the traits and skills that they, as individuals, truly possess.

We have already seen how human-resource professionals such as Martha can make faulty hiring decisions and inappropriate assignments because of stereotypical thinking. Another example might be the Middle Eastern entrepreneur whom the female sales representative is afraid to approach because of the stereotypical assumption that he will not be receptive to a female professional.

In both these cases, assumptions have been made about the other person's personality, skill, and cultural background. This sort of prejudgment results in losses for all concerned. In the case of workers, not only does management lose out on many fine employees, workers miss the opportunity of working in positions where their unique talents can be demonstrated. Asians, for example, tend to be passed over for management positions because of the stereotypical belief that they lack management ability, aren't authoritarian enough, and have poor communication skills. In the sales example, the female sales representative is missing out on a lucrative relationship and the Middle Eastern entrepreneur is losing the opportunity to purchase a valuable product or service.

Stereotypes can also be deeply offensive to the individual who feels that his or her individuality has been denied. Think of how you would feel if you heard someone say, "Don't worry, John won't lose his temper, he's from New England" or, "I'm sure Anne will get the job done, she's reliable, after all, she's from the Midwest." Although each of these statements is positive, it would still make you feel as though your unique talents were being ignored.

Finally, stereotypes can be self-fulfilling. When we assume because of prejudgments that workers are incapable of performing a task, we fail to give them the opportunity either to prove themselves or to learn the necessary skill. When we stereotype the needs and wishes of ethnic clients or customers, we promote to these groups what we expect them to want. We do not listen, as any good salesperson should, to the individual buyer. The end result is that every time we persuade the immigrant or ethnic buyer to purchase what we expected them to (regardless of what he or she wanted in the first place), we end up saying, for example, "See, I knew Hispanics preferred starchy foods to vegetables." The stereotype is self-fulfilling.

How Can We Eliminate Stereotypes?

The first step in eliminating stereotypical thinking is to become aware of the stereotypes we carry with us. The idea is to separate our genuine knowledge about particular groups from those inflexible notions that have become lodged in our brains because of past experiences, rumor, or media influences.

Exercise 1–2 is designed to facilitate this process. The instructions are simple. After the name of each group, write down those characteristics that immediately come to mind. Do not stop to think about your response and do not try to be fair, reasonable, or rational. What we are after is your immediate emotional reaction. No one will ever see the list, so you need not worry about appearing racist.

After each response, jot down the source of your information. Was it a childhood experience, an incident in your working environment, televi-

Exercise 1–2. Identifying Your Stereotypes

	Your First Response	Source
Hispanics		
Filipinos		
Southeast Asians		
Blacks/African-Americans		
Middle Easterners		
Mainstream Anglo-Americans		

sion, the movies, or something your parents used to say? Again, do not edit your reply. Be spontaneous and, above all, honest.

You probably noticed a couple of interesting things about this exercise. First, you may have had trouble thinking of a quick response to the "mainstream Anglo-American" category. The reason for this difficulty brings us to the importance of learning about groups in order to dispel stereotypes. Whether or not you yourself are of Anglo extraction, you probably know a great deal about Anglo-American culture and are also acquainted with many different Anglo-Americans. If you are Anglo, you know that in many ways you as an individual do not conform to prevailing stereotypes. Taken together, you realize that blanket statements simply do not apply.

Probably, too, the sources for the characteristics that you listed are quite feeble. Did you formulate your ideas about Hispanics from television or the movies? Did the evening news dictate your image of the Middle East, and did the coverage of the Vietnam War leave you with an impression of the Vietnamese as weak and downtrodden? Perhaps one or two experiences with African-Americans dictated your first response to that group.

Do not feel bad. It is just human nature. The point here is to learn to distinguish our inflexible stereotypes from well-founded, flexible information about a group. Once you are able to identify your stereotypes for what they are, it is not difficult to set them aside. Of course, they will still pop into your mind when you see a Hispanic surname or an Asian face, but the goal is to recognize them for what they are, shove them aside, and see the individual for who he or she really is.

Another means of diffusing stereotypes is to have multiple experiences with and in-depth knowledge of particular groups. We saw that our familiarity with Anglo-Americans makes it difficult to stereotype that group. The same process applies to any group with whom you have extensive contact.

The more you learn about a people, the less able you will be to lump individuals together. The Frenchman Michel de Montaigne said in the sixteenth century, "Nothing is so firmly believed as that which we least know." Acquiring knowledge can only weaken stereotypical thinking. It is ignorance and lack of familiarity that makes all those sailboats look alike.

Why Is Ethnocentrism a Problem?

The term *ethnocentrism* has many connotations. It carries with it implications of racial superiority, cultural elitism, and the insinuation that other cultures are exactly like ours or if not, ought to be.

For purposes of this discussion, ethnocentrism means that human beings tend to assume that the behaviors of others, no matter what their origins, can be interpreted according to the rules and values of one's own culture. It is as if our culture is the way of life toward which everyone else is striving.

The corollary of this perspective is that all people behave the way they do for identical reasons—that everybody's actions have the same meaning and arise from identical motivations. Psychologists call this a "self-reference criterion"—the unconscious process by which we evaluate everything according to that which we already know.

Here is the catch: This simply is not true. Identical actions can have very different meanings in different cultures. Nonetheless, ethnocentrism is part of the human condition. It is as if at birth we all don a pair of culturally tinted glasses through which we view and interpret the events of the world.

Ruth Benedict, an anthropologist, put it well when she said, "No man ever looks at the world with primitive eyes. He sees it edited by a definite set of customs and institutions and ways of thinking."[1] Benedict's "customs," "institutions," and "ways of thinking" are the pigments used to tint our cultural glasses.

How Does Ethnocentrism Cloud Our Perceptions?

There is nothing wrong with liking and even preferring one's own culture. The difficulty arises when we allow that culture to distort what we see. Such misinterpretations can cause serious problems as you do business with those of other cultures. Exercise 1–3 includes a case study that will show you how this process works.

If you checked "Agree" as your answer, you, like Mr. Burton, are in danger of losing the opportunity to cultivate long-lasting professional and personal relationships with Hispanic entrepreneurs. It is natural that Mr. Burton draw some conclusions about his Hispanic colleagues' obvious reluctance to talk business over lunch. The key question is on what basis did he draw these conclusions? It is obvious that Mr. Burton called upon the knowledge that was most available to him; that is, his own cultural assumptions about what it means when someone is reluctant to talk business.

In mainstream American business culture, when someone takes too long to "get down to business," they probably aren't interested. Mr. Burton's mistake was in applying this feature of American culture to the behavior of the Hispanic businessperson. The Hispanic clients obviously grew up in a culture that honors the importance of building well-rounded personal relationships *before* doing business. Mr. Burton would have done better to use this information about Hispanic culture when interpreting the behavior rather than project his own cultural idea of how a "hot prospect" behaves. This is just one example of how projecting the rules and expectations of one's own culture onto someone else can interfere with interpreting his or her behavior correctly.

Cultural projection, however, is not a one-way process. Just as native-born Americans can be ethnocentric toward culturally different

---

Exercise 1 – 3. Mr. Burton's Dilemma

Charles Burton is the owner of a small manufacturing company. As he is just getting the business started, it usually falls to him to conduct contract negotiations with the entrepreneurs in his area, many of whom have immigrated from Mexico. For some months, Mr. Burton has been arranging breakfast and luncheon meetings with several of these Mexican-American business owners. Although each is very gracious, none of them seems willing to talk business during their time together. It is obvious to Mr. Burton that this casual behavior means that they are not really interested in his product. Although he appreciates their warmth, he has made the decision to let these contacts go and put his time and energy into cultivating prospects that show signs of serious interest in what he has to offer.

WHAT DO YOU THINK ABOUT MR. BURTON'S CONCLUSION AND HIS DECISION TO MOVE ON TO OTHER PROSPECTS?

Agree _____   Disagree _____ customers, clients, and workers, members of immigrant and ethnic groups can also project their own rules of behavior and motivation onto American-born professionals. When American negotiators, for example, fail to bargain, some immigrant colleagues think of them as weak, unfriendly, and unintelligent, not nice or reasonable as you might expect. This may seem strange, but becomes logical when we remember that many immigrants are raised in cultures in which bargaining is an art and is not considered offensive or hostile.

Similarly, when American-born or assimilated managers ask foreign-born workers for their opinions about a project, the workers are likely to interpret this action as a sign of weakness and indecisiveness. This is because many immigrant workers are from cultures in which managers are more authoritarian and rarely, if ever, ask the advice of workers. In asking for suggestions, the manager is attempting to empower the workers, promote teamwork, and practice participative management. Unless these intentions are clearly spelled out, the message could be lost on the immigrant worker and the manager's good intentions thwarted.

Another example of cultural misunderstanding involves the fact that Americans, especially in certain parts of the country, tend to form friendships quickly and to speak relatively openly of intimate matters and feelings. To other native-born or assimilated Americans, this attitude is a sign of warmth and compassion. To people from cultures in which relationships are cultivated more slowly but in which friendships last a lifetime, such behavior might be interpreted as intrusive, frivolous, and even rude. Obviously, native-born and immigrant professionals need to learn about each other's culture in order to avoid the misunderstandings that ethnocentrism can create.

Why Do We Cling to Ethnocentrism?

Knowing that an ethnocentric attitude can create problems and distortions does not usually stop us from projecting our cultures onto other people. This is because it is comforting to believe that all behaviors, regardless of where they originate, can be understood according to familiar values that we, in most cases, respect and cherish.

If we accept the fact that this isn't the case, that we no longer have the luxury of looking at the world through our culturally tinted glasses, it means that we have more to learn. It also means that we must admit that our old ways do not necessarily work effectively in a culturally diverse environment.

Learning about Others: The First Step to Overcoming Ethnocentrism

There are two steps to overcoming ethnocentrism. You are in the process of accomplishing one of these right now: you are learning about different cultures. I am not saying that it is necessary to become an anthropologist in order to solve the problem of ethnocentrism or that you will be able to learn all the specific behaviors that characterize various cultures. What you will be able to learn, however, are some of the cultural values and patterns that lie behind and motivate those behaviors.

It is, for example, more important to know about the value many foreign-born and ethnic workers place on respect for authority than to memorize the details of how that respect is manifested. Once you have the general principle in hand, it is a relatively easy matter to apply it to the behaviors you see. You will, for example, be better able to understand why a Laotian worker might not take the initiative on tasks or why the Salvadoran is likely to refrain from taking issue with the trainer. You will not, as previously might have been the case, make the mistake of assuming these workers to be lazy, lacking in confidence, or uninterested in learning.

Similarly, by learning the general rule that some other cultures put emphasis on the group rather than on the individual, you will understand why purchasing decisions often involve many people and can take some time. This knowledge will help you avoid the faulty assumption that this slow process indicates inefficiency, lack of intelligence, or indecisiveness. In both these cases a little knowledge will give you the insights necessary to substitute the correct, culturally aware interpretation for the old habit of projecting your own culture onto the situation.

Learning about Your Own Culture: The Second Step to Overcoming Ethnocentrism

The second step to overcoming ethnocentrism is to become aware of those culturally tinted glasses that distort perception and cause us to misinterpret the behaviors of others. This does not mean that the glasses need to be removed but merely that we must know they are there so that we can compensate for the distortions they create.

Sunglasses make the world look dark and cloudy. Because we are aware we have them on, however, we know that it is not going to rain; we know that the cloudiness is an illusion created by the glasses. Because of this awareness, we do not react to the apparent overcast by running back in the house to retrieve an umbrella. On the other hand, if we did not know that our glasses were tinted, we could easily make that misjudgment and react inappropriately.

Knowing that you are wearing sunglasses may be no great challenge, but becoming conscious of your culture is not so easy. To paraphrase Ruth Benedict, "It is hard to become aware of the eyes through which we see."[2] Culture has been a part of us since the day we were born; it is in the makeup of our personalities, and it surrounds us like the air we breathe. We simply do not see it.

There are a number of techniques and exercises that can help you expedite this difficult process of cultural self-awareness. Each is designed to make you conscious of your own culturally specific points of view. The goal is similar to that which we have already accomplished with respect to stereotypes: to become aware of them so that they can be prevented from distorting your perception of particular groups.

One of the complexities in becoming culturally self-aware is that everyone has a number of cultures to get to know. National origin is only one of many categories of culture. We know that there are occupational cultures, regional or even neighborhood cultures, the culture of males and females, and cultures associated with hobbies and avocations. Just about any group designation you can think of shares some values, etiquette, rules of behavior, and an agreed-upon set of rules for living that constitute a culture.

Exercise 1–4 will help you become aware of those cultures that are part of your life and that you are likely to project unconsciously onto other people. The idea behind this exercise is for you to write down three cultures that influence your behavior and then enter three characteristics of those cultures. The cultures you pick might be from any of the categories that have been mentioned ranging from mainstream American culture to the values and rituals found in your own company. The characteristics might be values, rituals, customs, etiquette, jargon, or any other cultural feature you can think of. One entry has been filled in to get you started.

Exercise 1–4. What Cultures Do You Belong To?

Culture: Sales Professionals

Characteristics:

1. like people

2. good with words

3. self-starters

Culture:

Characteristics:

1.

2.

3.

Culture:

Characteristics:

1.

2.

3.

Culture:

Characteristics:

1.

2.

3.

Probably one of the cultures that many of you listed was that of "American culture." As you saw in question 4 of the "Cultural Diversity Quiz," American culture does have unique characteristics. There are, however, those who would argue that this is not so. Even Mark Twain commented that the only thing Americans have in common is a "fondness for ice water."

People talk about the "melting pot" and say that the United States is nothing but a conglomeration of cultures from around the world. It may be true that we are a "nation of immigrants," but there are still unique American characteristics that resulted from the synergy or coming together of these many cultures. It is from that very fabric that American culture grew—from the Puritan work ethic brought by the English to the "all-American" German hot dog, and such "American" French words as *rendezvous* and *hors d'oeuvres*.

Some rather strange comments have been made about American culture, many of them by foreigners. Alexis de Tocqueville, for example, commented that he knew "of no country, indeed, where the love of money has taken a stronger hold on the affections of man." A century and a half later, the Duke of Windsor was equally disparaging about a completely different aspect of American culture. His comment was that the thing that impressed him most about American society was the way the parents obeyed the children. At least Oscar Wilde seemed somewhat ambivalent about our way of life. He described America as a land of "unmatched vitality and vulgarity" and Americans as "a people who care not at all about values other than their own, and who, when they make up their minds, love you and hate you with a passionate zeal."

Colorful as these comments are, there is obviously a great deal more to our culture than obedient parents or the love of money. Exercise 1–5 is a starting point in understanding American culture and in becoming aware of the values that color, and sometimes distort, our perceptions. Proverbs and idioms embody the essence of a culture. Some of those listed in the figure may seem antiquated and quaint, but they represent the central tenets upon which American society is built. Look at them and write down the value that each saying represents to you.

Exercise 1–5. Taking a Look at American Culture

Proverbs and Idioms   **Value**

Everybody understands the bottom line.

Thanks a million.

The proof is in the pudding.

That makes sense.

There's no fool like an old fool.

God helps those who help themselves.

The early bird catches the worm.

A rolling stone gathers no moss.

Take the bull by the horns.

The sweetest grapes hang the highest.

If at first you don't succeed, try, try again.

There's more than one way to skin a cat.

A stitch in time saves nine.

Busy hands are happy hands.

All's well that ends well.

The details of American culture will be discussed throughout the book, but a quick look at the values reflected in each of these proverbs can serve as a starting point. The first saying, "Everybody understands the bottom line," reflects the American value placed on financial gain and materialism. The idiom, "Thanks a million," continues this theme and also illustrates the American desire to quantify everything. We see this in our need to measure intelligence with I.Q. (Intelligence Quotient) tests and knowledge with SAT tests. As infants, we don't even make it out of the delivery room without trying for a "perfect 10" in our Apgar score—a test which is used to measure our physical status at birth. For the negotiator and salesperson, it is important to remember that Hispanic and Asian clients are not necessarily impressed with our penchant to quantify the virtues of a product. Quality and aesthetic considerations are often more important.

"The proof is in the pudding" demonstrates the American belief that a product or service must be tested or personally experienced in order for it to be trusted and valued. American commercials, for example, show "real people" who have used a product successfully and who are prepared to testify to that effect.

Related to the desire to quantify everything, is the logical, linear, cause-and-effect thinking of most Americans. To say that an argument or position "makes sense" is high praise indeed. In French culture, in which aesthetic considerations are more important, or in Asian, Hispanic, and Middle Eastern cultures whose style of thinking tends to be more creative, this may not be as great a compliment as it might first appear.

The proverb, "There's no fool like an old fool," illustrates the value placed on youth in our nation. This perspective is in sharp contrast with the way in which other cultures respect and honor the elderly. The necessity of showing respect for those older than you is emphasized throughout these chapters.

"God helps those who help themselves" along with idioms like "stand on your own two feet," demonstrates the importance of independence of the individual. Again, this contrasts with the value many immigrant and ethnic families place on loyalty to and reliance on the extended family. This same proverb also illustrates the American belief in our ability and obligation to take control of our lives, a view that differs from that held by such cultures as the Filipino and Thai in which major life changes such as promotions and job transfers are best left up to fate.

"The early bird catches the worm" connotes both productivity and punctuality—the importance of being on time and getting work done promptly and on schedule. "Never put off 'til tomorrow what you can do today" supports this idea of the efficient use of time.

"A rolling stone gathers no moss," along with many other aphorisms such as "Don't let the grass grow under your feet," points to a preoccupation with horizontal and vertical mobility and speed. This differs from the perspective of many immigrant workers who recognize the benefits of putting down roots and staying in one home, company, and occupation for a long time. These workers are not always anxious to seek a promotion or move to another firm.

Curiously, the Japanese have a proverb that is almost identical to this one, but in their case it is an injunction against mobility, not a praise of it. For the Japanese, the moss symbolizes valued traditions. The idea is that if the individual is in constant motion and does not stop long enough to acquire tradition and custom, he or she will have missed something of great importance in life.

"Take the bull by the horns" continues the theme of assertiveness and action, and "The sweetest grapes hang the highest" connotes that striving for the top should always be the priority. This latter proverb might also be interpreted to mean that "The grass is always greener on the other side of the hill"—another way of stating the American desire for constant progress and movement. This is important for sales professionals and negotiators to keep in mind because, as we will see in Chapter 6, not all cultures place as high a value on products and services that promote mobility and change.

"If at first you don't succeed, try, try again" promotes the idea of perseverance, as do other proverbs such as, "You can't keep a good man down." "There's more than one way to skin a cat" is a call not only for perseverance but also for creativity and innovation. Mark Twain contrasted how Americans and Englishmen feel about the issue of innovation when he said, "An Englishman is a person who does things because they have been done before. An American is a person who does things because they haven't been done before."

Creativity is, of course, a universal human trait, but not everyone considers it a priority in the workplace. Some immigrant cultures feel that once a task is learned, changing the way in which it is performed is inappropriate and unwise. For this reason, it can sometimes take considerable persuasion to retrain workers who have become accustomed to doing a procedure in a particular way.

"A stitch in times saves nine" suggests the inclination for native-born and assimilated Americans to plan for the future. In 1955, Anne Morrow Lindbergh pointed out the negative side of the constant questing for the future that is so characteristic of American culture. She said, "America, which has the most glorious present still existing in the world today, hardly stops to enjoy it, in her insatiable appetite for the future."

This "insatiable appetite for the future" distinguishes the United States from many other cultures where the emphasis is on living in the present moment with dignity and honor. In the world of commerce, this attitude is seen in the hesitation of some consumers to buy products or services designed to control the future, such as insurance or long-term investments. In management, some immigrant and ethnic workers are reluctant to contribute to retirement funds or accumulate sick days.

"Busy hands are happy hands," along with the more antique saying, "Idle hands are the devil's workshop," brings us back to the theme of productivity. These proverbs are consistent with the large number of American idioms that emphasize perpetual activity. Examples include: "How are you doing?" along with the routine responses, "Keeping busy," "Doing fine." Benjamin Franklin's succinct comment, "Speak little, do much," sums this value up nicely.

Finally, "All's well that ends well" illustrates the value that American culture places on the end result; it is the goal, the product, that is important. This relates, of course, to the future orientation discussed above. The process that is going on in the present moment is considered less important than the end result that lies in the future.

As you can see from this exercise, there definitely *is* such a thing as

American culture. Certainly it is a way of life woven from the threads of diverse peoples, but it is, nonetheless, a true culture with its own values, style, and ways of looking at the world. More information on American culture will be found in subsequent chapters.

The two exercises that you have just taken serve two important functions. First, they help us become aware of our own cultures, and, in turn, improve our ability to perceive accurately the immigrant and ethnic colleague, customer, client, and worker. Second, the increased self-awareness these exercises encourage allows us to know ourselves better, make more informed choices, and appreciate the strengths and virtues of our own unique cultures.

Why Is It Important to Be Yourself in the Midst of Diversity?

As important as it is to become conscious of your culture and aware of your own cultural point of view, this does not mean that you are expected to change that culture radically or discard it. It is all right to like and value your own ways, and, in fact, studies have shown that appreciating one's own values and way of life does not make a person any more likely to be critical of other cultures.

Be reassured that, although you are being called upon to make adjustments and compromises in your interactions with culturally different people, you are not being asked to change your personality and cultural perspective. The point of this book is that there are adaptations to be made. The danger lies, however, in going too far too fast, in giving up cherished values or in adopting behaviors that are insincere and excessively uncomfortable. Some of the consequences of this "cultural overkill" are these:

1. *Immigrant and ethnic professionals and employees might feel patronized.* Culturally different people appreciate respect, understanding, and compromise. They do not, however, expect Americans to adopt the specific features of their culture or, to use the nineteenth-century phrase, "go native." To do things like look away just because the Asian is more comfortable with indirect eye contact or stand very close to the Middle Eastern male because that is the way it is done in the Middle East can be taken as patronizing and insincere.

2. *Misunderstandings might result.* In efforts to assimilate into our

culture, immigrants are learning about American values and behaviors just as we are learning about theirs. The Korean-born businessperson knows, for example, that it is considered a virtue in America to express openly one's confidence in one's own abilities. He also knows that an American who is not prepared to sing his or her own praises is very possibly lacking in ability and self-esteem. For you to attempt to please the Korean by being artificially self-effacing, is likely to elicit an unexpected reaction. The Korean is going to interpret your behavior in the context of American culture; after all you are a product of that culture. The result would be that the Korean would conclude that you are indeed lacking in confidence and possibly even ability.

3. *You are likely to feel resentment.* Just as immigrant and ethnic colleagues have a right to their values, so do native-born or assimilated professionals. When people pretend to be something they are not, it often creates resentment, which is eventually manifested in the form of negative feelings toward those whom they are trying to imitate. If, for example, managers begin eating Vietnamese food in the company cafeteria, not because they choose to, but because they feel pressured into it, a backlash might develop that could interfere with good working relationships.

4. *Resentment on the part of other groups will develop.* Giving preferential treatment to any one group can cause resentment among other groups. It is one thing to be culturally sensitive and respectful but quite another to go overboard on behalf of one culture. Chapter 2, for example, suggests that you learn a few words of the languages around you. If you do this, do it for every group so as to avoid the accusation of preferential treatment.

5. *The opportunity to teach the ways of American culture will be missed.* One of the best ways to teach the nuances of a culture is to model that culture—to live it in front of those whom you wish to teach. No amount of verbiage will pass on the true style of a culture along with its subtle rules and expectations as well as watching that style being acted out. By pretending to be something you are not, you lose a valuable chance to help others understand your culture better.

6. *Embarrassing mistakes can be made.* In many ways, learning about cultures is easy. There are rules and insights that can be readily applied and that make a real difference in how effectively we get along with others. On a deeper level, however, culture is subtle and replete with nuances of behavior that are difficult to grasp intellectually and almost

impossible to perform. Be yourself. By trying to be something you are not, you risk errors that can be embarrassing to all concerned. It is far more important that you put your energy into learning to understand other cultures, into making reasonable compromises, and into communicating respect for others and for yourself.

Summary

These first steps toward bridging cultural barriers are perhaps the most difficult. The good news is that by following the suggestions put forth in this chapter, you will develop a framework of cultural awareness within which the balance of the material can readily be understood.

- Remember that you are vulnerable to culture shock even at home.
- Acknowledge differences as well as commonalities.
- Become aware of and set aside stereotypes.
- Remember that stereotypes can be about both positive and negative characteristics.
- Get to know your own culture as well as the cultures of others.
- Do not project your culture onto others.
- Be yourself while communicating respect.
- Be reassured that we are all experienced in cultural diversity; every interaction involves some form of cross-cultural communication.

Solidifying Your Learning

At the close of each chapter, you will be asked to write down the three most important things you have learned and how you can apply them in your work. This process will help you clarify your thoughts and retain the knowledge that will make the greatest improvement in your cross-cultural interactions:

1.

2.

3.

Language and Accent Differences

How to Bridge the Communication Gap

The problem with communication is the illusion that it has been accomplished.

—*George Bernard Shaw*

English is a strange language. Did you ever notice that a "slim" and "fat" chance are the same thing and that you park your car in a "driveway," drive on the "parkway," and sit bumper to bumper during "rush hour"? Why is it that we duck our heads when someone cries "Heads up!" and bring a contract to life when we "execute" it? How is it possible that to be "bad" is to be good or "cool" in some circles, but that to be "hot" is also a desirable trait. What about the fact that "rough" is pronounced "ruff," but "dough" is "doe," and that you can buy a "whole" bag of seeds one "week," but be too "weak" to plant them in the "hole" by the time you get home? Why is it one thing to call your boss a "wise man," but quite a different matter to call him a "wise guy?"

If you note these peculiarities of English and add the fact that more than 140 other languages are spoken in the United States today, it becomes clear why good communication, especially in a multicultural setting, is a difficult task. Managers are concerned that workers do not comprehend instructions; sales and customer service personnel are having difficulty communicating their products' benefits; and business negotiators are worried that the details of important contracts are being misunderstood.

This chapter should help you overcome some of this confusion and achieve successful two-way communication despite the proliferation of accent and language differences. You will be surprised how much more easily you will be able to get along once you practice some of the simple techniques presented here.

What It Means Not to Speak English Well

The first step in improving communication is to gain an understanding of how your customers, clients, and workers feel when they have difficulty speaking or understanding English. Exercise 2–1 will help you see the situation from their perspective. Take a moment to recall a time when you, like the immigrant, were immersed in a foreign setting, surrounded by a strange culture, and confronted with an unfamiliar language. Although situations like these might generate some excitement, they also produce several uncomfortable emotions. Listed in the exercise are some of these feelings. Circle the numbers to indicate which of these emotions you have experienced when in another culture and to what degree. Mark the lowest numbers if you felt little or none of the feeling and higher numbers if the feeling was intense.

Exercise 2–1. What Is It Like Not to Speak the Dominant Language?

Loneliness	1	2	3	4	5	6	7	8	9	10
Fear	1	2	3	4	5	6	7	8	9	10
Passivity	1	2	3	4	5	6	7	8	9	10
Inadequacy	1	2	3	4	5	6	7	8	9	10

Those of you who circled 6 or higher in two or more of these categories have a good grasp of what it feels like to be surrounded by a culture and a language that are foreign and confusing. Remember, too, that the travels you have just recalled were probably temporary sojourns abroad. Imagine how magnified these feelings would have been if you were attempting to build a permanent home in a new land.

These emotions are not just unpleasant; they can also interfere with one's functioning in society. Loneliness, for example, and the desire for companionship are among the primary reasons for the speaking of foreign languages in the workplace.

Fear also has an effect on behavior. We are talking here about the kind of fear we have all felt when confronted with a strange environment—fear of not getting our needs met, fear of being misunderstood, fear of making mistakes, or even fear of being laughed at because of the way we express ourselves.

Fear can cause passivity. How often have you found yourself in a foreign country wanting to go to a new restaurant but too shy to risk the embarrassment of not being able to interpret the menu? For immigrants and international visitors, this can be far more serious than a missed meal. A foreign-born customer may not, for example, ask questions about a product for fear of not being able to understand the answer. A colleague may hesitate to speak up in a meeting or leave a message on an answering machine for fear of not being understood. An immigrant worker may fail to take independent initiative on a task partially because he or she is afraid that a supervisor's instructions might have been misunderstood.

Have you ever felt inadequate when you could not speak the language of those around you? When educated, intelligent, and accomplished people who rely on their ability to demonstrate those virtues verbally are unable to make themselves understood, they appear to others to be slow, unimaginative, and uneducated. Thousands of foreign-born professionals who are entering the United States today are experiencing this difficulty. Having been successful back home, they come here only to appear inarticulate and inexperienced—perceptions which often generate feelings of inadequacy and low self-esteem.

Lack of English-language facility can also interfere with the ability to understand instructions and important details, to grasp the values of American culture, to voice their own ideas, and to receive the promotions and praise they otherwise deserve. All of this too results in lowered confidence and self-worth.

Clearly the consequences of having little skill in English extend far beyond simply not being able to speak with others. Take a look at some of the misconceptions surrounding this problem before moving on to some specific ways in which communication can be improved.

The Myths of Undeveloped English-Language Facility

What happens when you hear colleagues, customers, or workers speak with foreign accents? Do you immediately assume that the speaker is uneducated and incapable of understanding what is being said? Do you find yourself judging the accent and not listening to the words? What about when an immigrant or international visitor declares that he or she understands what is being said only to have it turn out that this was not the case? Do you feel betrayed, embarrassed, and even a little angry? These and other misconceptions about what language and accent differences mean can interfere with efforts to communicate effectively. The following are the most common misunderstandings concerning language diversity:

> *Misconception:* Listeners believe that people with heavy foreign accents are likely to be uneducated, unassimilated into American culture, of low socioeconomic status, and ignorant of English vocabulary and grammar.
> *The True Picture:* A foreign accent tells us very little about the speaker.

Although there are times when these assumptions are accurate, more often than not they are rash and incorrect. When we hear a foreign accent, all that we can be certain of is that the speaker is at least bilingual—and in today's shrinking world, that is likely to be a definite asset.

Those of us who have attempted to learn foreign languages know, much to our dismay, that it is far easier to learn the vocabulary and grammar of a language than it is to master correct pronunciation. This is particularly true of those whose native tongues do not share the Germanic and Romantic roots of English. Asians, for example, have greater difficulty pronouncing English than do Hispanics.

This difficulty lies primarily in the fact that English employs sounds other languages lack. The Japanese have no sounds that correspond to our *l* or *r*. What they do have is one sound that falls somewhere in between. For this reason, many Japanese cannot hear, much less pronounce, the difference. Similarly, Arabic speakers have difficulty with the English *g* and *j;* Filipinos with *b, v, p,* and *ph;* and Farsi (Iranian)-speaking immigrants *v* and *w.*

This pronunciation problem is made worse by the highly irregular spelling of English. The correct pronunciation of words such as *charac-*

ter, school, and *handkerchief* can be a problem for even the most educated of immigrants.

To sum it up, English is difficult to pronounce and many competent professionals never completely overcome the challenges. What is certain is that when we come across anyone who speaks with a foreign accent, we need to resist the temptation to make any snap judgments about that person's background or abilities.

Misconception: If an immigrant cannot speak much English, he or she probably is unable to understand much either.

The True Picture: It is far easier to understand English than it is to speak it.

A person attempting to acquire a new language finds that the first thing that comes together is the ability to comprehend what is said. It takes some time for the skill of speaking the language to catch up with the ability to understand. In short, the fact that immigrants or international visitors may not speak much English does not mean that they do not understand what is being said.

Misconception: Once vocabulary and grammar are learned, the immigrant will always understand what is being said.

The True Picture: There is more to understanding a language than just knowing vocabulary and grammar.

It is a fairly simple matter to know the literal translation of English words but much more difficult to grasp the subtleties and shades of meaning in these words. English is riddled with subtleties, many of them difficult to grasp unless one is raised in this culture. The following pairs of sentences illustrate the complexity of English:

1. Barbara did not *come to* work today.
   Barbara did not *show up* for work today.
2. The speaker *elaborated* the point for an hour.
   The speaker *belabored* the point for an hour.
3. The worker *followed* the manager into the office.
   The worker *pursued* the manager into the office.

Although the nonnative speaker might know each word in these sentences, the dramatic differences in intention could easily be lost behind the subtleties of meaning.

Another nuance of English involves phrases that, if taken literally, can confuse the foreign born. "You can say that again" and "It's just one of those things," for example, are merely *idioms*. Cole Porter, the composer who popularized the latter phrase, never intended for the listener to respond by asking, "What things?" nor would it be appropriate to go ahead and "say it again." Similarly, "I have a lot of running around to do," could lead the nonnative speaker to think of you as a dedicated athlete. English is littered with such expressions, many of which can create painful embarrassment if taken literally.

To make matters worse, sometimes the same words have an opposite meaning depending on the context. To say, "I believe in this idea" connotes a firm commitment to the concept. On the other hand, to respond, "I believe so" to a question connotes some doubt about the matter. The questions "Would you like something to drink?" and "Would you like a drink?" carry with them quite different meanings. The first offers any kind of beverage, whereas the second signals the availability of alcohol.

Such social convention reaches an extreme in questions like "Why don't you read this over?" This statement, if taken at face value, would obviously be interpreted as a question to be answered. In fact, etiquette tells us that this is merely a gentle way of inviting the listener to read the material; it might be rephrased, "Please read this over." Similarly, the question "What's the meaning of this?" can be a simple request for more information or, in another social situation, an accusation of wrong-doing. As you can see, there is a great deal more to understanding what is intended than just knowing the vocabulary.

Misconception: Foreigners are often rude, harsh, and demanding.
The True Picture: Sometimes the intonation of the speaker's native language along with the lack of softening phrases can make the immigrant sound inadvertently rude in English.

Although the speaker may feel no hostility and does not intend to sound demanding or abrupt, the intonation of his or her original language may not convert well to English. When the speaker of a northern Indian dialect attempts English, the tone tends to sound harsh and abrupt to American ears. A Middle Easterner may sound a bit loud and brusk whereas the softer tone of many Asians may leave an equally inaccurate impression of meekness or fear. These examples illustrate the importance of understanding cultural differences in the style or tone of speech.

These misunderstandings may be amplified when the speaker is unfamiliar with how to use the softening words and phrases of English, devices important to the social process. Many languages do not have the equivalent of words like *could, might,* or *may* to cushion the impact of a demand. Note the difference in tone between the following pairs of sentences:

1. Fill the order right now.
   I'd appreciate your filling the order as soon as possible.
2. Give me the dress that it is the window.
   Would you please get me the dress that is in the window when you have a chance?
3. This contract is no good.
   There are some problems with this contract.

The tone of these sentences changes through the careful choice of words and phrases. In some languages, this softening effect is achieved not through the addition of words but through the adjustment of verbs, word order, and pronoun forms. French and German rely heavily on the choice of pronouns to achieve subtleties of meaning. Japanese varies verb forms to obtain the same results. In the Philippines, the prefix *paki-* is added to verbs in order to distinguish a request from a command.

Learning proper intonation is possibly the most difficult part of mastering a new language. If you add to this the necessity of understanding how and when to use softening words and phrases, it is no wonder that the emotions and intent of many foreign-born associates are often misunderstood.

> *Misconception:* When immigrants speak their native language around those who do not understand it, they do so out of laziness and/or out of a desire to exclude outsiders.
> *The True Picture:* Immigrants speak their native language usually as a means of relieving feelings of isolation and/or in response to a crisis.

Managers of foreign-born workers sometimes become concerned when they discover that foreign languages are spoken in the workplace. Depending on the setting, this behavior can cause fellow workers to feel excluded, customers and clients to lose confidence, and managers to feel incapable of communicating effectively. Similarly, when clients, colleagues, or customers speak their native language, those who are within earshot can feel anxious, angry, and offended.

As disruptive as this behavior can be, it usually does not arise out of a desire to be hostile or exclusive. Most likely, the speaking of a foreign language serves one or more of the following functions:

1. It helps to relieve feelings of isolation and loneliness.
2. It allows the immigrant to relax for a few moments; constantly speaking a new language can be a great strain.
3. It allows the speaker to function efficiently in a crisis (and as we saw in question 7 in the Quiz, a crisis can cause speakers to temporarily lose some of their ability to speak English).

I am not contending that speaking a foreign language around those who do not understand it does not sometimes create difficulties but merely that it is usually not a deliberately hostile act.

TIP: It is important that employers and managers keep in mind any legal restrictions against insisting that only English be spoken in the workplace.

Misconception: When immigrants and international visitors pretend to understand what has been said, they are doing so as an act of deceit.

The True Picture: Pretending to understand usually reflects a desire to avoid embarrassment for all concerned.

The problem with this behavior is that it leaves the speaker with no way of knowing whether a message has gotten across. Because of the importance of this topic, an entire section of this chapter has been devoted to techniques for assessing how much understanding has actually taken place. In addition, this problem will be touched upon throughout the book.

How to Make Yourself Understood

Now that you have a good grasp of what language diversity is all about, let us move on to some ways to minimize the impact of these differences.

Each of the following situations illustrates techniques that will help you communicate more successfully to associates, customers, and workers whose English is not fully developed. As you attempt to pick the answer that seems best, remember that some of the situations have more than one right solution and some of the answers are subject to debate. After you have chosen your answer or answers find out how well you have done by looking below each example at the discussion of the various options. Good luck, be creative, and trust your instincts.

Situation 1—The Simple Solutions: Deborah is a customer-service representative for a large utility company. In this capacity, she encounters many Southeast Asian customers who sometimes have difficulty understanding what she is saying. On one occasion, a middle-aged Vietnamese woman seemed especially confused. To relieve the situation, Deborah should have:

a. Spoken more loudly because the woman was probably hard of hearing
b. Spoken more slowly and distinctly
c. Spoken pidgin English and emphasized the key words so that it would be easier for the woman to understand
d. Allowed longer pauses in the conversation
e. Tried to keep the woman from reading her lips because to do so creates confusion

Evaluating the Options

a. Although the woman might have been hard of hearing, it is safer to assume that she is not. There is, of course, a natural tendency to raise one's voice when not being understood. The problem with doing so prematurely is that it can frighten an immigrant who is already intimidated by not understanding what you are saying.

This is particularly a problem when dealing with Asians, who regard a raised voice as disruptive of social harmony. In situations like this, the Asian is likely to speak softer as the American speaks louder. The cycle continues, much to the frustration and discomfort of both parties.

b. **This is a good answer.** Americans generally talk fast, a trait considered a sign of brightness and enthusiasm in the business world. Not only do we speak too rapidly for many immigrants to understand, but we also tend to run words together and pronounce words incompletely. To ask, for example, "Whatdjasay?" is all very well, but it will not elicit much information from someone who does not have a great deal of proficiency in English. Similarly, "Didjaeetyet?" will be meaningless to even the hungriest nonnative speaker. Try to be aware of your speech and to enunciate carefully even the most commonplace words.

TIP: While we are on the subject of enunciation, it is best to minimize the use of "uh uh" and "uh huh" for "no" and "yes." For one thing, these sounds can be indistinct and difficult to decipher and, for another, the Tagalog (Filipino) word for "yes" sounds dangerously close to the English "uh uh" sound for "no."

---

c. This one is a trick question. On the one hand, pidgin English should be avoided. Sentences like "You fill out form, pay money, get car" are not easier to understand and, to make matters worse, insult intelligent customers and clients. On the other hand, emphasizing key words can be very helpful to the immigrant who understands English but tends to get lost in all the verbiage. Be careful, however, not to raise your voice too much when emphasizing these words and ideas; that will be intimidating and discourage good communication.

d. **This is an excellent answer.** Just as mainstream American culture encourages rapid speech, it discourages pauses in the conversation. We think of silence as threatening and a sign of failure or lack of communication. But many other cultures regard silence as a demonstration of strength, as a way of communicating respect for what the speaker has just said, and as an opportunity to formulate well thought out comments and questions. The Japanese proverb, "He who speaks does not know; he who knows does not speak" exemplifies the perspective found in many Far Eastern countries. The practical use of a silence is to provide the nonnative speaker time to digest what you have said and formulate a response.

e. This is not such a good answer. There is nothing confusing about allowing the listener to see your lips as you speak. In fact, this is a good way to help the nonnative speaker decipher what you are saying.

TIP: If you find it difficult to maintain silence, use those few moments to take some deep breaths, compose a particularly intelligent comment of your own, or simply to enjoy a period of quiet. It might help to remember that Thomas Carlyle said, "Silence is more eloquent than words."

Situation 2—Training: Tom trains dozens of foreign-born and ethnic workers at the corporate office of a large midwestern bank. He has a great deal of enthusiasm for both the material and the training process. Although he is fairly unorganized, Tom brings lots of energy to the training class by interjecting interesting asides, anecdotes, and digressions. He also uses slides and handouts extensively. His supervisor has begun to complain that some of the trainees do not seem to be retaining much of the material. What could be the problem and how might it be solved?

    a. The problem probably lies with the slides. Too much sensory input can confuse foreign-born trainees.

    b. Tom should be more organized. His digressions, although interesting, can obscure the main points he is trying to make.

    c. Perhaps the difficulty lies with the handouts. Too many teaching aids can overwhelm students who do not speak English very well.

Evaluating the Options

    a. Probably this is not the problem. Visual aids that are legible, simple, and clear will help enhance understanding for all students. Each of us learns with the aid of our senses. The more senses that are utilized—in this case, hearing and sight—the more rapidly will learning take place.

    b. **This is the best answer.** Although spontaneity and enthusiasm are virtues in an instructor, excessive asides can be confusing to trainees struggling to understand what is being said. Also, the fact that Tom is "fairly unorganized" probably means that he is not allowing enough time at the end of the class in which to recap what has been covered. The process of review is important in any training setting; it is vital when dealing with immigrant workers.

    c. Again, probably not. As we shall see shortly, the written word is an important tool in cross-cultural communication. Any material the trainee misses in class, can be picked up by reading the handouts.

Situation 3—The Telephone: Doing business on the telephone is Richard's strength. He has always enjoyed the fine art of negotiating over the phone and even, much to the wonder of his colleagues, has no reluctance to make "cold calls." The only difficulty is that many of Richard's clients are in the process of learning English, and he sometimes does not know if his message has gotten across. The problem came to a head when Richard thought he had completed a lucrative deal only to discover on follow-up that the details had been badly misunderstood. What might Richard have done to prevent this costly misunderstanding?

   a. There is not much he could have done. Roughly 50 percent of all communication is visual, that is, through body language. Because of this, telephone conversations, even in the absence of language differences, are fraught with the risk of misunderstanding.
   b. The errors had nothing to do with language facility. This was the sort of mix-up that could have happened between any professional and client.
   c. Since this was such an important project and because Richard knew there was the danger of misunderstanding, he should have followed up each telephone call with a written memo spelling out the details of the deal.

Evaluating the Options

   a. Although conversation is more difficult on the telephone, there is still much that can be done to ensure accurate communication. Try another answer.

   b. In some ways, this is a good choice. It is important that we not get so preoccupied with cross-cultural issues that we forget about the ordinary principles of effective communication—principles which can be applied in any setting.

   c. **This is an excellent answer.** As mentioned above, it is easier to understand the written than the spoken word. In all areas of business, the use of written memos after important phone calls and conversations can alleviate many misunderstandings and disappointments. The same applies to meetings and interviews. A detailed agenda and follow-up document can go far toward minimizing the embarrassment and dismay that lack of understanding can cause. Posting important memos regarding benefits, policy changes, or company events on the bulletin board can also help minimize your cross-cultural communication problems.

Situation 4—Choosing Your Words: Jane manages a work force at a large hotel that is approximately 60 percent Hispanic, 10 percent Southeast Asian, and 20 percent Filipino. Some of the workers speak excellent English, but most are still more comfortable conversing in their native languages and often have difficulty understanding the instructions Jane has given.

Jane has devised some techniques for communicating better. She tries to communicate to the Hispanics by using a bit of her high-school Spanish along with English words that are similar to their Spanish equivalent; she tries to notice the English terms her workers use and understand and to use those same words when giving instructions; and, she is very careful, when demonstrating a procedure, to say what she is going to do, do it, and then repeat the instructions. What do you think of Jane's approach?

a. It seems to me that using her high-school Spanish is patronizing and, besides, it may offend the Vietnamese and Filipino workers who aren't getting the same treatment.

b. It seems to me that using English words with Spanish equivalents and words that the speaker already understands will only slow down the process of learning English.

c. I do not think there is any problem with Jane's using English words with Spanish equivalents, and it also seems as if this is a good way to boost the workers' confidence in their ability to understand English.

d. Repeating instructions before and after a procedure seems patronizing. It is as if Jane assumes that they won't understand.

Evaluating the Options

a. This answer is partly right and partly wrong. Whether or not the worker feels patronized depends on the tone and intent of Jane's use of the language. If she uses Spanish as a way of communicating respect, it will serve that purpose and will encourage the worker to meet her halfway and try to speak more English. If, on the other hand, Jane's attitude is one of "talking down" to these employees, her efforts will only further diminish good communication.

On the other hand, you are right: she should learn a few words of

Vietnamese and Tagalog (the primary language of the Filipinos) as well. When there is more than one nationality in the work force, it is important to communicate equal respect for all of them. This may involve learning just a few words of each language; a relatively small effort considering the resentment that can be avoided and the harmony that will be maintained.

TIP: Two cautions are in order: First, check with more than one native speaker of the language to make sure that the meaning and pronunciation of what you have to say is accurate. Tiny changes in inflection can radically alter the meaning of a word. In Mandarin Chinese, for example, the word *ma* can mean "horse" or "mother" depending on how the word is pronounced. Second, learn how to say "that's all I know"—only in this way can you spare yourself the embarrassment of not understanding a lengthy response.

---

b. This is not a good answer. Any technique that allows nonnative speakers to communicate successfully in English is a good one. The more they understand, the more confidence they will have and the more willing they will be to continue to speak English.

TIP: Some examples of Spanish words that are similar in English are *banco, client, doctor, hospital, hotel, distancia, diferente, complicado,* and *cancelar.* The English equivalents are just what they appear to be.

---

c. **This is an excellent answer.** Success breeds success. Not only will using techniques such as these encourage the speaking of English, but it will also lead to the successful completion of tasks and the building of confidence in all areas.

d. It is hard to be certain if this answer is correct. There is not enough information supplied in the scenario to tell us what Jane is feeling. If Jane is excessively pessimistic about her workers' abilities to understand, it will show, and her repetition of the instructions will probably be perceived of as patronizing. But if she has a genuine desire to help and to build a productive team, this feeling will be clear to the employees, and her careful approach will be seen as respectful and compassionate.

Situation 5—Making Meetings Work: Kitty is a senior buyer for a large retail department store chain in the Northeast. Because of the nature of the company, many of her suppliers speak English only as a second language. A large part of Kitty's job is to meet with these people periodically. Because these gatherings happen so infrequently, they are very long and deal with a great many issues at a sitting. At the end of each meeting, Kitty asks the participants if they understood all the issues. Often she discovers that they do not. What could be the problem and how might Kitty solve it?

   a. Rather than waiting until the end of the meeting to ask if the material is being understood, Kitty should do so at various points along the way.
   b. There would be more comprehension if the meetings were shorter. Even if Kitty could not cover every topic in a short time, she would probably come out with a much higher percentage of comprehension.
   c. Kitty should have put together a detailed agenda and follow-up document. This way she could have taken advantage of the written word to clarify the most important points.

Evaluating the Options

   a. **This is an excellent answer.** When there is any question of the group's comprehension, it is important to stop frequently to check for understanding. If a crucial point is missed along the way, any subsequent information that builds on that point will be lost as well.

   b. **This is also a good answer.** Those who do not speak English well are struggling to perform two tasks at once: they are trying to understand the words being said and to remember the important concepts. For this reason, fatigue is likely to set in fairly rapidly. Shorter sessions will prove more comfortable and more productive.

   c. **You cannot lose on this one.** As we have discovered, the written word is valuable in many cross-cultural situations. The agenda would have alerted the attendees as to what to listen for, and the follow-up document would have provided a second opportunity for understanding.

Situation 6—Using the System: Mollie supervises a work force that is approximately 15 percent Cambodian, 10 percent Laotian, 5 percent Korean, 30 percent Cuban, 10 percent Iranian, 15 percent Chinese, and the rest native-born Americans. Her workers range widely in their ability to understand English, although each group has a few informal leaders who are bilingual. Mollie's problem is that many of the workers are not taking advantage of the company's benefits partly because they do not understand them. What might she do to solve this difficulty?

    a. She should translate the benefits into the languages of her workers.
    b. She should explain the benefits to the bilingual group leaders and have them spread the information among their countrymen.
    c. She should call in interpreters and use them to explain the benefits to the workers.

Evaluating the Options

a. This is a satisfactory answer, although it is not always the panacea that it appears to be. Translation is difficult; dialects vary, idioms are confusing, and some words lack equivalents in other languages. There is also the logistical problem of having the information translated into the numerous languages Mollie has in her workplace. Remember that it will appear discriminatory to provide this service for only some of the groups.

b. **Good Answer!** Informal group leaders are a valuable resource for managers, supervisors, and human-resource professionals. They are likely to be bilingual and therefore able to communicate well, and they hold the respect of the group so they can function as valuable conduits between manager and worker.

c. Although not wrong, this answer has some of the problems of *a*. Using interpreters can be cumbersome; they may be hard to find; and, worse, they may not be very good. There is a great deal more to being a good interpreter than simply knowing two languages. It is also necessary to know the cultures and personalities involved so that the nuances of the information can be properly communicated.

Situation 7—Saying What You Mean: Gary owns a chain of restaurants in the Miami area. He does a pretty good job of communicating with the large numbers of Cuban employees, having traveled extensively in Spanish-speaking countries. On one occasion, however, while interviewing an apparently well qualified Cuban applicant, he asked what he thought was a very straightforward question: "How did you find your last position?" No matter how often he repeated the query, the prospect kept telling him that he got the job through his brother-in-law, but would reveal nothing about the conditions of the job. What could have been the problem and how might it have been solved?

    a. Probably the applicant was trying to hide something about his last position.
    b. The fellow obviously did not understand the question and probably did not speak English as well as Gary had thought.
    c. The meaning of the question would not be clear to anyone; it was poorly phrased.

Evaluating the Options

a. Of course this is a possibility. However, it would be more productive to assume that this is not the case and to pursue the matter from the standpoint of cultural and language diversity.

b. Obviously he does not understand the question, but that does not necessarily mean that he does not understand English. Let's try option *c*.

c. **This is it!** Gary's question is too ambiguous. To say "How did you *find* your last position?" could mean either, "How did you *locate* your last position?" or, "What was it *like* at your last position?" The applicant chose the first alternative and proceeded to supply the best answer he could. His inability to tell what Gary meant by "find" does not reflect on his intelligence or on his ability to speak English.

TIP: Be precise in your choice of words. Questions like "How did things go today?" or statements such as "This is really a sweet deal" and "The owner is really hot to sell" are both vague and idiomatic and can be easily misinterpreted.

Each of these case studies illustrates simple techniques that will allow you to communicate better with immigrant and foreign-language-speaking clients, workers, and colleagues. To review briefly:

- Do not shout.
- Speak slowly and distinctly.
- Avoid pidgin English.
- Emphasize key words.
- Allow pauses.
- Let the listener read your lips.
- Use visual aids.
- Organize your thoughts.
- Use the written word.
- Be aware of your tone of voice.
- Use familiar words.
- Repeat and recap frequently.
- Take care not to patronize.
- Check for understanding frequently.
- Do not cover too much information at one time.
- Be careful when translating.
- Choose interpreters carefully.
- Use bilingual group leaders.
- Say exactly what you mean to say.

The most important tip of all, however, was only touched on: Choose your words and construct your sentences carefully so that they communicate precisely what you want as clearly as possible. This task is not as easy as it sounds.

Some Ways to Clarify Your English

What is particularly useful about this section is that the tips provided here work in any interaction, not just those involving people whose native language is not English. Let's face it, we would all communicate better if we minimized jargon, were more concrete and organized when speaking, used shorter words, and kept our sentences uncomplicated. This discussion will help you do all of these things more easily.

Idioms, Slang, and Jargon

Idioms and slang have long been a part of the English language. In the nineteenth century, the peculiar query "How goes the enemy?" was a common way of asking for the time. Around 1900, to inquire "How's your belly for spots?" usually received a polite "I'm fine, thank you." In the second half of this century, Americans have been variously concerned with "What's cooking?" "What's up doc?" and "What's shaking?" Some have even been known to ask "What's your poison?" when offering a drink and "What's the damage?" when requesting the cost of a product or service.

Jargon, too, has been with us for centuries. Words we take for granted today were once industry terms designed to meet the needs of a new technology. Typewriter, airplane, and automobile are the most obvious examples. Today's jargon includes *printout, double-digit inflation, input,* and *telemarketing.* Even the field of cultural diversity has *multicultural, affirmative action,* and *English-as-a-second-language.*

If we add to this the proliferation of acronyms in our vocabulary, it is not surprising that even native English speakers at times have little idea of what is being said. For immigrants and international visitors the situation is worse. We tend to forget that jargon, slang, and idioms are rarely a part of English-as-a-second-language training nor are they taught in English classes overseas.

The problem with this informal vocabulary is that we use it too often and far too unconsciously. The passages in exercise 2–2 contain examples of idioms, slang, and jargon. See if you can find them all, circle them as you go, "take your time," "go for it," "have a ball," and "hang in there."

Exercise 2–2. Spotting the Idioms, Slang, and Jargon

Susan is a salesperson at a large store in a metropolitan area. Over the years, she has built a reputation as an outgoing employee who communicates well with customers and generates good relationships all around. Recently, however, she has been getting some feedback to the effect that things are not going so well. In short, she has begun to have difficulty making herself understood by the immigrant customers who are coming into the store in greater numbers. Apparently, her laid-back approach is not working very well. Here are some of the statements she has been heard to make.

1. Thanks a million for dropping by the store today. I'm pleased that every last one of you made up your minds to make the most of this back-to-school sale.

2. Without a doubt this dress will do the job for you. It looks dynamite on and you can count on it making you the belle of the ball.

3. When your child shows up wearing this jazzy new coat, you can bet that his buddies will be green with envy.

4. Needless to say, this wrench will save you a lot of elbow grease. It's really a cinch to use and won't cost an arm and a leg. You are much better off taking a chance on this one than making do with the one that you have used for so long.

5. This product is top-notch. If you could take the time right now to look it over, you will find that you'll have a head start on all your projects and never get behind schedule again.

6. Let me put your mind at rest. Of course the company backs up every product with any customer service and follow-up that is called for. We will see to it that you are satisfied with this cutting-edge product. High tech is our specialty and we put the full support of the company behind every purchase.

7. Certainly we guarantee that the product is delivered on time and in perfect shape. I know you have a lot on your mind and that your hands are full. Take my word for it, we will back you up all the way.

8. On the whole, I go along with your complaint. Beyond question, the product did not measure up to our high standards. My heartfelt apologies and appreciation for giving us this input.

9. This VCR is top of the line. Not only does it show your videotapes with clear definition, but it also can be programmed to record shows when you are away from home.

10. It would be very much to your advantage if you got your colors done. That way you could pick out a color scheme and mix and match your outfits to fit it. Once you have the scoop on your colors, it is a piece of cake to coordinate your separates, after-five clothes, and sportswear.

11. You had better give me a call if you run into any problems with this FAX. It is a pretty good machine, but some problems have turned up when the dedicated lines are connected. Believe you me, you are buying this at a cut-rate price and our profit margin on it is very small.

How did you do? Maybe it will help if you know that there are eighty-three examples of slang and idioms in the exercise, some of which are obvious and some more subtle. When you have circled your selections, look over the following list; you may be surprised at what you find:

thanks a million	dropping by
every last one	made up your minds
make the most of	back to school
without a doubt	do the job
looks dynamite	count on it
belle of the ball	shows up
jazzy	you can bet
buddies	green with envy
needless to say	elbow grease
cinch to use	cost an arm and a leg
better off	taking a chance
making do	topnotch
take the time	right now
look it over	head start
get behind schedule	put your mind at rest
of course	backs up
customer service	follow-up
called for	see to it
cutting-edge	high tech
on time	on your mind
hands are full	take my word for it
back you up	on the whole
go along with	beyond question
measure up	heartfelt
input	VCR

top-of-the-line	videotape
clear definition	programmed
to your advantage	colors done
pick out	color scheme
mix and match	the scoop
piece of cake	separates
after-five	sportswear
had better	give me a call
run into	FAX
pretty good	turned up
dedicated lines	believe you me
cut-rate	profit margin

If you had trouble finding all eighty-three items, take a look at the "Setting the Scene" paragraph—there are some idioms, jargon, and slang hidden in there. These include: *salesperson, over the years, outgoing, feedback, to the effect that, things are not going, in short, making herself understood, laid-back.* You might also have had some difficulty because words and phrases are constantly passing from jargon to legitimate language. Some would argue, for example, that *definition* and *videotape* are now as much a part of the language as *airplane* or *steamboat.* The point is, not how you categorize an expression, but whether or not it communicates what you want to say.

Some of the phrases in this exercise probably were easy to spot. We are fairly conscious of choosing idioms like *elbow grease* and *thanks a million.* Most idioms, however, are such an integral part of everyday speech that they are used unconsciously. Actually there is no problem with this as long as the usage is understood by the listener. Try to remember, however, that even the most worldly foreign-language speaker is likely to become muddled when told to *bide your time, play it cool,* or *give it your best shot.* Sadly, many workers have been *fired* or *let go,* only to return to the job the next day because they did not understand the jargon. It is not unusual to hear of cases in which prospective clients were told that a deal had *gone sour* or was *called off* only to have them act as if it were still *on.* Slang is dangerous. It can be readily misunderstood or even be offensive to someone who is unfamiliar with the spirit in which a term is used.

In addition to being alert to your choice of words, it can also be helpful to construct an easy-to-understand glossary of industry jargon for all employees and clients. We all find it embarrassing to have to ask the meaning of a term or acronym, particularly if we feel that it is something we ought to know. It would be most unpleasant, for example, for a hospital worker to become confused over the meaning of *LOC*, a term that in different parts of the country variously means "level of consciousness" or "laxative of choice." Similarly, the foreign-born client might become confused by a *sweet deal*, a quick *close*, or an *airtight* contract. A glossary would eliminate, or at least minimize, this problem. Your effort would be appreciated by those who are uncomfortable with the loss of face that accompanies having to inquire about the meaning of terms ranging from *flextime* to *deductible, lay away, revolving charge, IRA, exempt,* or, sadly, *laid-off.*

Keeping It Simple

Most of us have lost track of what simple, straightforward expression is all about. Big words, complex sentences, and, worst of all, too much verbiage have come to be the rule in our culture. Speaking and writing in complex sentences is a habit we usually indulge in unconsciously. Fortunately, practice, such as that provided in exercise 2–3 can help a great deal. It will make you aware of the bad habits that compromise your ability to communicate with the foreign-born. The instructions are simple, read over the passages and try to make each one simpler and more easily understood. When you are finished, examine the options provided and see how well you did.

Exercise 2–3. Simplifying Your English

1. "If you study this manual, follow the instructions provided by your supervisor, stick to the dress code, and are careful about punctuality, you will probably be considered for a promotion."

Your rephrasing:

---

2. "I was wondering what you think of our service. It is important we know how the public feels in order to meet our goals."

Your rephrasing:

3. "We are barely going to make that deadline. I almost think we ought to call in several additional workers."

Your rephrasing:

4. "This contract is one of the quintessential documents that I have ever perused. Although the verbiage is verbose and admittedly excessive, the significance behind the vocabulary is easily clarified and, in my judgment, will meet your every specification."

Your rephrasing:

5. "I was told by my boss that it was necessary for me to have you seen by a doctor to make sure you weren't hurt in that fall."

Your rephrasing:

6. "Don't forget that we won't be shipping that order to your office until Thursday."

Your rephrasing:

7. "This is the room that the management considers to be one of the finest in the hotel and that possesses all of the features that would be found in any high quality, first-rate property. We very much appreciate your repeated patronage for we realize that you have the choice of many good hotels in the area, and we hope you will visit our establishment again soon."

Your rephrasing:

8. "What matters in a situation such as this is that you never again fail to complete the patient's chart at the end of your shift. This effort will be greatly appreciated by myself and by my superiors and will most certainly be reflected in our feeling better about your work than we have in the past. It will also look extremely good on your record and in the eyes of your colleagues and may, eventually, result in a promotion or at least a better position."

Your rephrasing:

9. "This company has many benefits to offer. I am your customer-service representative. You probably have a great many questions to ask about your account. It is important, too, that you know that I have an assistant to whom you can turn if I am unavailable. Your account is in good hands with us. We've been in business for 15 years. Feel free to call me or my assistant if you have any questions."

Your rephrasing:

"Simplifying your English" is not as easy as it first appears. Examine some ways in which these passages might have been rewritten and then we'll discuss the particular problems found within each one:

1. *An Option:* "There are four things you need to do in order to be considered for a promotion: first, study the manual; second, follow instructions; third, follow the dress code; fourth, be punctual."
   The Issue: Mixing topics in one sentence can be confusing. Stick to one subject at a time or list them systematically.

2. *An Option:* "Do you like our service? It is important that we know how you feel if we are to succeed in business."
   The Issue: This passage is extremely vague. Phrases like "How do you feel about our service?" do not really say anything. "Feelings" can range from how the service makes them respond emotionally to what their opinion is of that service. Other examples of vague questions are "How did things go today?" and "How did things work out?" Also, the reference to "meeting goals" is too vague. Try to be concrete when you speak, and ask specifically for what you want.

3. *An Option:* "We will make that deadline but only by a few minutes. I am thinking about calling in three or four additional workers."
   The Issue: Modifiers such as *barely, almost, several, scarcely,* and *mostly* are difficult for nonnative English speakers to understand. It is very hard to learn exactly what words like these mean. What does it really mean to "almost think" or "barely make" something? One of the reasons that many immigrant students and workers do poorly on multiple-choice examinations is that such tests tend to use these vague modifiers. Because of this, multiple-choice quizzes end up testing the individual's knowledge of the subtleties of English far more than his or her actual grasp of the subject matter.

4. *An Option:* "This is a good contract. The words are complicated, but can easily be explained. I think you will like it."
   The Issue: Keep your choice of vocabulary simple but not patronizing. Winston Churchill, one of the greatest

communicators of the twentieth century, said, "Short words are best, and old words, when short, are best of all."

5. *An Option:* "My boss told me that you should see a doctor to make certain you didn't hurt yourself in that fall."
   The Issue: Use the active voice whenever possible. It is easier to understand and results in a simpler sentence structure.

6. *An Option:* "Remember that we will be shipping the order to your office on Thursday."
   The Issue: Do not use negative phrasing; it is complicated, requires more words, and can lead to misunderstandings. In the sentence above, for example, there is the danger that what will be heard is the "won't" and the "Thursday" leaving the impression that the delivery will *not* be made on Thursday. Also asking someone not to forget something is more confusing than simply saying "remember."

7. *An Option:* "This is a very fine room. It has all the features that you need. Thank you for choosing our hotel. We hope to see you again soon."
   The Issue: Keep your sentences short and simple. Run-on sentences are very difficult to understand, especially when spoken.

8. *An Option:* "Be certain to complete the patient's chart at the end of the day. I would appreciate it very much."
   The Issue: Do not use too many words, and do not talk too much. We see this happening especially when it is necessary to discipline a worker. Our discomfort shows itself in a tendency to jabber. More words are not clearer and, in fact, are likely to confuse nonnative English speakers. There is also a tendency to

---

TIP: When you are tempted to use too many words, remember that Thomas Jefferson almost succumbed to this temptation when, in an early draft of the *Declaration of Independence*, he wrote "We hold these truths to be sacred and undeniable. . . ." Rumor has it that it was Benjamin Franklin's suggestion to shorten the phrase to read, "We hold these truths to be self-evident. . . ." Which do you prefer?

say too much when answering the phone. Have you ever called a business, only to have the operator answer with a cheery, "Hello, this is Diana. Thank you for calling the Blabber Corporation. How can I be of service? . . . Have a nice day"? Even native English speakers can become confused with so much verbiage.

9. *An Option:* "I am here to answer your questions about the company's benefits. Please call me or my assistant if you have any problems.

The Issue: Put sentences in a logical order so they will be more easily understood. Organize your thoughts before you begin, and avoid the temptation of going off into tangents, no matter how interesting they might be.

It may seem like a monumental chore to keep all these rules in mind as you go about your already difficult task of communicating across accent and language barriers. Be assured, however, that speaking more clearly and concisely is a matter of habit and practice. If taken one step at a time, the task of good communication, like any other, can be easily accomplished. Here is a quick recap of the contents of this section:

- Avoid idioms, jargon, and slang.
- Talk about one topic at a time.
- Be concrete when you speak.
- Avoid vague modifiers.
- Use simple vocabulary and sentence structure.
- Use the active voice.
- Use positive phrasing.
- Use short sentences.
- Use as few words as possible.
- Keep your topics in a logical order.

How to Tell If You Have Been Understood

George Bernard Shaw once said, "The greatest problem with communication is the illusion that it has been accomplished." Never before has this been so true as in our multicultural society where misunderstandings are common and where it is not unusual for people to pretend to understand when, in fact, they have little idea of what has been said.

The practice of feigning understanding is, of course, not confined to foreign-language speakers. Occasionally we have all pretended to know what was going on when we were actually utterly confused. We usually do this for three reasons:

1. We do not want to appear foolish or ignorant.
2. We do not want to insult the speaker by implying that the material has not been explained well.
3. We are concerned that even if we ask for the material to be repeated, we will not understand it the second time.

You will notice that none of these motives involve malicious deceit, nor do they reflect a desire to make the speaker appear foolish. As business professionals, however, it is impossible to function effectively unless we can establish, beyond a doubt, whether we are being understood. The following suggestion will help you assess how much information has actually gotten across:

1. *Watch for nonverbal signs.* Although nonverbal signals can be very helpful in assessing how much has been understood, body language is by no means the same throughout the world. We will discuss this further in Chapter 3. A few examples here will be helpful. A blank expression may be a sign of poor understanding for most people but in the Far East, is more likely to reflect the Asian desire to avoid an overt display of emotion. Similarly, the avoidance of eye contact can indicate that the person is not following you but can also be an indication of respect.

I am not saying that body language is of no use in assessing understanding. It is still fairly safe to assume that when a listener narrows his or her eyes, stays focused on the speaker, and nods and smiles in appropriate spots, that he or she is generally grasping what you are saying. Beware, however, of perpetual nodding and smiling that does not relate directly to what you are saying. This behavior might reflect a desire to please and often indicates very little real comprehension.

In Filipino culture there is one nonverbal cue that can be particularly confusing. The Filipino is likely to move the head down as a way of indicating "no." You should be careful not to misinterpret this movement as an affirmative nod when asking the question, "Do you understand?"

2. *Notice a lack of interruptions.* Although some people misinterpret this as an indication of attentiveness, a complete lack of interruptions often means that the material is not being understood.

3. *Notice efforts to change the subject.* This could indicate that the listener is not understanding what you are saying so is anxious to talk about something more familiar.

4. *Note the complete absence of questions.* Paradoxically, this often means that the listener is not grasping what you are saying. Perhaps he or she is not understanding enough to allow for the formulation of questions.

5. *Notice inappropriate laughter.* A self-conscious giggle can indicate poor comprehension. Do not interpret laughter as a sign of disrespect for what you are saying. It more likely is a way of covering up embarrassment.

6. *Invite questions in private and in writing.* By providing the opportunity to ask questions in private or in writing, you spare the listener the humiliation of having to admit a lack of understanding in front of colleagues or friends. This suggestion is especially valuable during meetings or training sessions when the number of people present can make it particularly difficult for the individual to admit his or her confusion.

TIP: In the training room, loss of face can also be avoided by using self-graded quizzes.

---

7. *Allow enough time for questions to be formulated.* Remember that nonnative speakers need more time in which to construct questions. A person who is rushed may miss the opportunity to clear up an important point.

8. *Beware of the "yes" that means "Yes, I hear your question," not "Yes, I understand."* In Asia, it is appropriate to answer many question with an initial "yes." This positive response is often merely an acknowledgment that the question has been heard and understood; it is not an actual answer to a specific inquiry.

9. *Beware of a positive response to a negative question.* In English, when asked, "You don't understand, do you?" the appropriate response, if the listener does not understand, is to say, "No [I do not understand]." In many Asian languages, on the other hand, the way of communicating a negative response would be to say "Yes [I agree with

you that I do not understand]." Remember to phrase all questions in the positive that is, "Do you understand?," rather than, "You don't understand, do you?"

TIP: If asked a negatively phrased question by an Asian, answer it with a complete sentence. If you say just "yes" or "no," the meaning of your response could easily be taken as the opposite of what you intended.

---

10. *Beware of a qualified yes in response to the question, "Do you understand?"* Tentative answers such as "Yes, I think so" and "I suppose so" may be efforts to cushion the abruptness of a negative response and amount to a gentle way of saying "No, I do not understand [but I am not comfortable coming right out and saying so]."

11. *Have the listener repeat what you have said.* This is a simple way of assessing understanding. There are, however, a couple of pitfalls to this approach. First, if at all possible, it must be done in private to avoid loss of face in front of others. Second, you should be skeptical if you get back a word-for-word recitation of what you have just said. Rote repetition may indicate merely the ability to mouth the words, not a real understanding of the material.

12. *If your communication involves instructing workers, observe behavior and inspect production.* If the procedure that has been taught is done correctly the first time, the chances are good that your instructions have been understood and that they will continue to be carried out.

When checking for understanding it is important to avoid putting the immigrant in an uncomfortable or conspicuous position. By using the techniques provided here, it is possible to assess how much has been understood while preserving the dignity and pride of all concerned.

Some Tips on Translating the Written Word

Horror stories abound about errors in translation. The international marketing community will never get over the time when Pepsi Cola attempted to market its product overseas with the slogan "Come alive with Pepsi" only to have it translate into German as "Come out of the grave with Pepsi." Jimmy Carter probably still smarts when he thinks of how his wishes to "get to know" the Polish people were translated to say, "I desire the Poles carnally." Sometimes it is the subtle errors that can be the most painful, and the most damaging. For example, one large corporation went into China with marketing materials that boasted of the company's being an "old friend" of China, only to have them translate into Chinese as "former friend."

Now that I have made you thoroughly terrified of the translation process, you will be all the more receptive to the following suggestions. Whether you are translating contracts, advertising copy, pamphlets on how to do business with your organization, instructions to your employees, or whatever it might be, these guidelines will keep you from making too many grave mistakes.

1. *Choose your translators carefully.* The best translators have three characteristics. First, they are native speakers of the foreign language. The person who learns a language in school or later in life is not apt to be completely comfortable with the subtleties of particular words, nor with the complexities of idiom and slang. In addition to the errors cited above, think how badly you would feel were you the one responsible for the advertising copy that ended up saying, in Spanish, "eye lashes that *weld* to the eyes," or that attempted to sell cigarettes with "low asphalt." These same errors can be made when translating from foreign languages into English. One company was, for example, was dismayed to receive a FAX from France referring to its proposal as *c'est terrible,* literally, "it is terrible." What the American company did not realize was that this phrase is an idiomatic expression meaning "that's really terrific."

Second, the best translators are as proficient in English as they are in the foreign language. After all, they cannot translate accurately if they do not understand precisely what it is that you want to say.

Finally, any translator you choose should have knowledge of both cultures. As we shall see when we discuss working with interpreters, it is imperative that translators know what subjects are appropriate to mention, how things should be said, and what level of language should be used. For this reason, the translator needs to be a "culture broker" — someone who is familiar with both the American and foreign culture.

2. *Make certain you have the correct language and dialect.* This

may seem like an obvious suggestion, but all too often the wrong East Indian dialect has been chosen or the assumption made that Cambodian, Vietnamese, Laotian, and even Thai are the same language. With more than 140 languages spoken in the United States today there is the constant danger of making such an obvious error.

3. *Along the same lines, be sure that the idioms are appropriate to your target audience and that the level of sophistication is correct.* Idioms, for example, can be very different between the Spanish spoken in Cuba and that in Mexico. Some businesses use generic "Walter Cronkite" Spanish, which is usually acceptable, but if you have a very specific Cuban, Puerto Rican, or Mexican market, it would be wiser to tailor your translations to that specific audience.

4. *Be aware that translating is not an easy job.* We already know how easy it is to choose the wrong word or phrase and thereby create a nightmare of misunderstanding and embarrassment. There is the additional problem that many words simply do not translate into other languages. The English word for a state of emotional *depression,* for example, has no equivalent in many Asian languages. Other terms, such as the English *parallel* can be very tricky to translate. In English, *parallel* can be used to indicate two positions that are closely aligned. The Japanese language version of *parallel,* however, describes two points of view that will never meet. You can see how difficult a task translating can be; it goes far past sitting down with a foreign-language dictionary and looking up the words and phrases.

5. *Have one person translate the message into the foreign language and have someone else translate it back into English.* This extra step can save you a great deal of grief and embarrassment. It would, for example, have proved invaluable to the writing instrument company that mistakenly promised the Hispanic community that its ink would "prevent pregnancy," having meant to say that it would "prevent embarrassment" because it would never leak onto your shirt.

6. *Test your materials prior to mass distribution.* Have representatives from the community in question look over what you have done and make suggestions for accuracy, appropriateness, and clarity. If you are a part of a large company or public facility that has a lot of contact with ethnic or immigrant groups, you might arrange for "focus groups" of people from the community to help you out. This helps you clarify your translations, gives you and your staff the opportunity to get to know the community, and allows culturally different consumers to ask questions

and express their concerns about you, your product or service, and your organization.

How to Communicate through an Interpreter

The rules that you just learned regarding written translation also apply to the use of interpreters. There are, however, additional tips that can help you with the challenge of conversing across language barriers. Since the focus of this book is on doing business with diverse cultures within the boundaries of the United States, you probably will not work through an interpreter very often. When you do, however, there are certain errors that are important to avoid in order to minimize the danger of misunderstandings and hurt feelings.

Exercise 2–4 illustrates some of these errors. Elizabeth, our main character, is meeting a German client who is opening up a large manufacturing plant in the United States. This important meeting includes the discussion of delicate and confidential matters concerning the complexities of setting up business in a foreign country. Although Wilhelm speaks a little English, Elizabeth thought it best to bring in an interpreter to avoid any confusion. The scene in the exercise shows how she handled the situation and gives you a chance to list the things that you think she did right and those she did wrong.

Before you look ahead, I need to emphasize that all the material you have already learned about how to communicate with those whose English is not very developed apply when using an interpreter as well. To review just a couple of the most important points: keep your choice of words simple and concrete, take care not to raise your voice, and plan ahead of time exactly what it is you want to say.

TIP: In Chapter 5, we will look at differing rules of "conversational etiquette"; the tendency, for example, to talk *around* a subject. Be careful not to allow differences such as these to confuse your attempts to communicate through an interpreter.

Keeping your language simple serves two functions. First, it guarantees that the interpreter will understand what it is you want him or her to say,

Exercise 2–4. Using an Interpreter

When Wilhelm and his associates arrive at the company office, Elizabeth's secretary shows them into the conference room. Elizabeth herself is slightly delayed because she is finishing up the agenda for the meeting. She finally arrives a few minutes late and is followed, a short time later, by the interpreter Vicky, a colleague of Elizabeth's who had taken German in college and studied in Germany during her senior year in high school.

After making first-name introductions all around, Elizabeth begins the discussions. When speaking to the interpreter, Elizabeth is careful to look straight at her so as to maintain good eye contact. She also tries to say only a few sentences at a time so that Vicky will not have to translate too much material at once.

When it is Wilhelm's turn to speak, Elizabeth looks at him attentively, nods and smiles periodically, and then turns to Vicky for the translation. At one point in the proceedings, Elizabeth senses that the discussions are getting a bit intense so decides to "lighten things up" by joking with Wilhelm, through Vicky. She asks Vicky, in a joking tone, to tell Wilhelm that the world had better "watch out" now that Germany is reunified, that the Germans could take over Europe before we know it. Because she appreciates what Vicky is doing for her, Elizabeth takes a few moments out in the middle of the conversation to tell her what a good job she is doing.

Although one purpose of the meeting is to get at some fairly sensitive information about the status of Wilhelm's company in the United States, he seems reluctant to discuss the most delicate aspects of these considerations. Toward the end of the conversation, however, Vicky and Wilhelm begin talking animatedly about something which Elizabeth obviously does not understand. When she asks about it, Vicky says that it was not important, that they were just chatting.

After about an hour, Elizabeth has another appointment, so is forced to end the meeting even though not all the issues have been covered. She arranges for another time to meet and rushes out of the office.

Use these lines to list what you think Elizabeth did right and what she did wrong:

Right

1.

2.

3.

4.

5.

Wrong

1.

2.

```
3.


4.


5.
```

and, second, it increases the possibility that the foreign-language speaker will understand you even before the words are translated. Not raising your voice is important because, if your words are not understood, your tone of voice and body language are the only ways in which your intent can be read. A loud voice, even if it actually indicates enthusiasm, can be misinterpreted as anger or impatience, attitudes which can easily damage your relationship with the foreign-born colleague.

Among the positive behaviors that you might have put on your list is the fact that Elizabeth prepared an agenda for the meeting. This indicates that she had carefully thought out what she wanted to say and knew the value of providing a written document for Wilhelm and his colleagues to peruse. As we have seen, it is often easier to read English than to understand the spoken word; it is very likely that the German contingent would be able to decipher at least part of the agenda and could take it away with them for future reference.

It may seem like an obvious step that Elizabeth took the time to introduce the interpreter to Wilhelm, but all too often interpreters are ignored and treated as if they were invisible. Not only is this rude, but it diminishes the foreign-language speaker's faith in the expertise of the interpreter. If this person is so good at his or her job, the thinking might go, why is he or she being treated like a machine?

Another positive thing that Elizabeth did was to speak in short units. Covering too much material at a time can create confusion for both the interpreter and the foreign-language speaker. Finally, Elizabeth's attentiveness to Wilhelm, the fact that she looked at him while he was speaking, was both gracious and important to the success of the conversation. By looking at him, even though she did not understand what he was saying, Elizabeth was able to read his body language and communicate her interest in what he had to say.

Unfortunately, Elizabeth did a lot more wrong than she did right. The first things that she did wrong have more to do with cross-cultural etiquette than with the actual process of using an interpreter. The punctual and formal German probably did not look favorably on the fact that Elizabeth was not there to greet him, that she, and the interpreter, kept the group waiting in the conference room, and that she introduced everyone using first names. The interpreter's lateness also meant that Elizabeth did not have the opportunity to brief Vicky on the purpose of the meeting—an important step in minimizing the risk of misunderstanding.

Since this was obviously an important meeting in which some delicate and confidential matters were to be discussed, it would have been better if Elizabeth had allowed time in which the client could have gotten to know, and trust, the interpreter a bit more. Wilhelm had no reassurance, for example, that Vicky would not go off and talk to her colleagues about the contents of the meeting. This is probably the reason that he was reluctant to talk about the really delicate matters.

We have already learned that it would have been better had Elizabeth chosen an interpreter who spoke German as his or her native language and who was familiar with both American and German cultures. Spending a year in Germany is helpful, but does not qualify Vicky as an expert in German culture. Had Vicky known both cultures, she would have been able to caution Elizabeth about the poor taste of her "German reunification" joke.

Elizabeth also erred in not explaining to Vicky that it was important that Elizabeth know all that was being said during the meeting. It is good for the interpreter to take time to build the trust of the foreign-language speaker, but it becomes divisive for her to chat informally to the exclusion of the English-speaking party.

I realize that this may seem awkward, but Elizabeth would have communicated far better with Wilhelm had she spoken directly to him and not to Vicky. Even if he could not understand what she was saying, Elizabeth would be in a better position to communicate, nonverbally, the tone and intent of her words had she looked in his direction. Another reason why looking at the interpreter is not a good idea is that you risk making the other party feel left out of the conversation. In Elizabeth's case, this was exacerbated when she began to chat with Vicky about the good job she was doing. Positive reinforcement is important, but it should have waited until the meeting was over.

Finally, the presence of an interpreter makes conversations two or three times as long as they might normally be. Had Elizabeth realized this, she would have allowed the extra time and been able to complete her agenda in a relaxed unhurried atmosphere.

Admittedly, you do not always have the luxury of abiding by all these rules. You cannot always, for example, choose your interpreter. If you are on the sales floor, or in someone's home, for example, and the only person who speaks English is a child, you might have to rely on him or her to do the job. Although most children function well in this capacity, you need to be aware that the relationship between the child and the adult for whom he or she is interpreting can be a delicate one. Respect for authority and for elders is highly developed within most immigrant communities. Placing a child in a position of power can be awkward for all concerned. This is particularly true if the content of the conversation is in any way intimate or confidential. One way, as we saw in question 16 of the Quiz, to minimize this awkwardness is for you to look at the authority figure while you speak in order to communicate appropriate respect and keep the channels of communication open.

Guidelines to Understanding the Nonnative English Speaker

Now that we have explored ways in which to make ourselves understood, methods for knowing how successful we have been, and how to use a translator or interpreter when necessary, we are still faced with the challenge of understanding what a nonnative speaker is saying. This task varies in difficulty depending on the thickness of the accent, the country of origin, and your own familiarity with a particular accent.

If you feel especially frustrated by your inability to understand the accents of those around you, you might be encouraged by this last comment. You will be glad to know that the more you hear a particular accent, the easier it is to understand. Our ears and minds gradually adapt to new sounds and new ways of pronouncing words, and eventually, even the thickest accent becomes easily decipherable. In the meantime, however, there are some techniques that will help you better understand your foreign-born clients, customers, and employees.

1. *Share responsibility for poor communication.* If, for example, you speak on the telephone with immigrants whom you have difficulty understanding, you might comment from time to time on the bad connection or noise in the room that keeps you from being able to hear clearly. The purpose of a small deception such as this is to take the pressure off the immigrant, who may be self-conscious about his or her accent. The more responsibility you can accept for not understanding, the less stress the other person will feel and the more relaxed he or she will be. This allows the nonnative speaker to focus on pronunciation, speak more slowly, and communicate more successfully.

2. *Invite the immigrant to speak more slowly.* Just as it is important for you to avoid talking too fast when speaking with immigrants, speed is also one of the main reasons that the immigrant is hard to understand. Because we all talk faster when we are uncomfortable, it is important to make the nonnative English speaker as relaxed as possible.

Some immigrants, too, feel that if they speak English rapidly, they will appear more fluent in the language. Although speed certainly does represent a facility with vocabulary and grammar, it can also interfere with the ability to be understood.

3. *Repeat what you believe the immigrant has said.* Saying, for example, "As I understand it, you mean . . ." can be a quick and easy way to establish if you have heard correctly. This habit gives the speaker the opportunity to clarify what he or she meant and gives you a way of communicating the fact that you really care about what has been said.

4. *Encourage the nonnative speaker to use the written word.* The written word works both ways: it helps you communicate to the immigrant and it helps the immigrant communicate to you. It is, in many cases, not only easier to read English than to hear it but also easier to write it than to speak it. This brings us back to the point that some immigrants have a highly developed knowledge of English vocabulary and grammar, but have difficulty with pronunciation. The written word gets around this problem.

5. *Allow the speaker to spell difficult words.* It can be embarrass-

ing to ask speakers to spell out what they are trying to say. Nonetheless, this technique can substantially shorten what could be an otherwise long and painful exchange. Spelling is especially helpful when working with foreign names, many of which are unfamiliar to the native-born professional.

6. *Read the speaker's lips.* We have seen how helpful it is to allow the immigrant to see your lips in order to understand more easily. This same technique works in the other direction. Looking at the immigrant's lips can be useful in clarifying words that would otherwise be very difficult to decipher.

7. *Give the speaker plenty of time in which to communicate.* Nothing is more rattling than having to hurry. We already know how important it is to give the speaker enough time in which to formulate questions and responses. Create an atmosphere in which the conversation is leisurely and during which there is plenty of room for pauses, for collecting one's thoughts, and for relaxation.

8. *Listen to all that the speaker has to say before concluding that you do not understand.* In this instance, the rules are different for you than for the foreign-language speaker. I have mentioned how important it is for you not to speak too much before checking for understanding. In the case of your listening to the foreign-language speaker, it is better to do the opposite; listen to a large amount of what the speaker has to say. You will be amazed at how much you understand once you have evaluated the individual words and phrases in context.

9. *Observe body language.* Although the vocabulary of nonverbal language varies from culture to culture, it can still provide general clues as to the essence, if not the specifics, of what is being said. The client, for example, who is wringing his or her hands is obviously nervous, and the customer who is grimacing is probably angry or upset. Nonverbal signals such as these tell us far more about the emotions of the speaker than do the words themselves. They also give us clues to the meaning behind culturally different ways of expressing ideas. The Asian who does not want to hurt you by stating a definite "no" is likely to soften a negative reply by saying, "Maybe," or "We'll see." If you look carefully, you may notice that as these words are being said, the speaker's head will move down, a negative sign that counteracts the words being spoken.

10. *Remember to listen and expect to understand.* Studies have shown that most of us listen at only 30 percent of capacity and that this percentage drops still further when we do not expect to understand.

When we hear a foreign accent, for example, there is the danger of thinking, "I'll never understand what this person is saying," and then to conclude that there is no point in even trying to understand. The result is that we stop listening. Moreover, when we hear a foreign accent, we listen to the accent rather than to what is being said. Be aware of your listening habits. Are you truly listening to the words, or are you merely focusing on the way those words are pronounced?

How to Encourage the Speaking of English

English is a difficult language; it is replete with subtle idioms, words that sound one way and look another (*February, psychology,* and *laughter* are the classic examples), and single words with several different meanings. Did you ever stop to think, for example, that the word *check* has at least seven meanings ranging from the bill you receive in a restaurant to the tiny pattern in your suit?

To get some idea of how dangerous it is to speak English, examine these signs written by proprietors around the world for the benefit of English-speaking tourists. In a Hong Kong tailor shop, women are asked to "have a fit upstairs"; at a hotel in Japan, guests are invited to "take advantage of the chambermaid"; tourists are met in a Moscow hotel lobby with the greeting, "If this is your first trip to Moscow, you're welcome to it"; and, in a Bucharest hotel lobby, "The lift is being fixed for the next few days. During that time, we regret that you will be unbearable."[1] The frightening thing is that all of these sentences are literally and grammatically correct; yet their meaning is certainly not what the proprietors intended.

It is no wonder that immigrants and international business people are often hesitant to speak up in meetings, to ask questions, or to participate in simple English conversations. It is all too easy to make an embarrassing mistake. The fear of humiliation is combined with the concern that, if they begin to speak English, those around them will assume they know more than they do and, consequently, will launch into a long-winded conversation.

These are the reasons that so many nonnative English speakers, even those with a fair grasp of the language, are reluctant to use it. Certainly there are many times when it is none of your concern whether a colleague, client, or worker is speaking English. Indeed, it would be rude and in the case of the multicultural workplace probably illegal for you to insist on it. There are times, however, when it is appropriate to encourage the speaking of English in a gentle and nonjudgmental way. The following suggestions will give you some ideas as to how to go about this delicate process.

1. *Learn a few words of the immigrant's language.* It seems like a contradiction to learn the immigrants' language so they will be motivated to speak more English, but it is not as strange a suggestion as you may think. By learning just a few words of the languages to which you are exposed, you are showing a respect that they will be eager to return.

Perhaps this will be clearer if you think of a time when you were in a foreign country and someone made an effort to greet you in your own language. You probably felt relieved and grateful. Possibly you became just a little bit more willing to try a few words of the host country's language. By communicating this same respect to your foreign-born clients, workers, and colleagues, you encourage them to return the favor.

For those concerned that learning just a few words of a language is patronizing, remember that a behavior is patronizing only if you are acting out of that emotion. If learning to say "good morning" in Korean is motivated by a desire to show friendship and respect, it will serve that purpose. Like all the other suggestions in this book, it is your attitude that will dictate whether the immigrant or international visitor interprets a given approach as patronizing or as respectful and compassionate.

It may seem daunting to learn even a few words of such unfamiliar tongues as Tagalog, Vietnamese, or Farsi. To help you out, a few phrases have been included in the Appendix along with a phonetic rendering to help you with the pronunciation. Do not worry too much about the pronunciation. If you pronounce a word incorrectly, remember that your mistake will show the immigrant that it is all right to make an error from time to time. In the multicultural workplace, your errors, too, can give immigrant workers an opportunity to teach the manager something—a switch in roles that quickly promotes good communication and mutual respect.

TIP: You will notice from the list in the appendix that it is important to learn the phrase "That's all I know," in order to keep from getting lost in a lengthy conversation.

I mentioned above that if you are going to translate materials into other languages in the workplace or community, you must be certain to include all the languages found in your area. The same applies to learning a few words of a foreign language; just three or four phrases of *each* language will prevent any possible resentments or bad feelings.

2. *Smile, look enthusiastic, and be patient.* Use the same techniques that you would use when encouraging anyone to speak. Nod your head when appropriate, say encouraging phrases like "I understand" and "go on," and, above all else, do not show impatience. If the nonnative speaker appears embarrassed while attempting English, glance away from time to time. This will help the speaker to feel less in the spotlight and, therefore, less self-conscious.

I realize that you do not always have time for slow or lengthy conversations. When communicating with those who do not speak English well, try to do so at times when you will not be tempted to cut the conversation short or hurry it along. Allowing, for example, enough time for pauses and questions takes patience, or at least the impression of patience.

3. *Ask open-ended questions.* There is a temptation when speaking with those whose English is not highly developed to ask "yes" and "no" questions. We do this because it gives us the comforting illusion that we are having a successful two-way conversation. The truth is, however, that a "yes" or "no" answer can be misleading. In addition, giving immigrants the option of answering just "yes" or "no" discourages them from supplying lengthier answers.

Should you wish, for example, to find out how a foreign-born employee feels about his or her job, you would be better off inquiring, "Tell me about your job," than saying, "Do you like your job?" or even, "How is your job?" These latter queries allow the worker to answer with a brief "yes" or "no" or, equally unrevealing, "fine." Similarly, asking a customer, "What did you like about the product?" is better than "Did you like the product?"

When you phrase questions, see to it that they encourage and even demand more conversation. Not only will the immigrant have the opportunity to voice more ideas and practice more English, but you will get the chance to know that person better and to assess how much English he or she can speak and understand.

4. *Ask a series of short questions to keep the conversation going.* You may have noticed that some immigrants will answer a question and

then be silent, while many native-born or highly assimilated people will continue to talk as a way of showing how bright and enthusiastic they are. Whether the immigrant is falling silent out of respect for authority or because of a fear of speaking English, you can remedy the situation by asking a series of questions. Structure these questions so that they demand more than a one-word answer and you will facilitate a more successful two-way exchange.

5. *Do not laugh at a speaker's English, even if he or she does.* Sometimes when people laugh at themselves, we get the impression that it is all right for us to laugh as well. In the case of immigrants or international visitors who are struggling to speak English and making the occasional error in pronunciation or usage, it is best to assume that they would not appreciate even your good-natured laughter. Language facility is a very personal matter; it is one thing for a speaker to laugh at himself or herself, and quite another when someone else does, especially if that person is in a superior position.

6. *Positively reinforce good communication.* Excessive praise is *not* a universal motivator of behavior. Nevertheless, it is important to notice when someone is trying to speak English and to praise that effort quietly without calling undo attention to the individual.

Summary

It has been a long time since the days when the Founding Fathers wondered how to cope with a relatively small influx of German-speaking immigrants. Language diversity has come to be one of the greatest challenges facing the business professional today. Yet having workers who speak more than one language is a significant asset in our shrinking world as is the opportunity to do business with large numbers of culturally diverse vendors and clients. The information in this chapter, which is summarized below, will help business professionals minimize the frustrations of language and accent barriers and maximize the potential of a rich and diverse business environment.

- Understand the immigrant's perspective.
- Do not jump to conclusions about what undeveloped English-language facility means.
- Speak slowly, distinctly, simply, and concretely.
- Use familiar words and avoid jargon, slang, and idioms.

- Allow pauses, do not talk too much, and be organized.
- Use the written word.
- Utilize group leaders.
- Recap and check for understanding frequently.
- Avoid embarrassing the speaker when assessing understanding.
- Be cautious when using translators or interpreters.
- Share responsibility for mutual communication.
- Learn a few words of their language.
- Listen carefully.
- EXPECT TO SUCCEED!

Solidifying Your Learning

What are the three most important things you learned from this chapter and how might you apply them in your work?:

1.

2.

3.

The Unspoken Message

How to Decipher Body Language

When the eyes say one thing and the tongue another, a practical man relies on the language of the first.

—*Ralph Waldo Emerson*

What Makes Body Language So Eloquent?

Keep your *nose to the grindstone, shoulder the responsibility,* be *all ears* when the customer speaks, and you will have the boss *wrapped around your little finger.* Don't *look down your nose* at this *handful* of idioms because they serve as an *eye-opener* regarding the role of the body in the communication of images and ideas.

The use of the body, goes, however, far beyond the creation of picturesque imagery into the realm of what has been called *kinesics*—ways in which we use our bodies to send messages and communicate emotions. There are many reasons why it is important to learn as much about cultural differences in body language as about values, verbal language, and etiquette. Here are just a few of these reasons:

1. *Studies show that body language constitutes as much as 50 percent of the entire communication process.* Tone of voice is responsible for about 35 percent and the words themselves a mere 15 percent. The fact that vocabulary is of so little importance should come as an encouraging surprise. It means that you have tools available to you, tone of voice and physical movements, that can be very helpful when communicating with people who do not speak your language.

2. *Body language is more important to people from other cultures than it is to most mainstream Americans.* To native-born Americans, the words alone are considered by far the most important; in most other cultures, the way words are said and the gestures, posture, and facial expressions that accompany those words are of greater significance.

3. *The less English a person understands, the more apt he or she is to rely on body language.* When the verbal message is missing, the listener naturally relies on what is available.

4. *Immigrants are likely to become sensitive to body language as they become fatigued or disoriented.* This is because fatigue and confusion interfere with the ability to understand a new language. As a result, the listener relies more and more on how something is said and on the movements that accompany the message. It is when immigrants or international visitors are fatigued that you are in the greatest danger of causing offense or misleading them through an error in body language.

5. *Body language often contradicts the words that are being said.* The Asian, for example, who says "yes" while lowering the eyes possibly means "no," but is reluctant to disrupt the harmony of the relationship by saying so.

6. *Body language reflects emotions; words present facts.* In mainstream American culture, the folded arms of resolve, the grimace of pain or anger, the hand wringing of anxiety are all powerful communicators of emotions. Think about how much more convinced you are, for example, that a group of children are excited when they jump up and down than if they simply state, "We are very excited."

7. *We are often consciously unaware of body language.* Subconsciously, however, we react to the blank expression or slouching posture. By studying cultural variations in body language, we can learn to recognize the subtle signs that can improve communication.

8. *Body language gives us clues to cultural style.* Picture a southern European who is gesturing enthusiastically standing beside a more restrained Asian and you will see a clear contrast between an outgoing expressive culture and one which values physical understatement and quiet elegance.

Because this book is about cultural diversity within the United States, the differences in body language will be less dramatic and significant than if you were doing business in another country. Differences, however, do exist and to acknowledge them can tangibly improve your ability to form productive cross-cultural relationships.

How Should You Respond to Differences in Body Language?

What should you do when meeting someone who obviously has a different body language vocabulary? Do you make an effort to "speak the same language"—that is, to match his or her movements and ideas about space, touching, eye contact, and gestures, or do you simply notice what is going on and avoid doing anything that might offend? The answer to this question depends on your relationship to the other party and on how his or her body language differs from yours.

If, for example, the body language in question is more outgoing and expressive than yours, the best general rule is not to attempt to match it. If you are speaking with someone who stands closely and touches your arm during conversation, it would be unwise to try to match this behavior. Instead, observe the behavior, do not back away or rebuff the touch, and be reassured that this closeness does not imply an inappropriate relationship and is merely a way of showing his or her desire to communicate. If you back up, it can be insulting. Your ability to hold your ground will be a kindness that shows that you are confident and culturally aware.

On the other hand, when the other person stands further away than you ordinarily might and is more restrained with his or her touch, it is important that you honor this difference by modifying your behavior accordingly. The reason for this distinction is obvious; if you should err in the direction of too much intimacy, it is far more damaging than if you were to appear to be a bit withdrawn and reserved. The only exception to this rule, as we shall discuss shortly, is when you are talking with someone who seems uncomfortable with direct eye contact.

With respect to gestures, obviously you would avoid the use of any hand movements that are offensive or misleading. On the other hand, using gestures that communicate specifics, such as the finger wag of "no" in Mexican culture, can be a sign of respect for the other culture. We will be looking at several examples of each of these types of gestures in the following pages.

How Close Is Too Close?

Someone once said, "Whoever controls the space, controls the situation." The space we maintain around our bodies reflects a desire to control who gets close to us and under what circumstances. Ideas about appropriate distance vary from culture to culture and reflect the style and tone of the society at large. Table 3–1 will give you an idea of these variations. Although these guidelines are helpful, they are just that— guidelines. They cannot be applied to all relationships or circumstances, even within one cultural group. Middle Easterners of the same sex, for example, are likely to stand quite close to each other but to frown on public displays of affection between men and women.

Mainstream-American ideas of proper distance fall somewhere in the middle of those held by most cultures. The spread between 18 inches and 3 feet takes into consideration the nature of the relationship with the other person, from an intimate friendship between people of the opposite sex to a professional association.

With strangers, Americans tend to keep their distance. We leave, for example, one seat between us and the next person in the doctor's reception room, airport waiting area, or bus. On elevators, we become extremely uncomfortable if it is crowded and will not even enter if we have to stand "too close" to others. What we do not realize is that for

TABLE 3-1
Physical Distance

Under 18 Inches
Middle Easterners (with same sex only), Mediterraneans, and some Hispanic cultures

18 Inches to 3 Feet
Mainstream Americans and western Europeans

3 Feet or More
Asians (Japanese at arms length), many African cultures, Middle Eastern men with women (they will tend to stand sideways to women)

those cultures in which physical proximity is more comfortable, it can be considered an insult to sit a few feet away or to avoid this contact.

Few other areas of body language are more sensitive and, fortunately, easier to respect than ideas of how much space should be kept between parties in a conversation. There are, however, some circumstances under which notions of space are particularly important. These are the occasions when workers, colleagues, or clients are in danger of feeling emotionally or even physically threatened if their physical space is invaded, such as when a client is undergoing the stress of a difficult negotiation or when a customer is upset and angry about something.

Still more delicate are those times when a manager or employer is interviewing an applicant, must discipline a worker, or is conducting a performance review. Under those circumstances, it is especially important not to stand too close and to avoid standing over the worker, which can make the employee feel threatened and defensive. Workers who feel defensive naturally become nervous, have difficulty expressing themselves, and can even have trouble hearing what it is you have to say. This defensiveness is also apt to render them resistant to your suggestions and criticism. This same resistance can apply to customers, clients, and other business contacts.

When Is a Touch Appropriate?

As a general rule, touch should be minimized when doing business across cultural lines. Although some cultures are more liberal in their attitudes toward touching than others, even the most tactile groups have strict rules of propriety and etiquette. To touch at the wrong time can risk serious misunderstandings.

You will not be surprised to discover that the guidelines for distance already discussed apply to touch as well. In mainstream American culture, touching is, as a general rule, discouraged; native-born Americans tend to give up touching at an early age and substitute words as the primary means of communication. Northern Europeans, such as the Germans, Scandinavians, and British, too, are generally uncomfortable with touch from anyone other than intimate family members or friends.

Asians share a similar feeling and especially prefer not to be touched on the back, head, and shoulder. This applies particularly to small children. Frontline employees and sales professionals need, for instance, to resist the urge to tousle the hair of Asian or Southeast Asian children or to touch them on the shoulder. It is also inappropriate to put one's arm on the back of a chair in which an Asian is sitting or to pat a Korean on the back. On the other hand, to toss an object to a Filipino rather than hand it directly can be offensive in that it implies you might have some reluctance about touching him or her.

TIP: You may notice that Filipino females are very warm and tactile toward each other; holding hands while walking is not unusual. Do not let this display of comradeship confuse the issue; such signs of affection are confined to particular relationships and do not indicate a general receptivity to indiscriminate touching.

The British and Israelis have similar restrictions about touching. Those of you who have difficulty understanding the importance of this restraint might try imagining how you would feel if a stranger spontaneously put his or her arms around you; the sense of intrusion and impropriety is the same as that felt by the immigrant or international visitor.

Notions of appropriate touching are somewhat less clear cut in Hispanic and Middle Eastern cultures. As a general rule, these groups are comfortable with physical closeness; Mexican males, for example, are likely to stand close to a male colleague while speaking and to hold him by the lapel, shoulder, or forearm; this gesture is, as we saw in question 19 in the quiz, a sign of good communication. Similar behavior is found among Middle Eastern men although, if they are Muslims, care would be taken not to touch with the left, or "toilet," hand.

The situation changes, however, when the parties are of different sexes. Touching across gender lines should be strictly avoided in professional situations. A female who even casually puts her arm around the shoulder of an immigrant male is risking loss of respect and an embarrassing misunderstanding. Since so much is at risk if an error is made, the cardinal rule must be to avoid touching unless it is obviously appropriate. I am not suggesting that you need to appear cold and aloof but merely that you find alternative ways of communicating warmth.

What Do Variations in Eye Contact Really Mean?

Exercise 3–1 illustrates a problem that many professionals are facing today and which involves one of the most important aspects of body language, eye contact. Take a look at this situation and see how you would have handled it:

Exercise 3–1. The Windows of the Soul

Roberta holds a position in which she has extensive contact with her company's Asian-born clients and customers. Because of this, she frequently finds herself talking to people who look away during much of the conversation. At times this is very disconcerting and even irritating to her. How should she handle the situation?

a. Ask the client to please look her in the eye during their conversations because it makes it easier for Roberta to communicate.

b. Ignore it.

c. Avoid looking the client in the eye as a way of showing respect.

d. Make a joke about it in an attempt to lighten the situation.

The correct answer here is *b*—ignore the absence of eye contact. What difference does it make whether a client, customer, or worker looks you in the eye? In this day of frequent intercultural contacts, each of us must identify those behaviors that truly interfere with good communication and let the others go.

To ask a person, even an employee whom you are reprimanding, to look you straight in the eye is intrusive, rude, and humiliating. If you recall a time when a parent or teacher said to you, "Look at me when I talk to you," you will understand how offensive this suggestion can be and how incorrect option *a* is.

Alternative *c* is also wrong because to change your usual amount of eye contact just to accommodate the immigrant's behavior can create confusion and misunderstanding. The immigrant or international visitor probably expects you to maintain at least moderate eye contact. In mainstream American culture, eye contact is maintained for about 1 second before looking away. Those who keep eye contact longer than this are considered threatening and those who do not look us in the eye are thought of as uninterested, shy, or dishonest. One second may seem like a surprisingly short time but it actually represents a middle range compared to other cultural groups.

What can happen if you modify your usual habits of eye contact is that the immigrant, who understands the meaning of more direct eye contact in American culture, will assume that you, indeed, are not listening, are shy, or are hiding something. The only exception to this rule is when the person to whom you are speaking is visibly embarrassed about something. As you would with anyone, it is gracious to look briefly away as a means of taking the focus off the individual and relieving the awkward moment.

The final answer, make a joke of it, can be very dangerous. Although lightness and warmth are desirable in most intercultural relationships, jokes and sarcasm do not translate well, either verbally or culturally. Both can all too easily be taken as ridicule.

Table 3–2 lists some of the variations in eye contact that you are most apt to encounter as you do business across cultural lines. It also lists the misunderstandings that can arise because of these differences.

Middle Easterners, Hispanics, and southern Europeans generally maintain very direct eye contact. The exception to this is when Hispanics drop their eyes as a sign of respect. Females from these groups will be less inclined to look you straight in the eye than males. For other groups —East Asians, Southeast Asians, native Americans, East Indians— it is far more appropriate to look away. Cambodians, for example, consider it flirtatious to look at someone of the opposite sex in the eye.

As you can see, these insights throw doubt on some of the most cherished rules of how to read body language during sales calls. The notion, for example, that eyes wander when a delicate subject is brought up or when someone is about to tell a lie may not apply when selling to someone who normally would maintain little eye contact anyway.

> **TIP:** Although Asians prefer to avoid eye contact, it is, paradoxically, considered rude to wear dark glasses around a Korean.

To make things still more complicated, there is more to cultural variations in "eye language" than just the length of time a gaze is held. The Taiwanese tend to regard excessive blinking as rude, and immigrants from Hong Kong definitely frown on winking.

Another complexity has to do with the roles that the two parties play in the conversation. For example, Anglo-Americans and some African-Americans differ on the rhythm of eye contact. Anglo-Americans consider it proper to maintain eye contact when the other party is speaking but to let the eyes wander somewhat when they themselves are talking. For African-Americans, the situation is just the opposite: they maintain eye contact while talking and allow their eyes to wander when the other person begins to speak. Unfortunately, this can make the Anglo

TABLE 3-2
Eye Contact: Some Cultural Variations

Very direct eye contact

Groups: Middle Easterners (especially men), some Hispanic groups, southern Europeans
Misinterpretation: Hostility, aggressiveness, intrusiveness, bossiness
Correct Interpretation: A desire to express an interest, a desire to communicate effectively

Moderate eye contact

Groups: Mainstream Americans, northern Europeans, the British
Misinterpretation: Lack of interest in what is being said
Correct Interpretation: A desire not to appear aggressive or intrusive

Minimal eye contact

Groups: East Asians (Japanese at neck or side of your eyes, Koreans at the shoulder), Southeast Asians, East Indians, Native Americans
Misinterpretation: Lack of interest, lack of intelligence, dishonesty, lack of understanding, fear, shyness
Correct Interpretation: A desire to show respect, a desire to avoid intrusion

feel, mistakenly, that the African-American is aggressive when speaking but uninterested in what the Anglo has to say in return. By learning about and understanding such cultural differences, professionals can easily avoid this sort of misunderstanding and unnecessary tension.

What Can You Tell from a Facial Expression?

The human face can be the most expressive part of the body. Among southern European and Hispanic cultures, an animated expression is considered appropriate and desirable. When speaking with people from these cultures, it is fairly easy to assess, for example, how a client feels about an impending contract or a worker about the prospect of a transfer or promotion.

Asians, on the other hand, tend to be less expressive with their faces. A great deal has been said about the blank expression that many Asians maintain; admittedly, it can be difficult to know how an Asian feels about something. You will be glad to hear, however, that the more time you spend with Asians, the better able you will be to read the subtleties of their expressions. Small changes in the eyes, for example, combined with the context of the conversation can tell you a great deal.

What is important to remember is that the absence of expression is not intended to be manipulative nor does it mean that the listener is uninterested in what you have to say. All it does mean is that he or she has been culturally conditioned to avoid the display of strong emotions that could disrupt the harmony and balance of the situation while calling undue attention to oneself.

Is the Meaning of a Smile Universal?

Is smiling a universal way of communicating goodwill and cheerfulness? Probably. However, ideas about the importance of a smile and the fine points of when to smile do vary from culture to culture. Mainstream Americans, for example, generally smile freely. To them it represents goodwill and is a safe way of communicating friendliness and optimism. The Hispanic, too, places great importance on a smile. To many Soviet immigrants, on the other hand, a smile, especially if proffered by an authority figure, can signal a frivolity and lightness that is inappropriate to the situation. For Middle Easterners, a smile might be used to placate a colleague and avoid conflict. In France, to smile at someone on the street is considered an inappropriate intrusion or invitation.

For many Asians, a smile often covers up discomfort, embarrassment, or anger. We have seen, for example, that the Asian who does not understand what is being said might smile or laugh to conceal embarrassment. You will notice, too, that Asian immigrants and visitors will smile or giggle when granted a large concession or favor—for them, the balance of the relationship has been disrupted and this causes discomfort. The Korean proverb, "The man who smiles a lot is not a real man," illustrates the attitude Korean culture holds concerning the significance of a smile. The presence of a smile is not automatically a good thing nor is the absence of one an indication of bad feelings or emotional distance.

This is not to say that American-born professionals should in any way minimize their own culturally conditioned reliance on a smile. It merely means that we need to become aware that a smile does not carry a universal meaning.

How Do You "Read" a Handshake?

Body language helps us communicate, but it also allows the professional to read the personality, attitude, and intentions of a prospect or worker. The brusk handshake of the German leaves us with an assumption of sternness and commitment while the gentle grasp of most Asians can make us feel that they are weak or indecisive.

These impressions are, of course, likely to be incorrect. What we experience on these occasions is not the reflection of personality or character, but merely an indication of what that individual, and his or her culture, considers to be a proper handshake. Thus, the firm handshake that has always been a hallmark of a good sales or customer-service representative does not always "translate" across cultural lines. Table 3–3 shows how various cultures differ in their idea of a proper handshake.

Professionals must take care not to project their own idea of a good handshake onto others. The character or personality of the prospect, colleague, customer, or worker whose handshake is either firmer or gentler than the American norm should not be judged by his or her grasp.

In the case of handshakes, it is a good idea to match the style of the other person. Relax your usually firm grip when shaking the hand of an Asian. Adapt to the tighter grasp of the German. These adjustments can make both parties more comfortable and can guarantee a good first impression.

There is, however, more to the art of shaking hands than just the firmness of the grasp. Who do you shake hands with, when, and how often? Although table 3–3 contains some of this information, several key points need to be emphasized.

1. *Follow the lead of those around you.* When working with immigrants or international visitors, observe their handshaking habits: Do they shake hands with everyone in the room? Do they shake on arrival and departure? Do they pump your hand or simply shake it once? Follow their lead and it is unlikely that you will make any grievous errors.

2. *With women who have been in this country a short time, it is sometimes better not to extend your hand until they do.* Shake hands with the men and elders first and then see what happens. Obviously, this rule varies a great deal and depends upon how traditional the company or family is, how assimilated the individual is into mainstream American culture, and what the woman's position is in her community. As we will see in Chapter 6, many immigrant women are very strong and accomplished in the professions and would frown on being ignored. The best way around this is to watch what others do and wait to see if the woman extends her hand.

3. *Shake hands with and pay attention to the children.* This especially applies when working with families in a customer-service situation or during a sales call to the home.

TABLE 3-3

The Nature of a Handshake

Americans: Firm
Germans: Brusk, firm, repeated upon arrival and departure
French: Light, quick, not offered to superiors, repeated upon arrival and departure
British: Soft
Hispanics: Moderate grasp, repeated frequently
Middle Easterners: Gentle, repeated frequently
Asians: Gentle; for some, shaking hands is unfamiliar and uncomfortable (an exception to this is the Korean whose handshake is firmer than that of most other Asians)

This simple gesture communicates respect for the entire family and for the culture. Remember, children are often influential in making purchasing decisions and in establishing whether you are trusted and liked.

How Do You "Talk" with Your Hands?

Hand gestures are often the first thing that comes to mind when body language is mentioned. This is understandable as the signals we make with our hands can have a substantial impact on the success of nonverbal communication. The reason for this is that hand gestures serve three functions:

1. They represent and depict the style of a culture.
2. They communicate specific information.
3. They are used to express strong positive and negative emotions.

Because gestures serve these functions they can also create dangerous misunderstandings and bad feeling. For this reason, professionals tend to get very self-conscious about their hands and have been heard to say, "I sometimes feel that I have to sit on my hands to avoid offending someone." This section will help you overcome some of this fear by showing the meaning of those gestures you are most apt to encounter.

Amount of Gesturing

As with eye contact, distance, or touch, mainstream Americans generally make moderate use of hand gestures. We are prone to thinking that people who raise their elbows above their shoulders are too excitable and those who keep their elbows close to the side are too controlled.

Immigrants from Mexico, Italy, France, and Greece tend to gesture the most. The French, when in social situations, will express themselves with their hands, arms, and upper torso. When it comes to business encounters, however, most will be somewhat more restrained. In the United States, on the other hand, expressive movements are confined to the head and neck. Asian groups take this restraint one step further and keep the arms close to their sides.

Gestures, like so many of the other behaviors we have seen, reflect the style of the culture. The northern European who gestures little will also be more restrained about touching, more likely to be comfortable standing at a greater distance, and less inclined to plunge into crowds or sit next to someone in a crowded theatre.

There is, as with every other aspect of culture, a danger in misinterpreting the significance of the amount of gesturing. We might, for example, mistakenly assume that the more restrained person is cold or uncreative and that the elaborate movements of the southern European mean that the individual is hysterical, upset, or out of control. Just as in the case of the misinterpretations that accompany cultural variations in handshakes and eye contact, these conclusions are likely to be incorrect.

Pointing

Pointing is considered, if not insulting, at least as poor etiquette in most cultures throughout the world, including the United States. In Asian cultures, proscriptions against pointing are very strong. To point at an Asian with an index finger is considered both offensive and intrusive. Some Asian groups even consider it poor taste to point at an object.

In some cultures, pointing is considered so sensitive an issue that there are rules about how to point. In Thailand, China, and much of the rest of Asia, any necessary pointing is generally done with the entire hand, whereas, in Malaysia, it is proper to point with the thumb.

Because there are a lot of inconsistencies between cultures, the best thing to do is to follow the advice of your own upbringing and avoid pointing altogether. Why take a chance of offending someone when this simple restraint can easily solve the problem?

Beckoning

Mainstream Americans beckon to others with upturned fingers, palm facing the body—a gesture that is deeply offensive to Mexicans, Filipinos, and Vietnamese. In the Philippines, for example, this is the way to beckon to animals, underlings, and prostitutes. To understand how offensive this gesture can be, you might remember what it feels like to be called with a crooked index finger; it can be very humiliating and infuriating. This same feeling would be experienced by the next Asian customer in a line or the Filipino in a waiting room who is beckoned to with upturned fingers.

A more appropriate way to beckon, not only to Asians, but to Hispanics as well, is with the palm facing toward the ground and the fingers moving—a gesture that resembles the way Americans wave goodbye. The Middle Easterner will prefer the right hand out, palm facing up, and an open and closing movement.

Signs of Approval

Ironically, the American gestures of approval—the "OK" sign, the "hitchhiker's thumb" gesture, and the "V" for victory are among the most offensive to other cultures. All three have strong sexual connotations, as does our "thumbs-up" gesture. The "V" sign is particularly offensive if executed with the palm facing in. Even Winston Churchill used to make this mistake during World War II, no doubt, to the consternation of his aids and cabinet ministers.

To the Japanese, the "OK" sign means money. Ironically, the "thumbs-up" sign, which has since come to be considered obscene among many cultures, originated from the Roman signal to spare a beaten gladiator. For immigrants as diverse as Soviets and Hispanics and dozens in between, to use any of these gestures is to risk causing considerable embarrassment.

Although most immigrants and international visitors realize that you do not mean to be offensive when using these gestures, they still have a conditioned response to react with feelings of embarrassment and even anger. This is similar to the feeling you might experience if someone inadvertently extended his or her middle finger in your direction. Even if you realized it was done in error, you would at least feel a bit uncomfortable. You can easily avoid any difficulty by eliminating these gestures from your vocabulary of body language.

The Left Hand

Gesturing or handing something with the left hand is offensive to many Muslims, who regard this hand as the "toilet hand." You do not need to become excessively self-conscious about the use of this hand but do bear this restriction in mind when working with Muslim businesspersons and employees.

Professionals are prone to feeling especially self-conscious about the danger of making an offensive gesture. Although there is some reason for this fear, we can all take comfort from the fact that if an inappropriate hand signal is genuinely accidental or is made out of ignorance of cultural

> **TIP:** Placing the index finger to the lips and making a "shh" sound to signal silence is also considered obscene by many Middle Easterners and is amusing to the Korean who uses this technique to encourage the performance of small children on the toilet.

differences, it is likely that the immigrant or international visitor will realize this and not take offense.

Do I Have to Worry about My Legs and Feet Too?

American culture does not have much to say about the proper positioning of the legs and feet. About all that is ever mentioned is that it is inappropriate, particularly for women, to sprawl in a chair with one's knees open or feet on a desk. By contrast, other cultures have fairly stringent rules about the movement and placement of the legs and feet.

Most Asians and Middle Easterners, for example, regard crossing the legs as in poor taste. One of the reasons for this is that when the legs are crossed, the bottom of the foot is showing and the toe is pointing at someone—both of which are considered rude and offensive. Similarly, Iranians feel it is inappropriate to stretch the legs out in front of you. A Soviet variation on this restriction is that it is rude to place the ankle on the knee.

When doing business with persons from these countries, a safe rule is to maintain good posture and avoid too informal a pose. I would not, however, become self-conscious about the specifics of these rules when dealing with immigrants who are now residents of the United States and who have obviously made considerable adjustments to mainstream American culture.

Why Is Posture So Important?

Most of us have been taught to stand up straight and carry ourselves properly in formal or business situations. In many parts of the country, however, there is a tendency for many native-born Americans to be more casual in demeanor than their immigrant and international counterparts.

When doing business with immigrant professionals, I would suggest you make an effort to stand erect, avoid putting your hands in your pockets, or sprawling in a chair. Be careful, also, not to stretch or yawn or chew gum in public. Groups ranging from the Swedes to the Koreans will regard this behavior as a sign of inattentiveness and lack of interest. It also signals to them that you are apt to be as sloppy in your work as you are in your demeanor.

As a general rule, be formal in your body language. Do not lean up against a wall or back in your chair and be certain to stand when immigrant or international colleagues enter the room—an example of body language that communicates both respect and welcome.

When Is a "Yes" Not a "Yes"?

We have already seen that under certain circumstances it can be very difficult to tell whether an immigrant is responding with a "yes" or "no" to a question. One way to clear up this confusion is to rely on hand gestures. Mexican and Middle Eastern immigrants, for example, might indicate "no" with a back-and-forth movement of the index finger. Someone from Japan is likely to wave the entire hand in front of the face to indicate the negative. In Europe, a variation of our "waving goodbye" gesture can mean "no."

Movements of the head are the most common ways of communicating the positive and negative. In the United States and much of the Western world, a nod indicates "yes" and a shaking motion "no." Charles Darwin went so far as to explain these movements by saying that the nod originates when an infant moves the head down to accept food or breast milk. The shaking of the head, he reasoned, is the baby's effort to shove the food or breast aside.

The problem with Darwin's theory is that not all cultures have the same body language for "yes" and "no." In parts of the Middle East, India, and Pakistan, for example, the head is shaken to indicate "yes" and nodded for "no." In the Philippines, the head is often moved downward to indicate the negative—a movement readily misinterpreted by Western-ers as a positive nod. Alternatively, the head and brows will be raised for "yes." In the Middle East, too, sometimes the chin is held up slightly and a clicking sound made for "no," again a movement that could be misinterpreted in America as "yes." Most confusing of all is the figure eight of the head in East India to indicate "I am listening," "I understand."

Do not, however, let this potential for confusion disturb you too much. Those who have been in this country for some time or who are attempting to do business here are likely to adapt the more familiar American nod and shake of the head.

Summary

Body language can communicate more than words and can do so with extreme efficiency and economy of effort. Physical movements are capable of delivering both positive and negative messages with remarkable eloquence. You probably can recall a time when you reacted far more negatively to an obscene gesture than to a rude comment or far more positively to an unexpected smile than to a pleasant verbal greeting. If used properly and with an awareness of cultural differences and sensitivities, body language can be a very helpful tool in your efforts to communicate across cultural and language barriers. To summarize the key points of this chapter:

- Body language accounts for as much as 50 percent of the communication process.
- Many other cultures put greater weight on the visual accompaniment to a message than on the words themselves.
- When someone is fatigued, confused, or unable to understand the language, sensitivity to body language increases.
- Body language can contradict the words that are being spoken.
- Body language communicates emotions whereas words communicate facts.
- It is not always necessary to match the body language of others, just to be sensitive to it.
- Take cultural variations into consideration when interpreting the meaning of body language.
- Learn about and avoid the use of offensive gestures, but remember that immigrants and international visitors are quick to forgive should you make an error out of ignorance or forgetfulness.
- When in doubt, observe the behavior of others and err in the direction of formality.

Solidifying Your Learning

What are the three most important things you learned from this chapter and how might you apply them in your work?

1.

2.

3.

Values

How to Understand Cultural Differences

Observe a man's choices and you will know what he values in his heart.

— M. Barr

The Nature of Values

Values form the core of a culture. It is from values that the other elements of a culture arise; etiquette, lifestyle, even language are shaped by the values of a society. There would be, for example, no etiquette of calling strangers by their first names if it were not for the value that mainstream American culture places on informality and equality, nor would there be a term such as *self-reliance* if independence were not highly valued in the United States. Values also dictate behaviors and emotions. They tell us what to care about, what to strive for, and how to behave; they range all the way from notions of how to treat a client to what occupation to choose and what principles to fight for.

Some values are consistent among cultures. Few would deny, for example, that the desires for physical comfort and human companionship are universal. Other values are, if not unique to one people, at least ranked differently in its hierarchy of concerns. The value of independence from the family is, for example, highly treasured in the United States but is barely, if at all, appreciated in the Middle East or Asia.

Ideas about the importance of anticipating and controlling the future vary significantly from culture to culture. Whereas, for example, the native-born or assimilated American worker would place a high priority on planning for retirement, accumulating sick days, and purchasing insurance, the immigrant worker might be more concerned with meeting today's obligations and living in the present. These and other value differences can have a profound impact on how diverse workers are managed and on how potential clients and customers are best approached and cultivated.

The Importance of Learning about Values

"What's in it for me?" you are probably asking. Why is it so important to study culturally diverse values, especially if, as we saw in Chapter 1, we cannot be certain that all members of a particular group share the same values? What is there to gain from the effort? The answer is that these differing values can have profound effects on how business is done and on how business people relate to one another. Values have a major impact on how each human being behaves, reacts, and feels and affect our lives in four major and unavoidable ways:

1. **Values dictate felt needs.** Managers cannot accurately assess the needs and expectations of employees without first understanding their culturally specific values. Without this understanding of needs and desires, efforts to motivate productivity and cooperation can be seriously impaired. Similarly, values dictate purchasing decisions that must be understood if we are to market and sell successfully across cultural lines. A brewery can praise to the skies the value of "tasting the high country" to Hispanic consumers whose interest in the glories of the Rockies is minimal at best. How much beer do you suppose they would sell to the Hispanic community with that commercial?

2. **Values dictate what is defined as a problem.** An Asian could be embarrassed if praised in front of others, whereas a mainstream American would consider this a courtesy. An Asian employee might feel good about his or her tendency not to complain when dissatisfied or to ask questions when confused. The American-born manager, on the other hand, may see these behaviors as problems that reflect a lack of openness and an unwillingness to learn.

3. **Values dictate how problems are solved.** A Filipino worker might solve an interpersonal conflict by asking for a transfer to

another department in an effort to avoid the loss of harmony that would result from a direct confrontation. A native-born colleague, on the other hand, could regard this solution as cowardly and evasive, preferring instead to deal, in typical American fashion, with the problem directly.

4. **Values dictate expectations of behavior.** Hispanic business owners expect sales representatives to take time to chat and get to know them as human beings—to learn about their families, concerns, and interests. To behave differently can leave these prospects with an impression of cold aggressiveness that is not conducive to the building of productive, harmonious relationships.

Values must be understood if you are to work effectively with immigrant and ethnic groups. The values discussed in this chapter are central to that understanding. Some of these ideas are so important that many of them turn up throughout the book where their specific applications for sales, customer service, negotiations, and management are discussed.

The Value of Harmony and Balance

The desire for harmony and balance in all social and professional situations is a value held throughout most of the non-Western world. Although based on broad philosophical principles and rooted in both medicine and religion, this notion has specific, and significant, applications for the development of effective cross-cultural business relationships. Cultures that place great importance on harmony and balance maintain these values in three primary ways:

1. By avoiding direct or negative confrontations
2. By minimizing embarrassment to all participants in an interaction; that is, by saving face for all concerned
3. By not calling attention to the individual at the expense of the group

With a little practice, each of these can be recognized and understood so as to facilitate communication and minimize misunderstandings.

The Importance of Avoiding Confrontations

The value placed on avoiding negative confrontations is quite alien to mainstream American thinking. Expressed in Filipino culture by the term *pakikisama* ("smooth human relationships"), the desire to soften directly negative statements is common to many cultures throughout the world. This value is difficult for most Americans to grasp because we respect "telling it like it is."

Numerous American phrases, idioms, and proverbs reflect this desire for truth at all costs. Exercise 4–1 will help you become more aware of how much this perspective permeates American society. See how many

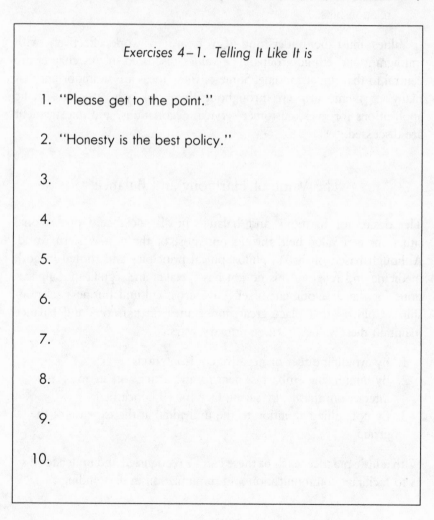

Exercises 4–1. Telling It Like It is

1. "Please get to the point."

2. "Honesty is the best policy."

3.

4.

5.

6.

7.

8.

9.

10.

phrases or proverbs you can think of that express this value. The list has been primed with two examples to get you started.

I could trace for pages the historical roots of this "tell it like it is," "straight talk" mentality, but our concern here is not so much the why of it, but the how: how can professionals deal with the often crippling confusion that results when two diametrically opposed values come into contact? The following dialogue between Harry, the purchasing agent for a large financial institution, and Arturo, the owner of the print shop that supplies much of the company's stationery, illustrates the kinds of problems that can arise.

Dialogue	*Speaker's Thoughts*
Harry: Arturo, will those new brochures be here by next Monday?	*Harry:* (They'd better be. We need to mail them on Tuesday.)[a]
Arturo: Don't worry, they'll be ready in plenty of time.[b]	*Arturo:* (Monday is cutting it a little close, I hope we make it.)[c]

(Monday comes and the brochures have still not arrived.)

Harry: What happened? You said the brochures would be delivered today.[d]	*Harry:* (Arturo is an unreliable vendor. He either lied to me or does not know how to judge time.)[e]
Arturo: (looking away) I'm sorry. We did the best we could.[f]	*Arturo:* (Why is he so angry? He knows we are good printers. Besides, I was only trying to spare Harry worry.)[g]
	Harry: (Arturo is so unreliable— you know how these Mexicans are about deadlines. I realize now, too, that he is dishonest. I can tell because he looks away when I talk to him.)[h]

What went wrong? Let us examine each element individually to see the misunderstandings illustrated here and how they might have been avoided:

Element a: Precise scheduling is of great importance in the United States but very much less so in Hispanic countries. We will look at the issue of time and punctuality again in the discussion of cultural variations in etiquette.

Elements b and c: These elements reflect Arturo's concern that the job may not be completed on time, but also his worry that if he states his doubts directly to the client, negative feelings and conflict might be created. This attitude would be amplified, among Hispanics as well as among Asians, to the extent that the client, colleague, or boss is regarded as an authority figure or superior. In that case, to say something negative is to defy that authority and to communicate disrespect. Thus, the Asian or Hispanic employee may hesitate to bring bad news to the boss or to admit that a task cannot be completed by a certain time. Again, this behavior arises not out of dishonesty, but out of desire to avoid a negative confrontation. Shakespeare might have agreed with Arturo when he said, "Though it be honest, it is never good to bring bad news."

American culture is not, by the way, devoid of behaviors designed to avoid confrontation. "Let's have lunch," "See you later," and "I'll try to make it to the party" are frequently nothing more than polite ways of ending a conversation when a speaker has no real intention of seeing the other person again. Statements like these are not considered lies, only gracious evasions. We are likely to comment on a poor "nice dinner" or even to say, "Don't call us, we'll call you," without considering ourselves guilty of any real dishonesty.

Elements d and e: Since Harry is unaware of the Hispanic preference to avoid directly negative statements, he draws the only conclusion he can: Arturo is either deliberately lying or is a poor businessman.

Element f: Arturo's first instinct is to look away from Harry in order to communicate respect and regret that the job was not competed on time. He does not, however, launch into a litany of apology, for that would serve only to heighten the confrontation and disrupt the balance by calling attention to himself.

Element g: Arturo's thoughts illustrate the importance of mutual cultural understanding between professionals of different cultures. If Arturo had known how important it was to inform Harry of the time problem, he would probably have realized that he was not helping his customer by keeping the difficulty from him. Harry certainly would have preferred to know that the brochures might be delayed so that he could adjust his own schedule. Also, if Harry had understood Arturo's perspective, he might have been less angry and more able to resolve the situation constructively.

Element h: In mainstream American culture, lack of eye contact is considered a sign of dishonesty, not respect. Harry assumes, particularly because Arturo does not defend himself, that he is indeed dishonest.

This dialogue reflects only one aspect of the desire to avoid direct confrontations: the hesitance to tell others, especially authority figures, of bad news. Other manifestations of this same value include the Asian practice of saying "no" in an indirect fashion and the reluctance of some immigrant and ethnic workers to complain about problems in the workplace.

This latter behavior may seem like a blessing. Perhaps you are thinking how lovely it would be if employees stopped complaining about poor relationships, inadequate equipment, or undesirable working conditions. The problem with this fantasy is that if owners and managers are not informed of difficulties in the workplace, there is no way that they can be resolved.

Asians in particular are likely to state complaints in such discrete terms that they become almost unrecognizable. The classic joke concerning this behavior involves the Japanese gentleman whose foot is being

---

Exercise 4–2. Solving a Workplace Dilemma

A usually outgoing and cheerful Filipino worker has recently become rather withdrawn and quiet on the job. You have heard rumors that she is upset because another worker has been hostile toward her, but she refuses to complain or even talk about the incident. How would you handle the situation?

a. I would assume that the worker has a personal reason for keeping the problem to herself and would not intrude. Eventually she will work it out or get over it.
b. I would tell the employee that she is overreacting.
c. I would ask fellow workers what the trouble might be.
d. I would gently explain to the employee that in order for me to do a good job, I need her to keep me informed of any difficulties.

stepped on by an American. Rather than abruptly ask the American to move, the Japanese man genteelly comments, "My foot is under yours." This approach to the problem is very different from that found in mainstream American culture, where speaking up for one's self is a virtue.

The dilemma depicted in exercise 4–2 explores some possible solutions to the difficulties created when a worker refuses to complain about a problem in the workplace. In Chapter 6 we will look at this issue again as it pertains to customers and clients who hesitate to let you know that there is a problem with a product or service. This case study is followed by a choice of possible responses to the dilemma. Choose the response you think best.

Let's take a moment to evaluate each of these options and see how you did:

a. Of course it is possible that the employee has personal reasons for keeping the problem a secret. Because of her cultural background, however, it is safer to assume that the Filipino value of not complaining to superiors is at play here. This wait-and-see attitude could cost you an opportunity to build a better, more open relationship with this woman.

b. This approach might work as a last resort with a native-born American who values a direct approach, but for most immigrant workers, this attitude would be taken as patronizing, insulting, and even cruel.

c. This might be a solution, but be careful not to betray any confidences. Hispanics and Asians in particular value discretion and would not wish for other employees to know of their difficulty. This is one reason that they generally prefer resolving conflicts in private.

d. **Good answer!** As we shall see shortly, many foreign-born and ethnic workers place great importance on preserving the dignity and meeting the needs of those around them. This approach calls on this value by inviting the worker to help you do a better job. In short, you are finding the correct fit between the worker's values and your own needs.

Throughout the book, you will encounter other examples of this desire to avoid direct confrontation. Please bear in mind that although this behavior can seem bewildering and frustrating, it usually arises out of a gracious desire to cultivate and sustain harmonious relationships.

The Value of Saving Face

The Chinese have a proverb: "If you disregard the question of face, life is pointless." This lies at the heart of the desire to maintain harmony and balance, the notion that no one in a relationship or situation should suffer embarrassment. It is this concern about the other person that is misunderstood within those cultures for which saving face is not a primary value. A Middle Eastern businessperson, for example, who is forced to grant a major concession in front of others will suffer a depth of humiliation that is difficult for most native-born Westerners to grasp. On the other hand, that same businessperson will be careful not to humiliate you in front of others by asking why you could not deliver on a promise.

If the doctrine of saving face is ignored, it can have a very immediate and destructive impact on those involved. A Korean who is passed over for promotion in favor of a younger countryman will suffer loss of *kibun* ("face") and is likely to quit rather than endure what is experienced as profound embarrassment. The Filipino worker may suffer what is known as *hiya* ("shame") should a suggestion for improvement be offered insensitively and, therefore, taken as an insult. Similarly, to criticize an Hispanic businessperson in front of others, even if it is done genteelly, is apt to do substantial damage to your working relationship. Again, however, the Hispanic would never embarrass you by saying something critical while others are within earshot.

Americans place nowhere near the emphasis on saving face as do the Asian, Middle Eastern, and Hispanic cultures. Native-born Americans are more prepared to "put themselves on the line"—to risk embarrassment—especially if the result of such a risk is perceived of as worthwhile.

The desire to save face is manifested in several behaviors and attitudes, each of which can have a profound impact on the success of personal and professional relationships and each of which reflects a different concern. Table 4–1 provides a sampling of these behaviors and the central fears associated with each.

The following situations will help you discover how to interpret several of these attitudes and behaviors. Each situation is an example of how the value of saving face can be seen in the multicultural business world and workplace, and each is followed by a selection of possible interventions. Identify the response you feel is best while remembering that there may be more than one correct answer to each dilemma. Evaluations of the options follow each example.

Situation 1—The Agreement: When a potential client who has emigrated from Mexico fails to ask questions regarding a sales agreement, contract, or other professional document, I:

a. Assume he or she understands the information and proceed on that basis
b. Am careful to repeat the material because I realize the client may not understand but is reluctant to say so because of fear of embarrassment
c. Recognize that the client may not understand but feel it is his or her responsibility to speak up and ask questions
d. Invite the client to contact me in the future if any questions do arise

TABLE 4-1
Face-Saving Behaviors

Behavior	Concern or Fear
A tendency to avoid stating a definite refusal although that is the intended meaning and a dislike for being refused directly	Causing the self or other party to feel at a disadvantage and therefore to experience loss of face
A reluctance to admit lack of understanding or to ask questions	Appearing ignorant and insulting the speaker
A sensitivity to being criticized, or criticizing, in the presence of other people	Being embarrassed or causing embarrassment
A reluctance to take the initiative on tasks or to perform a task in a new way	Doing the task wrong and appearing foolish or losing one's job
A tendency to avoid asking for promotions or other boons which might be refused	Humiliation if turned down along with putting the giver in an awkward position
A discomfort with being given a major concession, granted a large favor, or being complimented in front of others	Imbalance in the give and take between the parties
A reluctance to complain about a product or service	Causing the other party to feel as if he or she has failed

Evaluating the Options

a. You could, of course, be correct in this assumption; on the other hand, you could be wrong. What is at risk, for you and for the client, is the mutual understanding necessary for a successful, and smoothly operating, business arrangement.

b. **This is a good answer.** What is there to lose except maybe a few moments? Admittedly it can be irritating when a client, customer, or worker does not admit a lack of understanding, but it is important to realize that American culture values inquisitiveness; students are taught to ask questions at an early age. In many other cultures, on the other hand, asking questions is considered not only embarrassing but also rude and disrespectful in that it implies that the speaker has not explained himself or herself very well.

c. This answer may conform to the American emphasis on personal responsibility, but a hardnosed attitude like this will only be counterproductive for all concerned.

d. **This is an excellent answer.** By inviting the client to contact you later, you are giving him or her the time in which to contemplate what you have said, translate it into his or her native language if necessary, and then formulate an appropriate question. This technique also allows the client to ask the question in private where the nonnative English speaker will feel more comfortable.

Situation 2—Taking the Initiative: When a foreign-born employee fails to take the initiative on a task, I usually:

- a. Assume that he or she is lacking in self-esteem and recommend counseling
- b. Say that he or she will be penalized if it happens again
- c. Explain to the employee that taking the initiative is valued in the American corporation and that it is all right to learn from one's mistakes
- d. Enter into a pact with the employee that if he or she makes an error when taking the initiative, I promise not to get angry but to praise him or her for being willing to take a chance

Evaluating the Options

a. This is possible but unlikely. Probably the employee is a well-adjusted person who is acting the way his or her culture dictates.

b. Although many foreign-born workers are accustomed to an authoritarian boss, penalizing a behavior rooted in cultural misunderstanding will be unproductive.

c. **Good answer!** As we will see in Chapter 7, providing information about American culture is an important but often overlooked first step to successful cross-cultural management.

d. **This is another good answer.** It directly addresses cultural differences and includes both the manager and the worker in the solution.

Situation 3—Keeping the Balance: When an Asian-born colleague or worker does something particularly impressive or generous, I:

a. Make an effort to restrain my compliments as I recognize that positive judgments, if overstated, can be as embarrassing as negative ones

b. Take care to reward the achievement lavishly as I know that to do so conforms to the value which many Asians place on graciousness and generosity

c. Avoid saying anything at the time but wait and issue a lavish reward at a later date

Evaluating the Options

a. **Right the first time!** The issuing of lavish praise and gifts, especially if bestowed in front of others, is one way in which loss of face can happen. This may come as a surprise because we tend to think of embarrassment as being caused only by negative attention. One problem here is that the individual upon whom you are lavishing public attention has been put in the uncomfortable position of having received more than you and, therefore, of being in your debt. There is also the danger that your elaborate compliment will imply that you are surprised at the achievement.

Should you need to express praise or appreciation, do so as discretely as possible. You might, for example, put a memo in a good worker's file, quietly thank the person in private, or simply make a note to return the favor at a later time.

b. For the reasons that we have just explained, this is an incorrect answer. Perhaps this point will be clearer if you try to recall a time when

---

TIP: A clue that you have overdone it with an Asian is if he or she avoids eye contact with you, laughs or giggles, or vigorously denies the achievement.

---

someone has given you a generous gift on an occasion when you have come empty-handed. Rather than feeling good about what you received, you no doubt experienced grave feelings of embarrassment or loss of face.

c. The basic idea of waiting is not a bad one. Quietly rewarding the achievement or favor later with a note, returned favor, or small gift is an elegant and graceful way to handle this.

We all want dignity. Each culture achieves this in a different way. For the native-born American or those who have been assimilated into the culture, this need may be met through hard work, independence, patriotism, or the achievement of financial security. For many other cultures, dignity lies in the preservation of what the Greeks call *philotimo* ("self respect," "honor") or, what the Filipinos term *amor propio*—a phrase meaning "self worth." Preserving the *amor propio* of staff, colleagues, and clients is one of the most important steps that any professional can take toward effective cross-cultural communication and business dealings.

Not Calling Attention to the Individual

The Japanese proverb, "The nail that sticks out gets hammered down," illustrates another manifestation of the desire for harmony and balance. In sharp contrast to the American value of honoring the individual, this perspective holds that every effort must be made to maintain anonymity within a group.

This reluctance to call attention to oneself is manifested in several ways. Health professionals, for example, know that it is commonplace to encounter Asian and native American patients who do not complain of discomfort or even cry out when in pain. One of the primary reasons for this stoicism is the desire not to disrupt the harmony of the situation by calling attention to oneself. Managers and employers have found that some workers are reluctant to praise themselves during interviews for the same reason. Negotiators report working with immigrant professionals who appear to be uncomfortable calling attention to themselves or their product by excessively praising its virtues.

The following dialogue focuses on one of the most common situations in which this desire for anonymity is likely to be encountered—during a job interview.

Woo has come to a large company to interview for a supervisory position for which he is highly qualified and which he wants very much. Krista, the human resource director, is pleased with his application.

Dialogue	Speaker's Thoughts
Krista: Your schooling and work history are very impressive. What else can you tell me about your qualifications for the job?[a]	*Krista:* (This fellow is perfect. I'm eager to hear how he presents himself.)[b]
Woo: Well, I don't know. I'd just like to work for your company.[c]	*Woo:* (Why is she asking me? It's all on the application. I don't want to brag.)[d]
	Krista: (He sure is lacking in confidence. I wonder what that means for his ability to perform. Also, he doesn't seem to want the job very much. His background is so good, though, I'll give him a chance.)[e]

Krista hires Woo. He does such a good job that in six months he is being considered for a higher position. Yet despite his awareness of the new opening, Woo does not apply for the job.

Krista: Why haven't you applied for this higher position?[f]	*Krista:* (He is so unassertive or maybe he's lazy. Doesn't he care? This passive behavior does not fit with Woo's obvious love of his work.)[g]
Woo: I haven't applied because I feel that if the company wanted me for the job, you would offer it to me.[h]	*Woo:* (This is so strange. Don't they know what they want? It's not my place to ask for a higher position. My work speaks for itself.)[i]

Does Woo have an emotional problem? Is he lacking in self-esteem, confidence, and self-interest? Probably not. The following analysis indicates that a behavior that might be interpreted as neurotic in the context of one culture will appear normal when evaluated in the framework of the culture in which the behavior was taught.

Elements a and b: According to American business etiquette, it is desirable to speak up regarding one's achievements and qualifications.

Elements c and d: Woo does not understand why he is being put in the awkward position of having to sing his own praises. In Chinese culture, that is considered offensive and disharmonious. This applies to most other Asian, to native American, and, to a lesser extent, to most Hispanic cultures as well.

TIP: In many countries, jobs are acquired through family loyalty or personal affiliation, not through qualifications. In those cases, the issue of praising oneself doesn't even arise.

This desire not to "show off" is also manifested in the conference or training room where some immigrant and ethnic workers are hesitant to voice innovative ideas out of a concern of appearing arrogant and calling inordinate attention to themselves. Likewise, in social situations, the Asian might resist praising his or her cooking, home, or family. This does not mean that they do not have pride in such things, but merely that it is inappropriate to call attention to them.

Element e: Krista, because of her American background, does not understand Woo's reticence but instinctively knows he is right for the job. This is one of the many cases in which managers and employers of multicultural workers can and should rely on their instincts and experience when making decisions. The same applies to the sales representative, customer service professional, or negotiator. Use your instincts and your experience to look past the external, culturally dictated behaviors that you see before you.

Elements f and g: Krista does not realize that the Western value of always striving for a higher position is not universal. Some foreign-born and ethnic workers do not seek promotions because they feel that the new position will disrupt harmony by calling attention to themselves as individuals. This does not mean that managers should overlook these workers when trying to fill positions but merely that such employees will sometimes need to be sought out and encouraged to apply.

Elements h and i: Woo considers it the responsibility of his superiors to choose him for promotion. His goal, like that of many other immigrant workers, is to work for the good of the company, not for his own benefit. There is another reason why Woo might be hesitant to seek this promotion aggressively: He knows that in doing so he is risking loss of face should he be turned down, a humiliation that might necessitate his resigning in order to redress the balance.

Minimizing one's skills during an interview and not aggressively seeking a promotion reflect the value placed on not calling attention to the individual. Perhaps the most dramatic example of this attitude is seen in parts of Lebanon, where prospective employees sometimes bring along a companion to present the applicant's qualifications. In this way, the applicant does not have to suffer the embarrassment of doing so for himself or herself.

TIP: In other parts of the Middle East, however, self-praise is normal. Be careful not to generalize about immigrants from any region of the world.

The reluctance to call attention to oneself is another way in which the value placed on harmony and balance is manifested. It is found, not only in the area of cross-cultural management, but, as we shall see in Chapter 6, in the realm of customer service, sales, and negotiations as well.

The Value Placed on the Group over the Individual

Closely related to the issue of harmony and balance is the value that many cultures place on the group, company, or family. In 70 percent of cultures throughout the world, the needs of the family, community, and even corporation come before those of any one person. "The hand of God is with the group" is an Arab proverb that illustrates this perspective.

Loyalty in the Hispanic community goes first to God, then to the family, and, finally, to the individual. What is good for the group, it is thought, is good for the individual. In Japan, Americans are frequently surprised to hear a Japanese colleague use the plural when referring to a successfully completed task—"we did it"—even if the accomplishment was an individual effort.

TIP: In the United States, immigrant and ethnic consumers, as well as international visitors, are frequently members of a close-knit group within which word-of-mouth "advertising" is highly developed. Companies should take advantage of this network when promoting their product or service or when seeking to build a reputation as a good place to work.

Giving the priority to the family or the group runs contrary to many mainstream American values and can lead to confusion in the multicultural business world and workplace. The issues summarized in the following pages are perhaps best exemplified by the curious fact that English is the only major language in which the pronoun "I" is capitalized; the individual and his or her needs and achievements are clearly supreme.

Making Mistakes

THE MAINSTREAM AMERICAN PERSPECTIVE. A person's mistakes are important primarily because they make the individual look bad; any shame brought on the group is a secondary consideration.

THE PERSPECTIVE OF OTHER CULTURES. In many cultures, distress over a mistake results from concern for how the error will affect the group, not how it will reflect on the individual. This is most pronounced in Middle Eastern, Hispanic, and Asian groups.

IMPLICATIONS. One of the implications of this difference in priorities is the tendency for some workers to be reluctant to take the initiative on tasks or to voice ideas openly. They want to avoid making an error or saying something that would reflect on the abilities of the group as a whole. On the positive side, concern with the reputation of the group results in hard and conscientious work to ensure that colleagues and superiors evaluate the group favorably.

Similarly, potential clients and customers tend to resist giving out information that might reflect badly on family members or close associates. This reticence might, for example, create problems for the insurance salesperson who would have difficulty uncovering information about past health problems or personal habits. This is not dishonesty, but instead results from the same emotion that might cause you to resist speaking of a parent's severe dependency problem or a spouse's history of mental illness.

Finding One's Identity

THE AMERICAN PERSPECTIVE. A person's identity is determined by individual achievement, not by familial, geographic, or group affiliation.

THE PERSPECTIVE OF OTHER CULTURES. In countries such as Japan and Mexico, social and geographic links are all important. The Japanese term for this, *kankei,* roughly translates as "human relations," the sense of a bonding between people from the same locality or company. One Japanese asks another not "What do you do?" but "Whom do you work for?" In the United States, we ask "What do you do?" with the specific employer being of secondary interest.

IMPLICATIONS. In Mexico, being part of a company is being part of a family. For this reason, firing a person has serious implications and is to be avoided. This fact can create problems for managers and employers of Mexican-born workers in the United States unaccustomed to the sometimes casual way in which work forces are disbanded.

Managers might also notice a tendency for workers not to seek promotions that would separate them from the cultural group that generates their identity. Cases have even been reported in which individuals have been asked to be demoted so as to sustain group solidarity. The importance of the family is reflected in how positively many immigrant workers respond to inquiries about family welfare and to the employer who remembers specific family names and events. Among some Middle Eastern immigrants, you might encounter a reluctance to admit disliking a family member or to having placed an elderly relative in a nursing home; both of which, in Middle Eastern culture, represent disloyalty to the family unit.

Decision Making

THE AMERICAN PERSPECTIVE. In the United States, it is the individual who is responsible for making decisions. Doing so independently is considered a virtue and a sign of maturity and strength.

THE PERSPECTIVE OF OTHER CULTURES. In the Middle East and Asia, it is poor form to make a decision on one's own. Family members, other corporate personnel, and even community leaders are apt to be consulted in what can become a lengthy and complex decision-making process.

IMPLICATIONS. Sales personnel must learn to be patient when doing business with those families and professionals who favor group decision making. Be courteous if you find the entire family in attendance when you are accustomed to dealing only with a couple. Customer-service people also need to be alert to the fact that some immigrants and international visitors shop in large groups. You will find the group process strongest when making the larger purchases—homes, cars, insurance. Impatience or a patronizing attitude on your part is a certain way of alienating the customer and losing out on what might be a mutually beneficial relationship.

Assigning Responsibility

THE AMERICAN PERSPECTIVE. "The buck stops here." Although teamwork is often touted in America, ultimately one person is held responsible for a success or failure.

THE PERSPECTIVE OF OTHER CULTURES. Group responsibility is far more common among other cultures. As we saw in the discussion of the value placed on harmony and balance, it is in poor taste to call attention to the achievements or failures of the individual; it is the group that counts.

IMPLICATIONS. When negotiating with immigrant or international corporations, not having one individual to focus on can be confusing to the individualistic American. Also, group responsibility can prove frustrating for the native-born or assimilated American manager who, when faced with a situation, wants to find one person to blame, consult, or praise. Although the temptation to do so is very strong, to single out an individual for responsibility is likely to make an adversary out of that person and damage one's relations with the entire group.

When it is necessary to criticize the performance of a worker, for example, it is sometimes wiser to criticize the group as a whole than to pick out the one individual responsible. Similarly many immigrant and ethnic workers will respond more favorably to group praise than to the issuing of individual accolades. This is particularly true, as we have seen, of Asian and native American workers, who are uncomfortable having attention drawn to just one person.

The Meaning of Competition

THE AMERICAN PERSPECTIVE. Competition within a group promotes both creativity and productivity.

THE PERSPECTIVE OF OTHER CULTURES. Competition among individual members of a group is disruptive to productivity as well as to harmony. The group should work as a whole and for the whole.

IMPLICATIONS. When supervising culturally diverse workers, managers have tried to increase productivity by encouraging competition. In most cases, this has decreased efficiency and reduced morale. Managers and employers would do better to promote group pride rather than disrupt the group in the name of individual achievement. This is especially true of native American workers, many of whom are critical of the idea of competition. Offering a trip, for example, as an incentive to individuals may not be effective because only one person in the group stands to benefit. This same reluctance to compete is found in the meeting and training room, where voicing one's own ideas or answering questions creatively is considered rude and harmful to group solidarity. This is very different from the mainstream American practice of debating issues vigorously during a gathering only to emerge as friends after the process is completed.

In sales and negotiations, explore the situation carefully before you pit one merchant or businessperson of the same background against another in a competitive situation. In all probability, to do so will only cost you respect within the community.

The Setting of Goals

THE AMERICAN PERSPECTIVE. The goals and desires of the individual are paramount. For the group—whether family or corporation—to interfere with these goals is considered authoritarian and even morally wrong.

THE PERSPECTIVE OF OTHER CULTURES. In most cultures, the goals of the family or company come first. The individual who places his or her desires above the group is selfish and inconsiderate.

TIP: You might be able to remember this concept better if you know that the Japanese term for "individualism" (*kojinshugi*) has very negative and undesirable connotations.

IMPLICATIONS. In assessing the needs of consumers and potential clients, you must remember to stay aware of what will benefit the group as a whole and to put your focus on that. In situations like this we can fall into the trap of projecting our own cultural values onto others and assuming that the individual is most concerned about having his or her needs met. Remember, your prospect or client may have values and needs very different from your own.

If you are a manager or business owner, you may see this point of view reflected in the individual worker's willingness to forgo personal advancement if he or she feels that such a promotion does not fit with the goals of the organization at large. Management must remember that such an attitude by no means connotes low self-esteem or lack of assertiveness but, instead, reflects an honorable concern for the good of your company or business.

Achieving Independence

THE AMERICAN PERSPECTIVE. Independence from the family is desirable. To remain dependent on the family into adulthood is often considered neurotic. Eddie Rickenbacker, an American hero and World War I ace, said that one of the four cornerstones of character in the United States is independence of the individual. It is a sign of effective parenting to have one's children grow up to live largely separate lives.

THE PERSPECTIVE OF OTHER CULTURES. To set up a life entirely separate from the family indicates irresponsibility and even disloyalty. Adults in these cultures owe allegiance, maybe support, and certainly affection to parents and extended family members.

IMPLICATIONS. Managers and employers will encounter employees who wish to take extensive time off for family events or to return home for holidays and other special occasions. They must be aware that promotions that leave less time for relatives and spouses or that result in decreased opportunity for overtime income—income needed to send home to family members—are likely to be resisted.

In selling and marketing to immigrant and ethnic consumers, try to remember that some of the ways American advertisers depict the family are at best inaccurate and at worst offensive to consumers who value and maintain an extended family. We will take a closer look at this in Chapter 6 during our discussion of sales and marketing strategies.

Obviously there are many other manifestations of this value of placing the group's needs, goals, and reputation over the desires of the individual. One of these that has not been mentioned is the issue of the distinct national identities of many immigrant and ethnic groups. Professionals are often tempted to ignore these. Vietnamese, Cambodians, and Laotians, for example, regard themselves as separate entities and in some cases carry old animosities that can interfere with their ability to work and live together in harmony.

How attitudes like this are handled depends entirely on the situation. Whether managers and employers, for example, mix the groups in the workplace or put a supervisor from one group over members of another is up to their judgment. The issue is brought up here merely as a reminder that we need to be sensitive to the historical relationships that many groups have had to each other and to recognize that these relationships can affect the dynamics of the workplace.

Valuing the Whole Person

T. E. Lawrence ("Lawrence of Arabia") once said "Arabs believe in persons, not in institutions." In much of the Middle East, it is to individuals that businesspersons turn for support, not to organizations. This means that energy is put into cultivating relationships through the gradual development of mutual trust.

In the United States, the situation is different. It could be argued that one of the charms of the American personality is the ability to make friends quickly and to do so on fairly little evidence of common interests. This inclination to make and act on snap judgments is reflected in many aspects of our personal and professional lives.

Exercise 4–3 will help you discover how you feel about how relationships should be formed. The purpose of this exercise is to promote an awareness of your current behaviors so that you might more easily adjust to the requirements of building relationships across cultural lines. Circle the number that best indicates your degree of agreement with either statement in the pair: *1* if you strongly agree with the statement on the left; *2* if you agree with the statement on the left; *3* if you agree with the statement on the right; and *4* if you strongly agree with the statement on the right.

If you want to see how "American" you are in regard to this issue, add up all the numbers you circled and divide the total by 5. This will give you an average figure. If your average is 2.5 or below, you are very mainstream American in your thinking; the lower the number, the less concerned you are with evaluating the whole person in a professional or personal relationship. A score higher than 2.5 reveals a concern with more holistic business relationships similar to those fostered in such countries as Japan, Korea, and Mexico.

The statements in exercise 4–3 all focus on the question of how important it is to form well-rounded personal relationships in the workplace and in your business dealings. Statement 1, for example, points to the arguably sad reality that in the United States friendships tend to be formed quickly, to be based on fairly superficial associations, and to be dissolved just as fast. Outside the United States, friendships are not formed until the relationship has been slowly and systematically cemented.

In this connection, work is not considered separate from social life.

Exercise 4–3. How Do You Look at Relationships?

1. Friendships can be made fairly quickly on the basis of superficial knowledge and instinct.

   1 2 3 4

   Friendships last a lifetime so should be entered into only after careful investigation.

2. Successful hiring decisions can be made based primarily on the applicant's professional qualifications.

   1 2 3 4

   It is necessary to know all about a person—not just professional qualifications—before making a hiring decision.

3. When negotiating a major purchase or business deal, it is not usually necessary to know the salesperson or negotiator well before trust is achieved.

   1 2 3 4

   If possible, it is wise to develop a close relationship with a salesperson or negotiator before closing a deal.

4. Professionals are respected because of fairness and job skills. Their personalities, hobbies, talents, or social connections are of little importance.

   1 2 3 4

   Respect for professionals is based, not only on fairness and skill, but also on social connections and talents not directly applicable to the job.

5. To criticize a person's work does not usually reflect on the person as a whole.

   1 2 3 4

   To criticize a person's work is to criticize his or her whole being.

Whereas in the United States friendships are compartmentalized—"work friends" at work, for example, "church friends" in church—elsewhere a friend is part of all aspects of one's life.

Statement 2 deals with the fact that in the United States we tend to hire, not the whole person complete with loyalties, peripheral talents, and personality traits, but simply a skill or set of accomplishments. This hiring mode stems from the American value of evaluating people on the basis of their external achievements alone. This amounts to another example of how American culture quantifies anything significant be it intelligence, knowledge, or achievement.

In the Middle East, by contrast, employees are hired because of their social behavior, loyalty, and likableness, as well as because of their professional accomplishments. The likely question is "Would it please God to give this applicant the job?" In Japan, individuals are hired because of what they represent. This might include, as an important component, any past associations the applicants have had with key personnel of the corporation—such as having attended the same school, grown up in the same neighborhood, or belonged to the same organizations. *Jinmaku,* this cult of personal connections, can be vital to the success of any business relationship.

When hiring foreign-born workers, you must be alert to the fact that our insistence on concrete information regarding schooling, skills, and experience can appear rude and intrusive. This information must be obtained, but if the interviewer takes a few minutes to get to know an applicant, he or she will feel far more comfortable and probably far more communicative. Inquiring after a Hispanic or Middle Eastern worker's family is an effective way to show interest, communicate respect, and launch a potentially cooperative and productive relationship.

> **TIP:** Be cautious with Middle Eastern males when asking about female members of the family. In some instances, this can be offensive.

Statement 3 again addresses the issue of getting to know the whole person, but applies to sales and negotiations instead of to the hiring process. Take your time to build mutual trust in any business relationship.

The operative word here is "time"; the process requires patience. Look, for example, at the workings of a "business" lunch in Mexico; much of the time, such lunches are not opportunities to discuss business, but rather occasions during which mutual trust can be cultivated. In most other cultures, playing golf with one's colleagues, dining together, and visiting each other's homes are as essential to successful business negotiations as a professional conference or tour of a plant. In Japan, in fact, the size of an entertainment budget is in direct proportion to the importance of the business relationship.

Taking time to socialize runs against the native-born American's desire to "get going," "save time," "close the deal." This impatience must be suppressed if successful cross-cultural business relationships are the goal. By relaxing and taking the time to have a cup of coffee or a leisurely lunch—*without talking business*—you will greatly increase the chances of a mutually satisfactory business relationship.

TIP: Unless there is real urgency, do not bring up business until your immigrant or international colleague does or *at least* until there is a very long and awkward pause in the conversation.

Past associations or common affiliations are also important in sales and negotiations. Although it is unlikely that many of these connections will exist between sales staff and foreign-born clients in this country, they should be acknowledged wherever they are found. The same college, common professional organizations, mutual friends—all of these can boost the effectiveness of a relationship. These associations can often come from unexpected corners. An American businessman, for example, discovered that the chief representative of the Japanese firm with which he was negotiating had fired on the American's ship during World War II. When this information came to light, a bond, paradoxically, was formed and negotiations proceeded smoothly.

Statement 4 applies this holistic approach to the worth of any professional and especially to our attitude toward superiors. In the United States, we tend to hide our non–job-related achievements, especially if they seem artistic or academic. Quite the contrary is true in Germany or Mexico, where such accomplishments generate considerable respect

from both colleagues and employees. Reveal your achievements—
degrees, talents, interests, publications—to your foreign-born associates
and employees and you will gain respect and admiration.

TIP: Do not, however, brag about how you were born in poverty
and scrambled to the top against all odds. Such stories may
reflect the "up by your bootstraps" values of mainstream
American culture, but can be interpreted as arrogance by some,
or, by others, as an unsavory confession of your undistinguished,
lower-class background.

Statement 5 addresses a basic cross-cultural issue: how to discipline
immigrant and ethnic workers without causing alienation. In most of the
world, an employee's feeling of self-worth is closely tied to job
performance. To criticize an Iranian's work is to gravely insult him as a
human being. In short, work and the worker are one. You know that one
rule of constructive criticism is to present the issue as a mutual problem
rather than a direct attack on the individual. This is all the more
important when counseling and disciplining the foreign-born worker. In
addition, it is imperative that you make an extra effort to praise the
positive aspects of the employee's efforts and, if at all possible, to conduct
the conversation in private.

Americans rush through things. They (we) are concerned with
deadlines, efficiency, and rapid progress. To the foreign-born or ethnic
client, worker, or colleague, this can appear rude, pushy, and disrespectful. Take the time to form well-rounded friendships. You will substantially improve your cross-cultural relationships. Making the effort to get to
know a person can result in years of loyalty and productivity.

Varying Attitudes toward Authority

All cultures recognize authority figures. What varies among cultures are
who these leaders are, what their powers should be, and how they are to
be treated. For our purposes, authority figures might be the informal and
formal leaders within the ethnic community, or they might be the
managers, business owners, salespersons, government, public utilities,

or even frontline employees with whom immigrants come in contact. Culturally specific attitudes toward these roles affect how you conduct business in a multicultural environment and how you manage ethnic and immigrant employees.

Ethnic and Immigrant Group Leaders

Ethnic and immigrant groups have both informal leaders and community leaders. As professionals, it is important that you be familiar with these authority figures and understand their role within the community. Making the effort to get to know these leaders will benefit you in several ways:

1. It sends a signal to the ethnic or immigrant community that you respect its identity and culture.
2. It will allow you to utilize such leaders as conduits between employees and management in the multicultural workplace.
3. Your association with community leaders will make you accepted and trusted in business dealings.
4. You will be able to identify and cultivate those informal and formal leaders who influence decision making.

We need to learn how to identify the informal leaders within a particular ethnic or immigrant group. The idea of a powerful yet informal leader is often difficult for native-born Americans to grasp because American culture does not have an exact equivalent. Probably the closest is the American idea of the "the most popular kid in school" or the individual who takes the initiative in organizing activities and community efforts. Among ethnic and immigrant groups, however, this leadership role is far more powerful, which is not surprising considering the importance that many cultures place on the integrity of the group and its leadership hierarchy.

Although the dynamics of informal leadership will play a role in all your business dealings, these leaders are particularly important in the multicultural workplace. Workers who are reluctant to complain about problems on the job resolve this difficulty through the help of informal leaders. Among Hispanic workers, to cite just one example, complaints are often pooled and brought to management this way. Individuals are spared the embarrassment of complaining to an authority figure, and management is still able to learn of, and resolve, any problems that might exist. When this happens, it is important that employers and managers not judge this action as hostile or cowardly but merely as a culturally appropriate way of coping with a difficulty.

Unfortunately, there are no absolute rules by which to ascertain the identity of these informal group leaders. There are, however, some guidelines that can help.

1. **Age is often a factor.** Although age may no longer guarantee respect in American culture, it is still important in many immigrant and ethnic communities. For this reason, the informal leaders within these groups are often the eldest but not necessarily the most accomplished or senior on the job.

2. **Take notice of those who have held powerful positions in the past.** Among Southeast Asians or Central Americans this person might be a former military officer or an important figure from the homeland.

3. **Often, but not always, the most powerful informal leaders are male.** As we shall discuss in Chapter 6, women can hold far more powerful positions in many immigrant cultures than we sometimes realize. On the whole, however, informal leaders are men.

4. **Informal leaders often hold a formal position of some responsibility.** Among any group, the translator or sometimes assembly-line lead tends to take on informal-leadership responsibilities. There was a case, for example, in which a Vietnamese translator was passed over for promotion in favor of another Vietnamese worker. His loss of face was so grave that he resigned to minimize the humiliation. Ten valued workers resigned with him in support. This case reminds us not to be surprised when workers refuse promotions to keep from being elevated above a social superior.

5. **Observe what is going on around you.** If you have difficulty ascertaining the identity of informal leaders, watch the social dynamics around you. Watch for those individuals who get preferential treatment and are addressed by a formal pronoun or title. In the workplace, observe such simple things as which workers are given the best seating in the lunch room. Try to find out who is asked for advice most often and who is given the most decision-making power.

6. **Ask.** Finally, remember, just as it is all right to notice cultural differences, it is perfectly acceptable to acknowledge the existence of informal leadership and to ask immigrants who it is they particularly respect.

Although you may have difficulty ascertaining who the informal leaders are, try, for it is well worth the effort. Take, for example, the case of the corporation that had enough cultural awareness to give its largest Christmas bonus to the eldest member of its Asian work force. Although this gentleman had not been on the job the longest, he was obviously looked up to by the other workers. This simple gesture of respect for the workers' culture went far toward improving relations and sustaining teamwork in the workplace. Further, allowing newly arrived Cambodian workers to be accompanied on interviews by the informal leader or using leaders as conduits in your efforts to communicate to your workers are ways to work effectively with these groups.

TIP: When making these adjustments, be careful not to exhibit preferential treatment to one cultural group over another. This can be tricky but if you learn as much as you can about the cultures involved (including mainstream American culture), exhibit common sense, and use your instincts, you will most likely succeed.

The importance of communicating with and showing respect for immigrant leadership extends, however, beyond the multicultural workplace and into the broader world of doing business in a culturally diverse community. Identifying and cultivating the informal leadership within the community can be an effective business strategy. Whether you are making a sale or negotiating an important contract, be alert to the role that these leaders have in influencing decisions or the part they can play in securing you, and your company, a position of trust within the community.

Leadership within an ethnic or immigrant community, extends, however, beyond this informal hierarchy into formal roles that are a bit easier to identify and just as important to cultivate. Take the time to identify and get to know a community's political, religious, business, and media leadership. Editors of foreign-language papers, for example, have influence, knowledge, and connections helpful to anyone wishing to do business in his or her community. Religious leaders, too, can give you a stamp of approval that will ease your access to ethnic and immigrant consumers.

TIP: Some of the societal structures that you encounter may seem strange to you, but it is important that you communicate respect for even the most unfamiliar hierarchy of leadership. Samoan culture, for example, is a tribal society and even in the United States, it is not unusual to discover tribal leaders who wield considerable authority.

When cultivating both informal and formal leaders within ethnic and immigrant communities, remember that these individuals have far more power than their counterparts in mainstream American culture. Religious leaders, for example, might be involved in a family business decision. Less formal leaders might be turned to for counsel in times of trouble. In short, they are to be taken seriously.

Your Role as Authority Figure

In this age of participative management, the notion of authority has negative connotations in mainstream American culture. To be authoritarian conjures up images of dictatorships, discipline, and tyranny. Valid as this perspective might be, professionals and managers need to be aware that attitudes toward authority vary among cultures. Many immigrant workers and consumers are accustomed to deferring to and even fearing authority. In the workplace, for example, some workers are most comfortable with a structured hierarchy in which the boss is firmly in control. Table 4–2 lays out some of the attitudes toward authority that contrast with those held in mainstream American culture. Let's examine each pair of statements in the table to see how the differences between them affect how you operate in a multicultural environment.

STATEMENT 1. Age is still valued in many immigrant and ethnic cultures. For this reason, managers should find ways of communicating respect for the elderly leaders of these groups. Sales professionals, negotiators, and customer-service representatives will benefit by communicating respect for the elderly decision makers in families and corporations.

This respect for age works both ways. Many immigrants and international businesspeople are skeptical of the youthful decision maker, manager, or even clerk. In the Soviet Union young authority figures are not as respected as their seniors. In Japan, age is often a prerequisite for promotion, and in Mexico a younger employee is apt to defer to an older, more experienced worker.

TABLE 4-2
A Question of Authority

Mainstream America	Many Other Cultures
1. Age is only one factor in determining who is in authority. A younger person can readily be placed over someone older.	Age is to be respected. If possible, a younger person should not be placed over someone who is older.
2. Gender has little to do with who will be in authority.	As a general rule, males are most likely to be found in positions of authority.
3. Rules in business and government are largely inflexible and apply to everyone equally.	Rules in business and government are flexible and can change according to the consumer's status and connections.
4. Employees should be encouraged to participate in decision making.	The boss who does not make his or her own decisions is weak.
5. It is a good idea if the boss works beside employees.	The boss should keep a formal distance from employees.
6. Employees and consumers should feel comfortable questioning authority figures.	Employees and consumers should not question authority.
7. Workers are best motivated by persuasion.	Workers are best motivated by an authoritarian attitude.
8. Workers and consumers have the right and even the obligation to judge the performance of managers and vendors.	It is inappropriate for employees and consumers to judge the work of managers and vendors.
9. Governmental agencies and public services are largely to be trusted.	Governmental agencies and public services are sometimes to be feared.

The Difficulty. This attitude toward age can create difficulties when a younger manager supervises older immigrant or ethnic employees. The danger is that the employee will have trouble respecting the boss and might even suffer loss of face in being supervised by someone younger. In customer service, immigrant customers might try to push past the youthful clerk assuming that he or she has no decision-making power. In business negotiations, the more youthful American-born negotiator may be at a disadvantage when negotiating with or selling to a more senior immigrant colleague.

The Solution. In the workplace, we have seen one solution already. By giving the largest Christmas bonus to the eldest member of the group, the American-born management showed respect and minimized the danger of loss of face. Another remarkably easy approach is to address elder workers by their last names or, if appropriate to their culture, by the title Mr., Mrs., or Miss followed by a first name (for example, Mr. Peter).

When entering a client's office or home, defer to the elders by standing when they enter the room and looking at them as you speak, even if you are conversing through an interpreter. These gestures of respect are appreciated by those from cultures in which this courtesy is routine.

STATEMENT 2. American business is growing increasingly receptive to the idea of placing women in authority positions. In many other countries it is still unusual to find women who possess real power. There are, however, notable exceptions; for example, women hold many prestigious posts in East India, Korea, and the Philippines.

The Difficulty. Placing women in superior positions over immigrant men can sometimes create problems in eliciting the degree of respect necessary to do an adequate job; however, many foreign-born and ethnic workers realize that women enjoy more power in the United States than they do in most other countries. Because workers know this, they are better able to adjust to and accept this new relationship.

Just as being young can be a disadvantage in sales and negotiations, so can being female. The immigrant customer may ignore a female employee, thinking that she has no authority to make decisions. An international business contact might not take a female negotiator seriously.

The Solution. Women supervisors and managers should find as many ways as possible to show respect for the male worker without compromising their authority. Employing courtesies to make the worker feel more comfortable and cooperative, using the workers' last names, taking care to pronounce names correctly, and making an effort to get to know the strengths and interests of each individual are all effective ways of doing this.

Female sales and negotiation staff can do the same. They should also dress conservatively, pay special attention to the rules of formality presented in Chapter 5, and watch their body language.

STATEMENT 3. In most parts of the world, the rules of government agencies and corporations are very flexible. The well-connected or prestigious often find it easy to have the rules changed to fit their needs, especially if they can get past the frontline employees to someone who has authority to make these "adjustments."

The Difficulty. The problem is that immigrants sometimes think that this is the way business and government works in the United States as well. Of course, there is a certain amount of "not what you know, but who you know" going on. Even we say that "rules are made to be broken." However, in general, special privilege is frowned upon. Obviously it is disruptive to the business environment when consumers, no matter where they were born, try to bypass the frontline employee to reach someone who can bend the rules in their favor.

The Solution. The important thing to remember here is that many immigrants and international visitors are simply unfamiliar with the United States. Many will ask to see the boss, not out of arrogance, but merely because that is their custom. If the frontline employee is unable to persuade the customer that he or she does have the final say about a matter and that the rules cannot be bent, the best thing to do is allow the immigrant to speak with someone higher up in the organization. That individual, in turn, should reassure the customer that the person at the front desk or on the floor has the authority to take care of the matter. In most cases, a simple statement from someone highly placed will resolve the situation.

STATEMENT 4. Current management practice in the United States strongly encourages the participation of workers in many decision-making processes. Workers from other cultures consider it disrespectful even to propose an idea of one's own. Indeed, in countries such as Greece, only a weak boss leaves decisions up to employees. Often, even questioning the decisions of the boss is considered a violation of the proper order of things. There is a Thai proverb, "The leader has already been bathed in hot water," therefore, the sentence might continue, "he knows how to do the job."

The Difficulty. Managers and employers need to find ways to maintain the respect of immigrant workers while calling upon them to participate in their own management.

The Solution. Maintain as much of a position of authority as possible: have the worker address you by your last name; maintain an appropriate, but not cold, social distance; make it clear that although you are calling on the worker for help, the final decisions are yours. This may feel unnatural to most American managers and is not, of course, appropriate in all cases. It is, however, a compromise in management style that can be very much worth the effort.

STATEMENT 5. American managers feel that it raises productivity if they come down from their position of authority and roll up their sleeves to work beside employees. The native-born or assimilated worker perceives such a manager as a "regular" person. Many immigrant and ethnic workers, however, react quite differently.

The Difficulty. Asian workers in particular are inclined to interpret this as a sign of weakness or as an indication that the manager feels the worker is not doing an adequate job. This does not apply as much to Hispanic workers, who value the camaraderie with management, but should still be done with caution when the manager is a female and the Hispanic worker a male.

The Solution. Compromise. In this case, managers might explain to the Asian workers that their helping out does not reflect on the employee's performance but is merely a way of getting the job done faster. Another compromise is to maintain an otherwise fairly formal relationship with the Asian employees. Ways of doing this will be addressed during our discussion of cultural variations in etiquette.

STATEMENT 6. "Question authority" is a maxim that has survived the 1960s. American workers are expected and encouraged to question the decisions of their employers, consumers to debate the value of products and services. Elsewhere the situation is very different. For Asians, deference to authority begins in school where they are discouraged from questioning the wisdom of their teachers.

The Difficulty. It is in the health-care arena that the apparent passivity of immigrant groups is most often seen. Physicians and other health professionals are encountering patients who place full responsibility for all decisions onto the professional. Although this behavior is gratifying to the ego, it can interfere with the delivery of effective health care because the team involvement of professional and client is missing.

Managers are faced with a slightly different dilemma. Accustomed to having workers voice their ideas and speak up in meetings and in the training room, they find the apparent passivity of immigrant workers befuddling. Some managers think—erroneously—that these workers have no ideas of their own and are not committed to their jobs. Some immigrant workers miss out on chances for advancement due to this misunderstanding.

TIP: Not all immigrant groups exhibit this nonparticipative behavior. Swedes, for example, are accustomed to equal relationships with superiors and a healthy exchange. of ideas. Do not generalize.

The Solution. First, make certain that both consumers and workers know what you expect. Do not take it for granted that they are aware that you welcome questions and participation. In the workplace, tell the informal group leaders what you want and have them pass the request on to the other employees in a way that they will understand. Encourage the leaders to demonstrate publicly what it is you are after. This is often the most immediate way of giving workers permission to question authority. Another technique that is effective in the workplace is to allow employees to express their ideas in writing anonymously. Although this approach keeps you from knowing who had the idea, it is a way of allowing workers to voice their suggestions.

STATEMENT 7. Most American managers agree that persuasion is a more enlightened motivation strategy than coercion. However, persuasion is not an approach with which the immigrant worker is always familiar or even comfortable. Studies have shown that Italian, French, Mexican, German, South American, Middle Eastern, and British workers generally prefer an authoritarian boss. In the Middle East, for example, a worker rarely says "no" to a boss for any reason. Managers in Mexico and Asia however, do know not to carry this authoritarian attitude too far. If they, for example, lose their tempers or swear in front of their workers, they lose the respect they had previously enjoyed.

The Difficulty. Because of this, the "soft" approach of persuasion can be mistaken for weakness and indecisiveness. This misperception lowers the manager's standing and leaves the worker unsure of where responsibility lies.

The Solution. Explaining to workers the expectations and customs of American management is an obvious but often neglected solution to such difficulties. Simply tell the immigrant worker that motivation by persuasion is not a sign of weak management but rather the American way of doing things. You will be surprised how quickly workers respond to this different conception of management.

STATEMENT 8. If done with discretion, "keeping an eye" on the work of superiors, vendors, and big corporations is considered a virtue in American business. Whether it is complaining about a product or service or criticizing the boss, such behavior, within certain limits, is considered a sign of committment and involvement.

In most other cultures, criticizing superiors is taboo. In many Asian countries, it is even considered in poor taste to compliment a superior because such behavior implies that the worker has a right to judge that superior and that he or she is somehow surprised at the achievement. In Japan, for example, a compliment on a boss's report might be worded "I hope that many people have the opportunity to read this report," a roundabout way of stating how valuable the report is.

The Difficulty. The problems that arise because consumers do not complain about inadequate products or services are obvious; if you do not know there is a problem, there is no way that you can remedy it. As far as the reluctance to judge superiors is concerned, this behavior may, at first glance, seem harmless. However, management cannot know where it stands in the eyes of the employee who refuses to complain.

The Solution. We will examine some ways to promote consumer complaints in Chapter 6 when we discuss the issue of cross-cultural sales and service. With respect to management, however, inviting workers to submit critiques and compliments anonymously will encourage the silent employees to give management the benefit of their ideas and is a compromise that can go far toward solving the problem.

STATEMENT 9. Despite the fussing and complaining that goes on during income tax season, Americans generally trust their governmental bodies and public services. Many immigrants come from countries in which public bodies are not to be trusted. Add to this the fear of discovery that many newly legalized immigrants carry over from their days as illegal aliens and the causes for lack of trust are easy to understand.

The Difficulty. The greatest problem with this lack of trust is a reluctance to take advantage of public services and public programs. There are, for example, Vietnamese immigrants who hesitate to call the police because of confusion over how the system works. Many become upset when they see a suspect the police just arrested back on the street within hours. Because they do not understand the American system of bail, they assume the person has bribed an official and that the immigrant's need for security is being ignored.

The Solution. Education. Immigrant communities need to be taught how government, public utilities, and other organizations work, what their functions are, and how to use them. Whether this is done through the formation of community focus groups, public meetings, written materials, or with the help of community leaders, education of the immigrant community is the first step toward building trust and understanding.

Education efforts should not stop, however, with the immigrant community. Programs should also be designed to teach the frontline staff at government and public agencies how to meet the needs of those immigrants who do utilize their services. Word-of-mouth advertising is very strong within ethnic and immigrant groups. One instance of poor treatment, one avoidable misunderstanding, and the entire community is reluctant to use a service.

It is a mixed blessing that many foreign-born and ethnic consumers, clients, and workers have so much respect for authority. What matters is that you take the time to earn that respect, that you acknowledge its sincerity, and that you appreciate it for what it is.

Fatalism and Tradition versus Action and Change

Benjamin Franklin once wrote a tract entitled "*Information to Those Who Would Remove to America.*" In it, he said, "In America, people do not inquire concerning a stranger, what is he but what can he do? If he has a useful art, he is welcome." This concern with doing instead of simply being, contrasts sharply to the philosophical perspectives of Europe, Asia, Africa, and South America where one's ability to exist in harmony with others is considered at least as valuable as what one accomplishes.

In the United States, action is an imperative, not really a choice. Phrases like "How are you doing?," "I'm doing fine," "Keeping busy," and proverbs such as "Busy hands are happy hands" and "If it's worth doing, it's worth doing well" all reflect this emphasis on action, on becoming rather than being. This American desire for constant action is usually motivated by two goals: controlling the future and bringing about change.

Action in Order to Control the Future

Mainstream American culture is unusual in its belief that the future can be controlled. This view is not shared by many immigrants, who are far more able to make the most of the present moment and far less willing to believe that the future can, or even should, be controlled or changed.

The American illusion that all things can be controlled probably originated when the first pioneer set out to conquer the vast Western wilderness. Since then, American culture has focused on valuing action as a means of controlling both the environment and the future. This perspective is very different from the fatalistic view held by roughly seven-eighths of the world's population.

The idea that life will unfold as it will unfold is far more common and is reflected in the Arabic disclaimer, *In Sha' Allah* ("If God wills it"). By contrast, native-born Americans consider problems to be solvable by technology, intellectual skill, and sheer energy. They have what anthropologist Clyde Kluckhohn termed "effort-optimism," which means the belief that with action and doing—we can control the future.

TIP: The Middle Eastern belief that God's will is what controls all events is so strong that many consider it wrong to tell terminal patients the truth of their condition. To do so, in their eyes, is to predict the future, and, therefore, to defy the will of God.

These differing attitudes toward the future have implications for effective cross-cultural business relations. For one thing, it is often difficult for immigrant workers to aggressively seek promotions. These workers might accept a promotion if offered, but will take no direct action to bring it about. This does not indicate low self-esteem, but stems from a different set of values and priorities, values that leave such important life changes to fate.

Sales representatives must work around this when attempting to sell products that concern future eventualities. Life-insurance agents, for example, might promote the investment potential of a policy as opposed to the death benefit—death being an event the immigrant client might be reluctant to anticipate in any case.

Action in Order to Bring about Change

In the American view, change for the sake of change is a virtue. We invariably equate change with growth, improvement, evolution, development, and progress. Many other cultures feel that change should be carefully weighed against the virtues of tradition and continuity. Change is regarded by many immigrants as an option, not a necessity, as likely to be destructive as constructive.

Marketers and sales professionals know that this reluctance to change can create resistance to new products and services. The American tendency to discard the old in favor of the new is not necessarily admired by the immigrant whose brand loyalty, desire for quality, respect for durable goods, and lesser fascination with constant newness needs to be respected.

Employers, too, are encountering immigrant and ethnic workers who resist changing tried-and-true procedures and are particularly disturbed by structural changes within the organization. Managers have found it necessary to explain why a procedure needs to be changed, and how the new method is better than the old. The same principle applies to wholesale changes within the organization—changes which are, of course, understandably difficult for *any* employee to accept. In all situations involving change, the answer lies in improved communication and the transmission of detailed information on the "why" and "how" of any major adjustment.

Summary

Understanding the values of foreign-born and ethnic clients and workers is necessary if you are to know how to interpret their behaviors, motivate change, and appreciate their needs. Remember these essential points:

- Understand that a reluctance to complain or question can arise from a desire to maintain harmony and balance in the relationship.
- Respect the importance of saving face for all concerned.
- Do not call unnecessary and inappropriate attention to the individual at the expense of the group.
- Get to know clients, customers, and employees as complete human beings.
- Communicate respect for the informal hierarchy of leadership which is characteristic of many ethnic and immigrant groups.
- Be sensitive to the fact that participative management and an informal relationship with authority figures can make immigrant and ethnic people uncomfortable.

- Be certain to earn the respect that naturally comes your way.
- Recognize differing attitudes toward the future and toward the validity of change.

Solidifying Your Learning

What are the three most important things you learned from this chapter and how might you apply them in your work?

1.

2.

3.

Honoring Cultural Differences in Etiquette and Style

How to Avoid Alienation

Good business and good manners are identical when practiced with sincerity and care.

—Letitia Baldridge

How Can Proper Etiquette Help You Do Business?

Etiquette feels like second nature. It seems as if we are born knowing that it is rude to shove in line, important to say "please" and "thank you," and wrong to take a seat in someone's office until invited to do so. Only when we encounter people from other cultures who do not share our etiquette do we remember that these rules are not inborn but are, instead, a part of our cultural conditioning.

The Vietnamese client who does not hesitate to ask the price of a colleague's clothing, the Hispanic employee who refuses to call a manager by his or her first name, or the Japanese business owner who is insulted by a compliment—each of these behaviors can distress the mainstream American professional. On the other hand, the immigrant is likely to feel disoriented and offended when you automatically call him by his first name, refuse well-intended gifts, or discuss inappropriately personal subjects on short acquaintance.

The purpose of this chapter is to clear up some of this confusion. Why a whole chapter? After all etiquette might be considered the poor relation of culture; it does not dictate our life choices like values do or, like language, allow us to communicate our loftiest thoughts. Why so much emphasis on such seemingly inconsequential things as gift giving and who pays the check in a restaurant? The answer is that these behaviors are not inconsequential. Every culture possesses rules of etiquette, and each of these rules serves a number of very important functions without which society would be far more chaotic:

1. **Etiquette allows us to express the style of our culture.** By *style* is meant the values, atmosphere, and tone of a culture. The Asian desire for personal dignity and harmony is reflected in a quiet tone of voice and a reluctance to interrupt another speaker. Similarly, the egalitarian American expresses his or her culture in the use of first names and casual dress. Etiquette symbolizes the larger values that make a culture unique.

2. **Etiquette lets us know what to expect in the behavior of others.** This works only when everyone is following the same rules—that is, when they have the same cultural background. A sales representative, for example, is likely to become confused when foreign-born prospects are not punctual for meetings despite the fact that they seem genuinely interested in making a deal.

3. **Etiquette tells us how to make a good first impression on others.** In America, we know what fork to use at the dinner table and what sort of gift to bring the hostess. Again, however, everyone must be practicing the same etiquette for this system to work. A Middle Easterner might expect the native-born customer-service representative to be pleased when he showers elaborate compliments on a product. Unfortunately, the representative may misinterpret this enthusiasm as questionable flattery. Because of differing rules of etiquette, the desired favorable first impression is not achieved.

4. **Etiquette allows us to feel confident in unfamiliar settings within our own culture.** When keeping an appointment with another professional, we know we are expected to be on time or certainly no more than five minutes late. That is the etiquette of corporate America. Even though we have not met the individual before, we have no doubt about how we are expected to behave. On the other hand, in cultures where time is more flexible, our punctuality might be perceived of as excessively fastidious, anxious, and even aggressive.

Etiquette is powerful. Violations can easily offend and compliance can easily please. Before you become too apprehensive about what can happen if you commit a *faux pas* in the multicultural business world, here is some reassurance.

First, it is the spirit of etiquette that matters, not the letter. Grasp the general values and style of the immigrant's culture and have a basic respect for that style. If you violate the formality that so many immigrants prefer by deliberately neglecting to use a colleague's title, it is likely that the colleague will be offended. But if you genuinely appreciate the colleague's perspective and neglect the title out of ignorance or forgetfulness, the immigrant will probably sense the innocence of the error and react accordingly.

Second, it is all right to ask about etiquette differences. Acknowledging and discussing the reality of diversity is an acceptable and practical way to minimize the risk of misunderstanding. I am amazed at how often we neglect this simple solution. By inquiring after the other person's needs and perspective, we not only learn how to avoid misunderstanding and conflict but also communicate a respect that can only strengthen our working relationship.

Third, it is all right to observe the other person's actions. Have you ever been to a formal dinner with no idea of which utensil to pick up first? Your confusion, was no doubt eliminated when you saw the hostess reach for her salad fork. In the same way, by watching the behavior of culturally diverse employees, colleagues, and clients, professionals can quickly learn what is acceptable to them and what is not. If done in a way that does not cause self-consciousness, this technique can provide you with much information about differences in etiquette and notions of proper behavior.

Fourth, it is all right to apologize. This is another obvious solution that tends to get overlooked. Perhaps it is pride, perhaps absentmindedness that makes us forget that, if someone is inadvertently offended, a quick solution is to simply apologize. Due to the nature of many immigrant cultures, the other person, in order to avoid embarassing you, is likely to deny that he or she felt offended. Nonetheless, your apology will have been heard and silently appreciated.

How Do You React to Etiquette Differences?

Before we describe the etiquette of various cultures, you might be interested in finding out how you feel about the behaviors encountered in the multicultural business world. You probably find some of these culturally rooted behaviors charming, some bewildering, and some irritating. We all have our pet peeves. Maybe you hate it when someone talks too much or are uncomfortable around "up-tight" formality; perhaps vague answers drive you crazy. No matter what your particular irritation, the important point is to identify it, learn more about it, and thereby gain the power to control your reactions.

Exercise 5-1 will help you begin this task by asking you to identify your feelings about each behavior on the list. Circle the number that most closely reflects your emotional response.

Now that you are aware of just what variations in etiquette are a problem for you, you are better equipped to read the following pages with an eye toward learning as much as possible about those particular behaviors. Watch for those issues that make you feel the most uncomfortable.

"Remembering Your Manners": Was Grandmother Right All Along?

American culture is a "low context culture." This means, among other things, that the society has relatively few rules of proper behavior. Perhaps this is a corollary of our free society, but, whatever the reason, we have fewer strictures regarding how an individual must behave in a given situation than do most other cultures.

Traditional formality, or, as grandmother would say, "minding your p's and q's," is regarded with varying degrees of disfavor in different parts of the United States. The general trend, however, is to think of any type of formal behavior as cold and distant. This attitude—whether it is manifested in casual dress, relaxed posture, disconcerting openness about ourselves, or informal terms of address—tends to make colleagues from other countries question the seriousness of our demands and culturally diverse workers feel confused about how much authority the American manager really has.

American informality can create problems when working with individuals who feel more comfortable in structured relationships. The desire for formality varies, of course, among different groups. Koreans, for example, are slightly less formal than the Japanese, and the Russians somewhat less than the French. But in general, it is safer to err in the direction of propriety.

Formality becomes particularly important when the immigrant is under emotional stress. Employers should not drop old-fashioned courtesy during an initial job interview or when criticizing, coaching, or

---

Exercise 5–1. Finding Your Etiquette Pet Peeves

People Who Call Me by My Last Name

| Bothers Me a Little | 1 | 2 | 3 | 4 | 5 | Bothers Me a Lot |

People Who Ask Me Personal Questions

| Bothers Me a Little | 1 | 2 | 3 | 4 | 5 | Bothers Me a Lot |

Slowness in Building Relationships

| Bothers Me a Little | 1 | 2 | 3 | 4 | 5 | Bothers Me a Lot |

Extreme Formality

| Bothers Me a Little | 1 | 2 | 3 | 4 | 5 | Bothers Me a Lot |

People Who Allow Pauses in the Conversation

| Bothers Me a Little | 1 | 2 | 3 | 4 | 5 | Bothers Me a Lot |

People Who Talk a Great Deal

| Bothers Me a Little | 1 | 2 | 3 | 4 | 5 | Bothers Me a Lot |

People Who Speak Very Softly

| Bothers Me a Little | 1 | 2 | 3 | 4 | 5 | Bothers Me a Lot |

People Who Speak Loudly

| Bothers Me a Little | 1 | 2 | 3 | 4 | 5 | Bothers Me a Lot |

Vague Answers to Questions

| Bothers Me a Little | 1 | 2 | 3 | 4 | 5 | Bothers Me a Lot |

Relaxed View of Time/Deadlines

| Bothers Me a Little | 1 | 2 | 3 | 4 | 5 | Bothers Me a Lot |

evaluating a worker. A good manager or human-resource professional will try to make employees feel more comfortable under such circumstances. The trick is not to project your own idea of comfort onto others. While a casual, familiar attitude may suit the native-born applicant or worker very nicely, formality is more likely to put the immigrant employee at ease. Similarly, when negotiating the final stages of a sale, it is generally a good idea to exhibit proper behavior as it makes all parties feel less intimidated by the pressure of the situation.

In Chapter 3, we saw some of the ways formality and propriety can be expressed by cultural variations in body language. Making certain not to slouch, talk with your hands in your pockets, or lean your chair back during a conversation are some examples. There are many other ways, however, to express good manners and formality. The following case study illustrates several of these. Although set in the multicultural workplace and involving a manager's relationship to her workers, the principles are applicable to cross-cultural customer service, sales, or negotiations. Pay careful attention to those items followed by a superscript letter:

> As manager of fifty workers at a small manufacturing firm in the Northeast, Nancy is constantly hiring new employees of different cultural backgrounds. Being very friendly and easygoing, she always greets the workers—many of them Korean and Puerto Rican—with great warmth and friendliness. Nancy has even been known to ask new employees to lunch on their first day in order to make them feel welcome.[a]
>
> At lunch, Nancy asks lots of questions as a way of getting to know each worker quickly. She inquires after their personal lives[b] and tries to set a casual tone by making jokes and laughing.[c] Nancy makes every effort to be egalitarian by using first names[d] and builds each worker's confidence by issuing compliments whenever possible.[e] She is careful to avoid alienating anyone, so refuses to accept the gifts that are sometimes offered by the immigrant workers.[f] Above all else, she prides herself on treating everyone alike regardless of his or her age or position in the community.[g]

On the surface, Nancy is a wonderful manager. The trouble is, she is unaware that some cultures wish to be treated differently from others. Let us take a closer look at how the gaps in Nancy's cultural awareness are reflected in the key points of her dilemma.

a. *Take your time developing relationships.* Like Nancy, native-born and assimilated Americans tend to form friendships quickly and to base those friendships on a fairly superficial knowledge of the other person. We think of individuals who are slow to open up as cold and reclusive. The situation is very different in cultures where the speedy formation of friendships is considered intrusive, unwise, and rude. In this case, Nancy's vigorous efforts to form good relationships probably backfired.

Probably one reason Nancy makes so many errors in cross-cultural etiquette is that she does not put herself in the place of the worker; she does not try to understand what the employee feels when Nancy is so "friendly." One way to avoid falling into this trap is to ask yourself how you would feel if the boss came up to you on your first day, put his or her arm around you, and began to gossip about company personnel? The immigrant workers in our case study felt decidedly uncomfortable. No doubt, you would too, and, like them, you would lose some respect for the boss. You would probably feel the same about a professional colleague or sales person who became prematurely familiar.

Forming relationships slowly may take some restraint, but it will prove beneficial in the long run. Taking the time to get to know someone from another culture can yield substantial dividends. Relationships that are formed slowly are deeper, last longer, and inspire more loyalty than those cultivated overnight. To the Asian, Hispanic, or Middle Easterner, the person who rushes into camaraderie is probably superficial, untrustworthy, and even weak. Asians interpret the premature revelation of information about oneself and the implied intimacy that goes with it as a sign of insincerity. Take it slow—the long-term benefits of doing so will be worth the restraint.

b. *Do not ask intrusive questions.* Because ideas of what is intrusive vary from culture to culture, it is difficult to specify which questions are inappropriate in a particular situation. Asking a woman her age is almost universally offensive but other topics will elicit varying responses. A fairly innocent inquiry about a person's home life can appear rude to the native American Indian whereas a Hispanic would welcome any interest you show in his or her family. Filipinos and Middle Easterners are inclined to ask fairly personal questions, which can be misinterpreted, even by the friendliest American, as intrusive. An Arab immigrant, for example, might ask you why you are not married or when you plan to have children. In fact, such queries are intended to show warmth and respect.

The idea is to learn what is appropriate before asking questions that might make someone uncomfortable. To understand how such intrusive questions make the immigrant feel, put yourself in his or her position. When an intrusive question is asked, the immigrant feels the same sense of violation that you would experience if your boss asked about your love life.

TIP: If you must ask personal questions, explain why you need the information and make it clear that whatever is revealed is in the strictest confidence. This will relieve a lot of resentment by communicating that you are aware of, and respect, the immigrant's point of view.

---

c. *Avoid using jokes and sarcasm around people of diverse cultural backgrounds.* The problem with Nancy's playfulness is not only that jokes tend to set an informal and intimate tone that can make others uncomfortable but that humor generated out of American culture may not be understood by people from other backgrounds. Although humor is universal, the specifics of what makes things funny vary from culture to culture. Because of this, jokes, and sarcasm in particular, can offend someone who does not "get" the joke.

Sarcasm is especially dangerous because it is not found in every culture. To say playfully to a Middle Easterner, "You're a nut," or "You're crazy," is to risk compromising the relationship. Sarcasm is also a form of humor that smacks of intimacy. This sort of behavior is particularly offensive to the Chinese-born employee who finds humor of any sort inappropriate between managers and workers.

d. *Be receptive to the use of last names and titles.* Attitudes toward the use of last names vary, of course, in different parts of the country. In California, it is commonplace for managers and even chief executive officers (CEOs) to be addressed by their first names. This informality is difficult for the more formal foreign-born and ethnic professional or worker to accept. In Korea, only children, family, and one's closest friends are addressed by their first names. It is not unusual for workers to stop using the manager's name altogether rather than to address him or her in a manner they consider disrespectful and intimate.

Formality is one way of defining relationships. Most immigrants are accustomed to regarding superiors with respect. Thai workers are consistently formal with business owners and managers, even in a social setting. To call on an immigrant worker to use the more intimate first name is like asking an American manager to summon the CEO with "Hey, boss." This informality would be alien even to the most casual southern Californians.

Fortunately, there is a compromise between these two points of view. Asian and Middle Eastern workers, for example, are often comfortable calling the boss by the salutation "Mr.," "Miss," "Ms.," "Dr.," or "Mrs." and then the first name (Mr. Roy, Dr. Andy, Ms. Jenna, Mr. Paul) a usage that may seem strange and even patronizing to native-born Americans. This is a compromise that contributes to harmonious cross-cultural relationships. The reason that this works so well is that in many parts of Asia and the Middle East, respect is communicated in just this way: title and then first name.

TIP: Whichever name you use, make certain that you pronounce it correctly. This courtesy is an important and easy way of communicating respect for the individual and the culture.

---

   e. *Be restrained with compliments.* I am not saying that sincere praise is not considered good etiquette in most cultures, merely that Nancy should not have assumed that everyone regards it as appropriate. Calling attention to an individual's virtues is sometimes considered poor taste, particularly by Asians. The British also consider it better manners to state compliments in restrained terms and, if possible, in private.

If you do get overly zealous and issue elaborate flattery to an Asian, be aware that you are likely to be met with a denial, which is designed to maintain social harmony and should not be interpreted as evidence of low self-esteem. The Asian might even respond with a laugh or giggle to conceal his or her embarrassment. Flowery compliments issued in front of others is likely to make an Asian feel the way you would should you walk into a meeting, only to have the entire staff break into a standing ovation. Admittedly, some of you would love this, but most would consider such behavior excessive and embarrassing. As we saw in question 15 of the Quiz, not everyone likes to be complimented in front of others.

Middle Easterners are inclined to feel very differently about compliments. As a general rule, they are quick to flatter and pleased to be flattered. The key here is not to project your own cultural-specific ideas about propriety onto others. If you are observant and not afraid to ask questions, you will have a good idea of what to do.

f. *Respect and observe the small rituals of relationships.* Social rituals, whether in the home or in the workplace, form an important part of the culture of many ethnic groups. The exchange of food, for example, means far more than the satisfaction of hunger. Sharing food symbolizes, and cements, relationships. To refuse an offer of food because you are on a diet is to reject the person doing the offering.

Dining out can also have pitfalls when it comes to cross-cultural etiquette. Generally, when doing business with foreign-born colleagues, whoever extends the invitation pays. If a group of people eat together and it is unclear who is responsible, do not go through the cumbersome, and inelegant, process of dividing the bill; simply have one party pay and reimburse him or her later. Middle Eastern professionals are apt to be very gracious in wanting to pay for the meal. The best way to handle this is to let them have the check and arrange to reciprocate at a later date.

When inviting immigrant and international colleagues to a meal, do not be surprised or hurt if they refuse you the first time or two. It is not because they do not want to go, but merely that it is, in many cultures, more gracious to decline the first two or three times an invitation is extended. This is similar to the American practice of not wanting to be the first in the buffet line or the one to take the last cookie off the plate. Just continue to extend the invitation—three times is usually the magic number—and your persistence will be rewarded.

The ritualistic proffering of gifts can lead to considerable misunderstanding in the American workplace. In the United States, giving gifts to the boss is usually interpreted as bribery. In other cultures this is proper social behavior and represents gratitude and deference, not a request for special privilege.

There are no absolute answers concerning valuable gifts; how you respond depends largely on the policy of the specific company and the value of the present. Generally, however, to refuse the gift will be interpreted as an insult to the giver. If the giver is an employee, this can be minimized by educating immigrant workers regarding management's policy toward gift giving. In the meantime, every attempt should be made to turn the gift down with sensitivity and good judgement.

Although most applicable to international business and beyond the scope of this book, the issue of business cards should be addressed briefly. Much has been said about the importance of handling business cards with respect when doing business with Asians. This applies especially to the Japanese. First, do not offer your card until asked—to do otherwise is to appear excessively forward. Second, as a general rule, take the card with the right hand and give yours with the left. Finally, once you have your counterpart's card in hand, do not instantly stuff it away, but treat it with respect by laying it on the table in front of you. This can also rescue you if you happen to forget the name of your Asian colleague.

Entire volumes could be written on the small rituals of etiquette. One general rule can prevent you from making most of the fatal mistakes: be formal and restrained. Remember the more formal behaviors you have been taught and those that you have observed and you will be safe. If, for example, you light a cigarette, offer one to everyone present. If a superior or elder enters the room, stand up. When visitors leave your office, see them to the door. Proceed in this vein and the chances of your offending someone, no matter how formal their culture, are very slim.

TIP: If you think about it, it is far easier to become more casual in your behavior once you learn that the immigrant prefers it that way than it is to back up and be formal once you have offended someone.

---

g. *Respect the older members of a group.* Respect for the elderly has become less of a priority in American society. Despite a similar trend in other cultures, it is still largely accepted that the eldest of a group should be treated with deference and respect.

This means that you should treat the elder members of an immigrant group with added formality. Managers like Nancy might protest that too much formality toward the oldest workers will cause them to lose respect for her as an authority figure. Quite the contrary, it will increase that respect—respect given to others is usually returned. Moreover, the elderly often have considerable influence as decision makers and can also serve as valuable allies in your efforts to work with the members of immigrant and ethnic communities.

The Spoken Word: What Do You Say and How Do You Say It?

In Chapter 2 we discussed techniques for bridging language barriers. There is another aspect of communication—conversational etiquette. In other words, what to say and how and when to say it. Often the manner of speech can be more important than the content. The excited New Yorker who interrupts a more sedate southern colleague is likely to offend the southerner, for the southerner probably interprets that interruption as rudeness. Even if they agree on what is being discussed, the conversation is in danger of ending badly. These misunderstandings can be avoided by taking the following steps:

1. Learn about cultural differences in conversational etiquette.
2. When appropriate, match the communication style of the other person.
3. Avoid projecting your own cultural interpretations onto the behavior of others.

The subject of language etiquette can be divided into seven components: interruptions, pauses and silences, spontaneity, volume of speech, degree of directness, degree of embellishment, and ritualistic phrases.

Interruptions

Many cultures regard interruptions during conversation as extremely rude. This is part of the formality common to many Asian cultures. For the normally outspoken American, a certain number of interruptions is normal. It is, however, important to resist this temptation with Asian-born colleagues, clients, or workers. If you do interrupt, the Asian is apt to fall silent out of courtesy to you, and you will have difficulty finding out what it is he or she was going to say.

French, Italian, and Arabic cultures are very different from Asian cultures in this regard. Members of these groups are comfortable with interruptions and with several people talking at once. This style of communicating is considered an expression of enthusiasm and commit-

> **TIP:** As in so many areas, Koreans and some Chinese are the exception to this rule and will be more apt to interrupt than will other Far Easterners.

ment to the life of the conversation. With someone who feels this way, recognize that such conversational gusto does not mean that the speaker is uninterested in what you are saying.

It is situations like these that call into play rules 2 and 3 above. Match the communication style of the Asian by resisting the urge to interrupt, and avoid misinterpreting your talkative colleague's behavior as a sign of rudeness or self-involvement.

Pauses and Silence

Mainstream Americans have strong feelings about pauses. Exercise 5–2 gives you a chance to write down how you feel about unexpected pauses in a conversation. Do they give you a chance to think or do they make you uncomfortable because you feel the other person is angry? After writing down your feelings, try to redefine what a pause can mean. Maybe silence gives you a chance to show how confident you are, or maybe the other person's pause is simply an indication that he or she is contemplating what you have just said. See how many positive interpretations of pauses and silences you can come up with.

The answers which you gave to the first question probably included such comments as, "A long pause feels really awkward," "It usually means that the other person disagrees with me," or "I feel like such an idiot when I can't think of anything to say." Although there are times when these feelings are appropriate, pauses also can indicate several positive things and can be utilized to achieve better communication. There are other ways of looking at silence. Consider the following suggestions:

Pauses indicate confidence on the part of the speaker who knows that there is no need to say anything else.
Pauses give the nonnative English speaker time in which to translate what you have said and formulate a question or response.

Pauses can indicate that the other person regards what you have said as so important that he or she wants to take a minute to contemplate it.

Pauses serve as a quiet moment in which to organize one's thoughts.

Pauses can communicate respect for what you have said.

Pauses can indicate that the other party is trying to figure out a way to give you what you just asked for.

As we have seen, the Japanese proverb, "He who knows does not speak, and he who speaks does not know," summarizes the very different attitude Asian cultures have toward the etiquette of silence. It is, for them, not something to be avoided or feared. For mainstream Americans, however, sudden conversational pauses can be very painful especially if they occur in the middle of an important negotiation when it is necessary to know exactly where one stands.

It is important that you find ways to diffuse this discomfort. If you do not, there is always the danger that you might weaken during one of these pauses and begin to jabber aimlessly in a desperate attempt to fill the gap. Others will take this as a sign of weakness, fear, or lack of focus. Here are a few suggestions to help you avoid that temptation:

Exercise 5-2. Silence Is Golden?

1. How do you feel about pauses and silences during a conversation?

2. What positive purposes can they serve?

---

1. Use the silence to think about what has just been said and to figure out what it is you will say next. Pauses can buy you valuable time in which to devise a strategy, overcome an objection, or think up a tactful way to demonstrate the superiority of your product or service.
2. Think about the list of positive functions and meanings of silence that you just came up with. Realize, for example, that your silence will communicate strength, not weakness, to the other party. Remember, too, that the other party's silence may indicate respect for what you have just said, not criticism.
3. If the other person suddenly falls silent, remind yourself that it might mean that he or she is seriously considering what you have just proposed—the longer you keep quiet the more time he or she has to come around to your way of thinking.
4. Give the golden gift of silence to the other party. We have seen that the nonnative speaker may need that time to translate what you have said or to formulate a response or question. Your patience will be well rewarded in better communication and mutual understanding.
5. Share the silence with the other party. Use it as a way of getting closer and building a relationship. This idea may be hard to grasp for the mainstream American to whom words are the best way to form lasting friendships, but after a little practice you will realize how unifying silence can be.
6. Spend the silence contemplating the Japanese advertising slogan, "Men Keep Silent and Drink Sapporo Beer." Although this may make you want a beer to relieve the tension of the situation, it will also serve as a reminder that silence is valued in Asian cultures, not feared.

This discussion would not be complete, nor would it be very honest, if I failed to mention that pauses can sometimes indicate that something has gone wrong. They can, for example, signal a veiled criticism or disagreement with what you have proposed. A silence sometimes, but not always, is one way of turning you down without having to rebuff you directly. The answer here is: Do not assume the worst. The pause could just as easily be a way of sending a positive message as a negative one.

For managers and business owners who work with large numbers of Asian immigrant and ethnic workers, you may have noticed that some of these employees tend to remain silent when in the presence of authority figures, which can lead to the faulty impression that the worker is afraid or excessively shy. More often such silences are signs of respect and deference to the superior.

As far as your behavior is concerned, too much talk and too few pauses can be taken as meaningless jabber. Asians, for example, are inclined to believe that little thought goes into what you say, that you lack confidence, and that you are unfocused in your thinking. The solution is to watch others and match their style when communicating with them—allow, for example, pauses when speaking with Asians and avoid them when conversing with Middle Easterners.

Spontaneity of Speech

Related to the issues of interruptions and silence is the spontaneity and rhythm with which particular groups speak. Asians, for instance, are inclined to speak only after careful deliberation. To blurt out a spontaneous idea in a brainstorming session would be considered both rude and unwise.

Mainstream American culture, on the other hand, as well as the Italian, the French, and many of the Hispanic cultures, values spontaneity as a sign of creativity and enthusiasm. The problem lies in the meaning assigned to each speech pattern. The deliberate and careful speaker is in danger of being thought less intelligent and energetic than the more spontaneous and outspoken person.

Remember, just as an accent tells us nothing about the intelligence of a person, spontaneity and pace has little to do with brightness or creativity or even enthusiasm. It is simply a reflection of the individual's culturally dictated style of expression.

Volume of Speech

We saw in Chapter 2 that tone of voice can cause immigrants and international visitors to appear rude or demanding when in fact they are merely expressing a wish or request. Volume of speech can be equally misleading. Indeed how loud to speak is a particularly noticeable cultural difference. In the mainstream American culture, for example, individuals should neither talk "too" loudly nor "too" softly. This middle-range position makes it seem that how loud a person speaks is not very important in American etiquette. Think of how often you hear the commands, "speak up" or "pipe down," and you will realize that this issue is as important in American culture as it is elsewhere.

Asian cultures favor speaking softly and avoiding loud and raucous laughter. Listeners from "louder" cultures sometimes regard Asians as meek and socially retiring. At the other end of the spectrum, the southern Europeans and Middle Easterners speak louder. Outsiders often assume them to be aggressive, crass, and pushy. To function effectively in a multicultural world, you must learn to avoid jumping to conclusions based on how loudly, or softly a person speaks.

Try the rule mentioned earlier that urges you to "match the conversational style." Matching the volume of a colleague's, client's or worker's speech results in increased rapport especially when conversing with Asian or Hispanic females who tend to be soft-spoken. If the native-born American speaks louder, the Asian progressively speaks softer, which causes the American to raise his or her voice still further. The difficulty is obvious, the solution simple: match the speaker's tone and you have solved the problem. When talking with someone who speaks loudly remember the rule that urges you to "avoid projecting your own cultural interpretations" of what this behavior means; a loud tone of voice does not necessarily mean that the speaker is angry, upset, or demanding.

Degree of Directness

Cultures possess differing notions about how direct one should be when speaking of negative things or giving negative answers. Asians, Hispanics, and East Indians tend to soften the negative. An Asian might, for example, avoid saying "no" by answering your inquiry or request with another question. Koreans are, however, an exception to this rule; under certain circumstances they will surprise you with their bluntness. Hispanics, like most Asians, will turn you down gently as a way of saving face for all concerned. Middle Easterners, too, although capable of being very direct, will, when asked for a favor they cannot grant, rebuff you gently by saying something like, "Maybe I can do it, I'll let you know," even though he or she knows it is impossible.

Although we have discussed this issue elsewhere, it needs to be reemphasized as a reminder not to misinterpret the meaning behind this seemingly evasive behavior; it is not weak or dishonest just as the directness of most Americans is not unkindness. Most often both

> **TIP:** One way to get a specific answer out of clients or customers who give you a qualified "yes" when they really mean "no" is to avoid asking "yes" or "no" questions, but instead to provide a choice among several options. In this way, they can reject what they do not want without feeling they have offended you or disrupted the harmony of your relationship.

behaviors are a matter of cultural style and have little to do with the speaker's feelings or intent.

The issue of how direct a person is in speech goes beyond the question of qualified refusals into the realm of how any topic is approached. The French tend to talk around a subject rather than confront it directly. Germans, despite their forthright style, often postpone the main point to the end of the conversation, while Americans start right in with the primary subject. Because of this difference, it can be helpful, when doing business with Germans, for American-born professionals to be alert to what is said at the end of a conversation and to reemphasize their main point when the discussion is finished.

The Japanese, too, tend to approach the primary subject in a roundabout way. They talk about other things while slowly circling in on their central point. Chinese colleagues respond to direct questions by seeming to ignore them. After a question has been asked, a few minutes might pass in which they continue to talk about other matters. Finally, having allowed themselves time to formulate a response, they return to the subject of the question and give you an answer.

In most cases, these apparently evasive styles of conversing are not meant to be hostile or manipulative. The best way to handle them is to "go with the flow," say encouraging things like "Of course," "I understand," and "Yes," and listen attentively. Your patience will be amply rewarded.

Degree of Embellishment and Emphasis

Compared to other cultures, Americans are fond of plain speech. We greet people with a perfunctory "Hi." Respond with a succinct "Nope." When asked how we are, we briefly say "Fine" or "OK." Of course, this varies with the individual, but to be a man or woman of few words is generally considered a virtue.

Mainstream Americans also tend to avoid exaggeration. Although we are prone to speak of our "highest" building, "tallest" mountain, and "highest-grossing" company (there are no "small" eggs in the grocery store), we are very unlike the southern European, Middle Eastern, or Irish person who takes pride in his or her ability to create flowery, embellished statements. Even the Japanese, who tend to use words economically, may say about an overpriced object, "I am overpowered with admiration," rather than simply stating that it is "too expensive."

Middle Easterners, in particular, value language and its power. They tend to repeat and embellish statements to the point that native-born Americans are inclined to question their credibility. Middle Eastern-born businesspersons and customers might repeat a request so many times that you might begin to feel angry. Similarly, they are likely to feel that unless they, and you, say "yes" or "no" repeatedly, it will not have any real impact or meaning. You need to know that this repetition is meant to convey sincerity, and that the person from the Middle East may not realize your sincerity unless you repeat yourself also.

Professionals must be careful not to overreact to the elaborate statements that some cultures prefer. Such exaggerations and repetitions are usually not intended to intimidate or deceive, but, instead, reflect what is regarded as a traditional, gracious, and artistic form of expression.

Ritualistic Phrases

The English language is filled with phrases designed to fulfill routine social functions. Statements such as "I'll see you later" or "Let's get together sometime" are mere social amenities not to be taken literally. How do you feel when you greet someone with "How are you?" and he or she actually tells you—at length and in detail? In America, this question is no more than a greeting. To the Dutch, on the other hand, not stopping and listening to the answer is considered rude and self-centered.

A problem in the multicultural business world is that the person raised in another culture may take such phrases seriously. There have been cases in which employees were told to "come to dinner sometime," only to have the worker show up without a more specific invitation. This illustrates their understandable ignorance of American social norms. I am not saying that you need to curtail your use of such ritual expressions, only that you be aware that some immigrants and international visitors might, out of ignorance of American etiquette, take them literally.

Does Your Clock Run or Does It Walk?

In northern European cultures, "Punctuality is the politeness of princes." Since the eighteenth century punctuality has come to be considered a sign of productivity, reliability, and even intelligence.

Nowhere else, except perhaps in Germany, has this edict been more accepted than in corporate America. Time is precious to mainstream Americans; it can be "used," "saved," "spent," "wasted," "lost," and even "killed." Although this varies across the nation, it is generally thought that to be late to work, late for an appointment, or late with a deadline is to be lazy, sloppy, and rude. In many parts of the country, 5 minutes is considered a significant unit of time—that is, the point after which it is acceptable to feel offended or anxious at having been kept waiting. The French are only slightly more relaxed; they can wait 15 minutes before becoming impatient.

Most of the rest of the world has a more casual attitude toward time. In much of the Middle East and in Hispanic countries, to keep someone waiting for an appointment is not considered a sign of disinterest or rudeness; the clock is simply not that important. The Arabic proverb, "Haste comes from the devil," sums up these differences, as does the linguistic oddity that in the English language clocks are said to "run," in Spanish to "walk," and in native American dialects simply to "tick."

The cultures most relaxed about time are the Hispanic cultures, the Caribbean groups, some Middle Eastern cultures, and the Filipinos—the latter largely as a result of 300 years of Spanish rule. Northern Europeans and Asians generally value punctuality. The most likely exception are the Koreans, whose punctuality varies according to the situation and relationship.

This does not mean that it is acceptable for employees to be chronically late for work, appointments, meetings, or deadlines. What it does mean is that employers must understand why a worker is chronically late if they are to change that behavior. Recognizing that chronic lateness might not be based in laziness, lack of commitment, or stupidity but, instead, in culturally rooted misunderstandings about the expectations of American management, employers can design effective strategies for remedying the situation.

Nor do I intend to suggest that sales representatives and negotiators should become lax when doing business with people from these cultures. Do not get in the habit of being late yourself. If an immigrant client or

TIP: Most immigrants who are working successfully in this country have adjusted to the punctuality that is valued by American culture. Do not assume that the person will be chronically late until you have actually experienced it with that particular individual.

customer is casual about appointments, you cannot assume that he or she is uninterested in what you have to offer, nor that he or she is being intentionally rude. Get in the habit of double-checking appointments with the client. If all else fails, and the person continues to have a relaxed view of time, all you can do is accept it, recognize that it is nothing personal, and bring something enjoyable to read while you wait.

Punctuality is not the only way in which varying attitudes toward time are manifested. Those cultures which value punctuality are also concerned with meeting deadlines and keeping to schedules. Germans for example, are punctual and fastidious about precise scheduling whereas Hispanics are more casual in both areas.

Again, this relaxed attitude has largely disappeared among those who are successfully doing business in the United States. When you encounter it, compensate for these differences by allowing extra lead time in your own schedule. The more effort you make to build a substantial relationship with the individual, the more he or she will feel a personal obligation to meet your time constraints.

Summary

Although he lived and wrote in turn-of-the-century Ireland, George Bernard Shaw had a good grasp of the complexities of cultural differences when he modified the Golden Rule to read, "Do not do unto others as you would they should do unto you. Their tastes may not be the same." Just because we are equal does not mean we are the same. One of the greatest areas of diversity lies in what might seem like the inconsequential area of etiquette—the small rules that can have a big impact on relationships.

Even in the absence of specific knowledge about every cultural variation in etiquette, the following general rules will help diminish the chance of conflicts and misunderstandings:

- Etiquette makes a real difference in your professional relationships.
- The spirit of the rules is more important than the letter.
- Ask your immigrant and international contacts for details about their etiquette practices.
- Observe behaviors.
- Apologize if you make an error.
- Become aware of what bothers you.
- Proceed slowly when developing relationships.
- Err in the direction of formality.
- Match behaviors when appropriate.
- Do not overreact to varying cultural styles.
- Avoid projecting your own culture onto others.

Solidifying Your Learning

What are the three most important things you learned from this chapter and how might you apply them in your work?

1.

2.

3.

6

Cross-Cultural Customer Service and Sales

How to Achieve Client Satisfaction

Friendship first, business second.
—*Chinese Proverb*

Defining the Challenge

Mr. Shiomichi, a Japanese businessman, is flying coach class to Europe. As he is about to board, a flight attendant, Edward, offers him a vacant seat in business class. Much to Edward's surprise, the passenger declines, explaining that the move would be inappropriate since his immediate superior is already in business class. The attendant takes that in stride and proposes that Mr. Shiomichi's boss move to first class. You guessed it: the vice-president of the company was already in first class, thus thwarting Edward's well-intended efforts to deliver culturally aware customer service to his passenger. This incident, similar to one that occurred on an SAS flight some years ago, shows how complex cross-cultural customer service can be.[1]

Sales, customer service, and negotiation are difficult even in a homogenous marketplace. Each of these tasks requires the ability to communicate with human beings whose particular personalities, tastes, and needs are unique. This challenge is far greater when the marketplace in which you are working is culturally diverse. The purpose of this chapter is to help you compensate for some of this diversity and find ways to apply your skills to customers and clients regardless of their cultural background.

The following are the six basic requirements of successful sales, customer service, and negotiations. Keep these in mind as you read and watch for ways in which each of them can be met in the multicultural marketplace:

1. You must build trust.
2. You need to be at least somewhat liked.
3. You need to be able to communicate.
4. You need to know and satisfy the prospect's needs and expectations.
5. You need to make the prospect feel comfortable.
6. You must make it easy for the client or customer to buy.

The challenge of meeting these goals is increased when doing business with prospects whose expectations and needs might be different, whose knowledge of the simplest mechanics of buying—exchanges, sales tax, layaways—may be limited and whose language may preclude easy communication. If you apply what you learn in this chapter, you will soon discover that immigrant and international customers appreciate every small effort you and your frontline staff make to understand them, to meet their needs, and to make it easy for them to do business with you.

Before looking at this information, you will find it helpful to review how well you have done in the past at delivering customer service and

---

Exercise 6–1. Cross-Cultural Sales and Customer Service Experiences

1. A Successful Experience   What went right?

2. An Unsuccessful Experience   What went wrong?

sales across cultural and language barriers. Take a look at exercise 6–1 and recall an incident in which you functioned well across cultural and language barriers and a time when you had difficulty. Ask yourself what you did right in the first case and what went wrong in the second.

Now that you are aware of the times when you have and have not succeeded, you are better equipped to use the information in the following discussion to avoid the same problems in the future.

Understanding the Decision-Making Process

Any sales, customer-service, or negotiation strategy requires knowing who makes the decisions and how those decisions are made. This may be obvious when dealing with a homogenous and familiar population, but can be far more complex when faced with Asian or Hispanic immigrants who shop in large groups or when selling to a family-owned business in which many family members are involved in the decision-making process.

Who Makes the Decisions?

Why is it so important to identify precisely who the decision makers are within the immigrant and ethnic community, company, or family? The most obvious answer is efficiency. If you have no idea whom to approach, and whom to persuade, you are in danger of losing valuable time cultivating someone who has little influence on the final decision.

More important, however, is that if you approach the wrong person, particularly in the immigrant and international community, you may offend the actual decision maker. On the other hand, if you take the time to understand your prospect's culture and learn who the decision makers are, you will make a favorable first impression that can only strengthen your position.

Observation is one of the most effective ways to identify the decision makers within a community, company, or family. Observe how the members of the group relate to each other, who appears to be the leader, who dominates the conversation, and to whom the others turn for advice.

As you gain more intercultural experience, you will notice that it is often the eldest person who has the most power to make decisions. In Middle Eastern cultures, for example, it might be the eldest brother of the family or, in some cases, the eldest female. In Samoa, the eldest brother or, for those who have preserved the tribal system, an older tribal leader. Any respect you show older members of the group will be noticed and appreciated. Stand when older immigrants enter the room, shake their hands first, and address them before speaking with anyone else.

In some cultures, the decision maker is more difficult to identify. He or she might appear to be passive, uninvolved, and subservient, but in fact holds a great deal of power. Males seem to have the most power in immigrant families and businesses. Behind the scenes, however, it is often a woman who actually holds the purse strings. Watch for the Hispanic, East Indian, Japanese, Filipino, Korean, Middle Eastern, or Chinese woman who, in public, appears to have little influence but, when behind closed doors, makes important decisions regarding how the household dollar is spent. This is particularly true of the mother-in-law or eldest female.

Here's the tricky part. Although you may know that the outwardly passive female is really the one to cultivate, it is a good idea to allow the male to appear dominant in front of others. Address him directly, shake his hand, and treat him as if he holds all the power. I realize that this may be hard for you to swallow. You might think that this behavior is at best patronizing and sexist and at worst downright hypocritical. Perhaps. But, it is also true that by honoring the male's pride, you are simply adapting to his needs and to the values of his culture.

How Are Decisions Made?

In addition to identifying who makes the decisions, you also need some knowledge of how those decisions are made. Although some cultures have unusual ways of making decisions—most Japanese corporations for example, require a group consensus—immigrant groups within the United States are most likely to rely on one of two methods.

Sometimes decisions are made by the group as a whole. Because there are so many variables involved, including the degree of assimilation and nature of the decision, it is impossible to list all the specific groups that fall into this pattern. You will, however, see it most often when working with Hispanic and Middle Eastern immigrants.

The problem with the group process is that it can take time. Sometimes decisions regarding a purchase or business transaction can drag on for weeks. Remember to be patient and not push for a close too quickly. That will communicate a lack of respect for the prospect's culture and will make you appear weak and obnoxious.

If you are present while a decision is being made by those who have a flamboyant cultural style—Middle Easterners, Italians, or Hispanics, for example—do not be concerned if the discussion gets a bit heated. Raised voices and emphatic statements are just a mode of expression and in most cases do not indicate real hostility or bad feeling.

The second decision-making style is that in which one individual decides after having listened to the needs and preferences of others. From your point of view, this approach has two advantages. First, although it is important to show respect for the entire group, this system allows you to identify one individual whom you can approach and cultivate. Second, decisions are usually made faster when one person is in charge. For the mainstream American, for whom time is always a consideration, this is a distinct advantage.

Assessing Needs and Desires

Francis Bacon would probably not be surprised to hear that his comments on how to influence the decisions of other human beings are as applicable today as they were in the sixteenth century. He said of him whom we wish to persuade, "You must either know his nature and fashions and so lead him . . . or his ends and so persuade him." Nowhere is this more true than when doing business with people whose "nature," "fashions," and "ends" are unfamiliar and confusing.

What does the foreign-born or ethnic prospect want and need? Some experts in intercultural and international marketing would have us believe that, as one has put it, "a headache is a headache no matter whose it is." This may be true, perhaps "a headache is a headache," but it does not automatically follow that the headache *means* the same thing to everyone who has it or that everyone treats the pain in the same way.

Many other scholars in the field of cultural diversity contend that there are only two universal needs: sanctity of the family and freedom from physical pain. Beyond that, cultures differ. These various needs can be categorized at three levels: simple needs and wants, preferences that grow out of cultural and societal values, and needs and desires that are a reflection of broad world views and philosophical beliefs. Although a detailed discussion of the needs and wants of different groups is beyond the scope of this book, examples from each of these categories will give you an idea of what to watch for in the culturally diverse marketplace.

Simple Needs and Desires

By looking around, you can see what people in your culture or subculture tend to purchase. If you are a "yuppy," I would guess that perhaps you and your friends buy lots of yogurt, designer shampoos, and running shoes. Fortunately, guesswork like this became obsolete long ago and extensive marketing surveys came into use that reveal the specific tastes of various groups. Such surveys show, for example, that Hispanics tend to eat more canned spaghetti than other populations and to favor soft drinks, cereal, fruit nectar, and white bread. They also buy large quantities of beauty products and spend money on holidays and celebrations rather than on vacations. Hispanics, too, tend to be brand loyal, to resist the use of coupons, and to favor high-quality products that last a long time. Many Hispanics consider price to be an indication of quality.

This is just a sample of the kind of information that ethnically targeted marketing surveys can provide. Such surveys are helpful, but they are valid only as general overviews of the needs of particular groups. Remember that each individual within those groups has a unique set of needs and desires that no survey can possibly document.

Needs and Desires Related to Cultural Values

Values influence purchasing decisions and should determine appropriate marketing and advertising strategies. Advertising that depicts a Hispanic family with disobedient children and a grandmother in a nursing home will elicit little business from Hispanics, who value a traditional extended family.

Societal values dictate spending patterns as well. Hispanics and Asians, for example, tend to save and pay cash. If you work in banking or financial planning, this is something for you to consider. If you sell insurance, annuities, or retirement plans, take note of the cultural variations in attitudes toward the future. Try to redefine your product for the buyer who may feel that attempting to control the future is, at best, futile, and, at worst, blasphemous. You might emphasize how your product benefits the family by allowing the male prospect to continue fulfilling his role as provider even after he has passed away. This approach appeals to the value of family loyalty and to the importance many immigrant males place on their responsibility to the family.

Change, disposable products, new ways of doing things; these are all values with which most mainstream Americans are comfortable. Many immigrant cultures, on the other hand, value tradition more than change. They will buy a new product or do things a new way only if they are convinced that change is necessary and represents a real and tangible improvement. Do not assume, however, that they will respond to newness as intrinsicly good.

These are just a few examples of purchasing patterns that relate to culturally specific values. Take a look at the discussion of values in Chapter 4 and do some serious thinking about how you might adjust your marketing and sales approaches to accommodate these differences.

Needs and Desires Related to Cultural World Views

A "world view" is how an individual or a culture looks at the world and the conclusions they draw about what they see. "Is there a God?," "What is my purpose in life?," and "Do we have control of the events in our lives?" are the kinds of questions answered in the context of a world view.

The aspect of world view on which I would like to focus is one that is widely misunderstood and, therefore, likely to interfere with good cross-cultural understanding—superstition. Superstitions are part of world view because they reflect a belief that one can control events in supernatural ways. The term "superstition" is a biased one because it carries with it the implication that the believer is unintelligent or unsophisticated, both of which are rarely true.

In any case, superstitions can influence purchasing decisions in any

---

TIP: Just because someone gives lip service to a belief ("Oops! I just broke a mirror. I'd better throw salt over my shoulder") does not mean that he or she *completely* believes in it. Such a comment most likely only indicates that the person feels a slight anxiety associated with the superstition and wants, you might say, to "play it safe."

group. I must caution you, however, to use this information sparingly. You cannot generalize about who will hold a particular belief and who will not. If you assume, for example, that an Asian customer will not buy shoes for a friend because it would cause the friend to walk away or that a Hispanic will avoid purchasing anything involving the number thirteen, the odds are that you will be wrong. To assume that these beliefs are held by all members of any group is as foolish as maintaining that all mainstream Americans are afraid of black cats.

Before you become too judgmental of those who are, to whatever degree, "superstitious," remember that superstitions—even those strong enough to influence purchasing decisions—are not confined to immigrant and foreign cultures. Exercise 6–2 will give you a chance to find out just how superstitious you are. Check the "yes" column after those

---

Exercise 6–2. How Superstitious Are You?

	Yes	No
1. If I had a choice between row thirteen or fourteen on an airplane, I would feel safer in row fourteen.		
2. When in a challenging situation (job interview, exam, giving a presentation), I am more confident when I carry my lucky charm, use a lucky pen, or wear particular clothes.		
3. When I say something good about my life, I have an urge to knock on wood.		
4. When blowing out the candles on my birthday cake, I really make a wish even though no one would ever know if I just pretended to.		
5. When I walk under a ladder, I feel just a little bit anxious.		
6. As a child, if I stepped on a crack in the sidewalk, I worried about my mother's back.		

beliefs that make you even a little anxious. You do not have to believe completely in the superstition, but just feel a bit uncomfortable when the conditions of the belief are violated. You will probably be surprised at how many strange beliefs have a hold on you.

If you, like me, answered "yes" to even one of these questions, think twice before judging too harshly the Asian home buyer who prefers not to live on a street that forms a "T," in a cul de sac, or in a house with a tree in the front yard—all of which can attract an unlucky presence. An immigrant who mentions such a belief may not feel any more strongly about it than you do about the number thirteen—it is just a somewhat uncomfortable association.

Other examples include sanctions against purchasing a house built facing north and south, one in which the inside stairway leads straight to the front door, or one with the number four in the address. The number four is an inauspicious number throughout most of Asia whereas the number eight is auspicious.

TIP: Almost all of these superstitions have counterparts in mainstream American culture. The Asian, for example, who is hesitant to give shoes as a gift for fear of losing a friend is using the same superstitious "logic" as the mainstream American who will not give a knife as it might symbolically cut the friendship. Some Americans are still known to include a penny along with the knife to counteract any negative consequences.[2]

Needs and tastes are a part of culture. Whether it is the Japanese traveler who requests a bathtub in his hotel room or the Englishman who must have his cup of tea, the unique wants of individual groups need to be studied and understood if your marketing and sales strategies are to be effective.

How to Approach the Culturally Different Prospect

Picture this: You are a small business owner who is thinking of purchasing new carpeting for the reception room of your offices. You have contacted several carpet showrooms and invited sales representatives to bid for the job. One afternoon, you have an appointment with a very promising outlet. The salesman arrives, however, almost 45 minutes late, does not apologize, sits on your desk, fiddles with your pens, and asks you intimate questions about your family and background.

What are the chances of you buying carpet from this fellow? Not very good. Your decision to go elsewhere has nothing to do with quality, price, or service; it has everything to do with the fact that the sales representative violated nearly every standard of what mainstream American culture dictates is appropriate in a situation like this. This is exactly the same thing that can happen if sales, service, and negotiation professionals are ignorant of what can make the immigrant, ethnic, or international prospect uncomfortable.

Building the Relationship

In ancient Greece, Hermes, the god of cunning and trickery, was the patron deity of merchants and traders. The old Italian word for retail meant a tendency to cheat. Throughout most of the world, "merchants and traders," and let's face it, that's what many of us are, are automatically distrusted. You have the power to earn that trust, but it takes time and the careful cultivation of many relationships; as the Chinese say, "Friendship first, business second."

The problem is that native-born Americans tend to be impatient. We imagine that taking hours, days, or even months to build trust is a waste of a precious commodity. If you stop, however, and think about the development of any relationship, you will realize that those that take the longest to build, be they friendships, romances, or business associations, are the strongest, most meaningful, and most productive.

How have you done in the past? Do you take the time to become a *buena gente* ("a nice person") as they say in Puerto Rico, or do you rush into things and expect to be trusted on the basis of your credentials alone? Exercise 6–3 will tell the tale.

The more times you checked "Always" or "Usually," the more aware you are of the importance of cultivating relationships. Some of the principles discussed in this book can be applied to all immigrant and ethnic groups, while others cannot. Taking time to build relationships is one of the suggestions that can be quite safely applied to a wide variety of cultures. The trust you generate with culturally diverse clients is as important as your expertise.

If an Arab-born immigrant or businessperson hasn't gotten to know you, he or she is not apt to listen to what you have to say. If you have taken the time to develop the relationship, he or she will be receptive to your ideas. The importance of relationships in the Arab community comes clear when your Arabic counterpart asks you to enter into a business arrangement in the name of friendship—"Do it for me." This is not an attempt to presume on your friendship, it is merely the way business is conducted in the Middle East. It also means that, once a relationship has been developed, you, too, can appeal to friendship.

There are four primary ways in which these relationships can be cultivated. These are (1) be formal; (2) take an interest in the other person; (3) share of yourself; and (4) use your connections.

1. **Be formal.** We discussed formality in Chapter 5, but the topic is so important that it deserves review. In many communities, for example,

---

Exercise 6–3. Taking Your Time

1. Even though a Mexican-born businessperson seems anxious to buy my service, I still spend a lot of time with him socially before trying to close the deal.

Always	Usually	Sometimes	Seldom	Never
____	____	____	____	____

2. When doing business with people from other cultures, I make an effort to learn about their interests and families as a way of building the relationship.

Always	Usually	Sometimes	Seldom	Never
____	____	____	____	____

3. When socializing with immigrant and international prospects, I am able to wait until the other party brings up the subject of business even if it is not until after several meetings.

Always	Usually	Sometimes	Seldom	Never

---

casual dress in a business situation can signal the other party that you do not respect them, that you will be equally casual with deadlines and attention to detail, and that the client and the business transaction are not important enough to warrant dressing up. Pay attention to your dress and to the other rules of formality already discussed.

2. **Take an interest in the other person.** This means everything from pronouncing the client's name correctly to communicating an interest in other aspects of his or her life. When working with a Puerto Rican or Middle Easterner, this means to make inquiries after family members and personal interests. In the latter case, however, it is a good rule of thumb to avoid asking specific questions about female members of the family. Although this practice is far more acceptable among Middle Eastern immigrants in the United States than it would be abroad, I would caution you to play safe and keep your inquiries general.

TIP: It is perfectly all right to ask for the correct pronunciation of someone's name. There is no need to feel embarrassed about this, nor to be concerned that the other party will be offended. Your asking will be appreciated because it shows that you care and signals that it is all right for the immigrant to ask similar questions about you and about American culture.

The amount of personal information that individuals are prepared to share will vary substantially among immigrant groups. Arabic immigrants, will, with the exception mentioned above, reveal more about themselves than most Asians or Europeans. In general, avoid asking anyone about politics or religion, or making extremely personal queries such as, "Why haven't you been married?" or "Are you going to have children?"

3. **Share of yourself.** Do not be surprised or offended, however, if some immigrants (Filipinos, for example) ask some quite intimate questions in return. They do not intend to be rude or nosy; they are merely showing an interest in your life. How much you reveal is up to you. If you are not comfortable answering a question, simply deflect it by changing the subject.

As usual, we cannot generalize. Some cultures are comfortable with discussing fairly intimate facts and, if you are too reserved, will conclude that you are hiding something. Others, such as Asians and most Europeans, will be embarrassed by such openness and consider it a sign of weakness and naivete.

4. Use your connections. The key to building relationships that last is using previous associations to start the process. Avoid the cold call. If you do not know anyone within a given ethnic or cultural group, make it your business to get to know the community, its leaders, its expectations, and its way of doing things. In the course of building connections that may prove valuable in the future, you will end up in a better position to utilize these new associations when the time comes.

Build your business friendships slowly; once they are acquired, you will have not only a lucrative customer or client, but an ally for years. Among the Japanese, for example, once a personal relationship has been formed, so too have personal obligations. A Thai will buy from a friend just to help out and Middle Easterners place great stock on previous associations. Look on your efforts as an investment in the future—they are certain to pay off.

Presenting the Material

Once you have built a good relationship, you must design the most effective way to present your product or service. Before looking at how to adapt presentation styles to various cultures, use exercise 6–4 to examine briefly the conventional wisdom about good sales and service techniques as they are practiced in the United States.

Probably you wrote down that you give lots of hard data, emphasize short- and long-term benefits, point out ways your product or service is superior to that of your competitors, take an objective approach, and minimize emotional appeals. You will see shortly that these techniques, although basically solid, are not effective with all cultures. The following nine suggestions will sometimes be more appropriate.

1. **Present your product or service in person if possible.** Doing business on the telephone can be very difficult in view of accent and language barriers. As you know, 50 percent of the impact of your message is based on body language and the other 35 percent on tone of

voice. Body language is completely lost on the telephone and tone of voice seriously compromised.

Meeting in person also allows you to continue the process of building trust. Personal meetings have the added benefit of allowing you to meet associates, relatives, and other members of the community, all of whom can strengthen your connections and increase the opportunities of doing additional business.

2. **Do not make your presentation too soon.** If you have arranged what you expect to be a business lunch, but the client seems reluctant to bring up business, wait until he or she introduces the subject. To discuss

---

Exercise 6–4. Traditional Presentation Styles

In the space below, jot down three ideas about the basics of sales and service. It might be something like: listen to the prospect's needs, be prepared to overcome objections, etc. When you are finished, we will discuss some approaches that might come as a surprise and that differ very much from those to which you are accustomed:

1.

2.

3.

---

business prematurely will appear pushy and rude and can even leave the impression that you are overanxious, desperate, and insecure.

Do not chance losing the relationship by moving too fast now. *You* know that your haste comes from how important the deal is to you; the prospect may see it differently. To him or her, your rush may indicate that the transaction does not mean very much to you and is not worth your time and patience. Recognize and accept the fact that you might have to attend several meetings before business is even discussed. Preliminary gatherings are often intended, not as actual "business" meetings, but more as opportunities for the parties to get to know one another better.

TIP: If this "courting" stage takes too long and you need to move it along for practical reasons, at least wait until there is a lengthy lull in the conversation before plunging in.

---

3. **Do not present too much detail at one time.** Native-born and assimilated Americans value rational thinking; the more logical the argument, the harder the data, the more concrete the detail, the more impressed we are. The German prospect responds well to hard data, but the Hispanic or Thai might become impatient with too much documentation. Members of these groups feel that too many details distort the larger picture, which is more clearly seen by discussing the broader benefits of a product.

Do not spell everything out. Asians, for example, will respond better if you provide the general picture first. Do not try to wrap up each point as you go along. There is an old joke, "Ask an American the time and he'll tell you how to build a clock." This attention to detail often gives the impression that you are showing off.

Mainstream Americans feel a need to support every idea and thought with a fact. We have less confidence in the power and validity of abstract thought than others do. European cultures, on the other hand, have great faith in reasoning from one general concept to another. Non-Western cultures take this further and approach the world through intuition and direct experience. They often consider masses of specific information not only unnecessary, but distorting of the true picture.

4. Consider using emotional and personal appeals. Related to these differing attitudes toward concrete details is the fact that mainstream Americans are suspicious of emotional appeals. They rely heavily on hard evidence, tend to quantify benefits, and place great value on financial gain. American-born buyers generally respond best to rational and logical sales approaches. They appreciate ad campaigns that show that the product has been thoroughly tested and testimonials from "real people" who are "satisfied customers" give the American buyer the proof that their rational instincts crave. In response to this attitude, sales professionals and front-line employees are often guilty of ignoring the mood of the prospect, neglecting to comment on any aesthetic and emotional value that a product might possess, and plunging ahead with the concrete figures and statistics that they themselves would like to hear.

In contrast, sales and customer-service efforts that are based on emotions and aesthetics are more successful with many immigrant and ethnic groups. Even the Japanese, who respect hard data, appreciate a more subjective approach. Most groups respect a presentation that also points up the benefits of a product to the prospect's associates and friends or even to the entire community. Hispanic businesspersons will generally respond favorably to a proposal that promises to create jobs, homes, and recreational opportunities.

Hispanics also tend to buy on impulse and instinct. For this reason, appeals to subjective factors, aesthetics, and sentiment can be far more effective with Hispanic buyers than the hard facts that appeal to mainstream Americans. Middle Easterners and, to a lesser extent, Asians can also be influenced by these considerations.

5. Praise the competition, or, at least, refrain from criticizing it. This suggestion is really nothing more than good judgment and good manners. If you praise the competition, your prospect will know that you have confidence in your own product, that you are gracious, and that you are honest. The latter, in particular, is the key to having successful cross-cultural business relationships.

6. Refrain from bragging about your importance or your influence. It is one thing to be confident and open and quite another to be arrogant. The first two are appreciated and respected, the last is frowned upon. Flaunting your strengths will only cause you to lose respect. It can also cause the prospect, who may not be as well-connected or accomplished as you are, to lose face.

7. Persuade, do not push. If, in the course of a sale or negotiation, you hit a stumbling block, let it go for the moment. Never back the prospect into a corner. The decision-making process can take time. Rushing it can easily make you appear pushy, rude, and overanxious. The prospect could drag his or her feet to compensate for your urgency or back out of the transaction altogether. This applies, by the way, as much to a customer in a retail store as it does to negotiations between multinational corporations.

Saving face is the issue here. Most immigrant businesspersons and customers are concerned that no one suffer embarrassment. If you push for a close, he or she will be forced either to back down or turn you down abruptly. In either case, the loss of harmony and face can do permanent damage to your relationship and to your reputation within the community.

TIP: When selling or negotiating across cultural lines, allow enough time for the contingencies of a long decision-making process, the need to cultivate relationships, and the possibility of stalled negotiations. Expect the process to take longer, and it will be far easier for you to restrain your impatience and allow the colleague or customer to proceed at his or her culturally appropriate pace.

---

8. **Refrain from getting upset.** Or at least refrain from showing that you are upset. Even cultures that have a high tolerance for overt displays of emotion, will be unimpressed if you become visibly angry, anxious, or impatient. No matter what, stay calm. To do otherwise is to leave the impression that you are weak, undisciplined, and unprofessional.

9. **Question prospects cautiously and respectfully.** It is often necessary to gather personal information from prospects and clients. Requesting information, for example, about one's medical history is routine when selling insurance and questions about finances and employment must be asked when applying for a loan.

In the United States, revealing information about oneself and one's family is fairly commonplace. We have come to accept it as a normal part of living in a complex and bureaucratic society. We generally trust the corporations and governments who ask how much we make a year or where we lived 10 years ago to use that information for the stated purpose and nothing else.

In many immigrant and ethnic cultures, the attitude is very different. Distrust of large organizations and ignorance of their workings makes immigrants reluctant to reveal even the most innocuous bits of information about themselves and their families. For those who are, or at one time were, illegal aliens this situation is exacerbated by a no longer appropriate fear of "exposure."

In addition to this fear, revealing information about oneself and one's family is taboo in many cultures. For this reason health professionals sometimes have difficulty taking medical histories from immigrant patients and insurance agents have trouble learning of previous accidents, illnesses, and other misfortunes. Much of this reticence comes from a profound sense of privacy of self, family members, and community.

Above all, there is a reluctance to mention anything that might reflect negatively on the family. We have already seen how important the family is within immigrant and ethnic communities. This reluctance to reveal information is just another manifestation of that value. It is sometimes surprising to the person asking the questions that things a mainstream American might think nothing of are often revealed very reluctantly. Failed businesses, previous periods of poverty, severe illnesses, minor psychological problems—each of these is an example of the kind of information that might be concealed out of fear, pride, and protectiveness.

To avoid difficulty gathering information from immigrant and ethnic prospects, first explain why you need the information. Often we are asked things that seem nonsensical to us, but we answer because we assume that there must be some reason for the query. The immigrant does not make this assumption. If you need a financial statement or a particularly intimate piece of medical history, tell the client to what use that information will be put and why it is absolutely necessary that you obtain it. Do not just say, "I *have* to have it"; give the very specific reason *why* you must obtain the information.

Make it clear that the information is confidential and will be used for no other purpose than that which you just stated. If there is any chance of the revelation being used for something else, or seen by anyone else, say so. Honesty is the only approach. It will improve the client's attitude toward you and help him or her better understand the system.

Finally, if possible, conduct your questioning in private. This might mean the exclusion of family members. Asians and Hispanics, for example, are discreet about gynecological disease and might be uncomfortable discussing it in front of children, relatives, or neighbors of the opposite sex. Give your client a choice between being alone or having someone else there. Do not project your own idea of comfort onto the other person. Whereas you might be very open with family members and consider it an insult to exclude them, the immigrant may not want to have a relative involved in so intimate a conversation.

Concessions and Bargaining

Mainstream Americans look down on bargaining. We tend to regard it as crass, greedy, and low class. The conviction that bargaining is in poor taste is an example of the ethnocentrism discussed in Chapter 1. Much of the rest of the world regards bargaining as a sign of sophistication and good business acumen. In fact, Mexican, Middle Eastern, Korean, Chinese, and Southeast Asian customers and businesspersons are likely to consider you cold and unimaginative if you do not bargain.

If, in your dealings with immigrant customers and businesspeople, you encounter someone who wishes to bargain over the price of a product or service, remember that this does not mean the person is greedy or dishonest. Corporate America "bargains" too in the form of seeking concessions in business transactions. It is more a matter of setting (a corporate office versus a clothing store) than of behavior.

Whether faced with a customer who wishes to bargain on the price of your product or a buyer who seeks one last concession minutes before closing a real-estate deal, realize that this behavior is a part of an age-old way of doing business and is motivated by a desire to exhibit negotiating skill and save face by obtaining concessions from the other party. Even the smallest concession on your part will save face for the client and preserve a good working relationship for you both.

Having said this, do not make concessions too soon. Most immigrant prospects or colleagues will regard that as a sign of weakness. Some Asians, for example, will doubt your integrity if you back down on a position quickly. Let them make the first concession.

What to Expect from the Prospect

Learning to build relationships and present your product or service to the culturally different prospect are only the first steps to success. The next is to learn what negotiation strategies, style, and demeanor to expect from the other person.

What I have done here is to quickly review material covered in greater detail throughout the book while applying it to the specific topics of customer service, sales, and negotiations. Examined below are those behaviors you are most likely to encounter and that carry with them the greatest risk of misunderstanding.

1. *Lateness to appointments and interruptions in meetings do not mean that the client is not interested in what you have to offer.* In Chapter 5, we discussed the significance of lateness among immigrant groups and the fact that just because a prospect or client is casual about punctuality, it does not mean that he or she is uninterested in you or your proposal.

The same applies to those prospects who allow and even encourage interruptions during business meetings. Perhaps you've seen a Hispanic family crowd around during a visit to the prospect's home or the Middle Eastern professional keep the door open during your time together. Both these behaviors reflect a warmer and more casual attitude than that usually encountered in mainstream American culture.

Allowing interruptions during meetings also reflects a differing attitude toward the proper use of time. In the United States, it is generally agreed that a person should do one thing at a time. To flit from task to task is considered inefficient and a sign of poor concentration. In many other countries, on the other hand, doing several things at once is the norm—thus the interruptions and multiple encounters during your sales meeting.

2. *When an Asian client or prospect is self-deprecating, it does not mean that he or she is lacking in confidence.* Do not assume that the client is fishing for a compliment or manipulating you into feeling sorry for them. More likely, it is a sign of social graciousness designed to maintain harmony and avoid calling attention to the individual. If you have complimented a colleague, for example, and he or she vehemently denies the truth of your praise, quietly rebut the denial once and briefly, and move on to the next subject.

3. *Do not overreact to the assertive style of the Korean, German, Middle Eastern, and Chinese customer or client.* Remember what you found out in Chapter 5 about variations in cultural style. Behavior is not always an accurate indication of a person's intent or feelings; often it is just a reflection of the individual's cultural style. A Chinese male immigrant, might, for example, feel perfectly calm while he tries to make his point by speaking loudly and harshly. So too, as we have seen, might the Middle Easterner repeat himself, interrupt, and exaggerate in an attempt to get his ideas across.

Misunderstandings also arise when immigrants attempt verbally to bypass frontline employees to get what they hope to be preferential treatment from superiors. As we saw in our discussion of attitudes toward authority, rules are often very flexible in other countries. It becomes routine for dissatisfied customers to ask to see someone higher up who may be willing to listen to the customer's needs and make the necessary adjustments. This behavior usually represents no more than a misunderstanding about how American business functions.

4. *Asian, Hispanic, and Middle Eastern prospects will sometimes turn you down so gently that you will be unsure of their intent.* When unhappy about your proposal, Asian, Hispanic, or Middle Eastern prospects will often answer with vague statements like, "This could be difficult," "This will take time," or "I'll have to check with my superiors." There might also be unreturned phone calls, delayed meetings, or your offer might be countered with a question that ignores the subject all together.

TIP: Koreans and Iraqis are the exception to this rule and usually will let you know exactly where you stand.

These gentle rebuffs are not designed to lead you on or humiliate you, but, quite the opposite, to save face for all parties. When you hear them, do not continue to hammer away with arguments and figures; back away. To do otherwise will eliminate any chance of salvaging the deal and possibly even doing future business.

Before you judge these vague answers too harshly, have you ever been asked to a party, knew perfectly well that you could not go (or did not want to), but still responded to the invitation with a hearty, "My goodness, I'd love to, I'll certainly try to make it"? You did this, no doubt, in order to let the hostess down easy. This is no different from when the Hispanic says, "I'll see what I can do" knowing full well that your demand cannot be met.

The problem is that it is sometimes difficult to decipher when a gentle statement or evasive action is a refusal and when it is not. If you are unsure of the meaning of one of these softened rebuffs, consult with someone else who is either from the same country or who has worked with these individuals.

Also, take a cue from your immigrant counterpart and get in the habit of softening your refusals as well. Save face and build solid relationships by giving up some of the trademark directness that is characteristic of corporate America. Rather than saying, "That offer isn't good enough," comment instead that, "It *might be difficult* to sell it to you for that price" or "Perhaps some adjustments are necessary."

5. *Asian and Hispanic customers tend to complain in very softened terms.* Professionals in retail and in the service industries realize that customers who complain are a blessing. Without them, there is no way to know how well you are doing or where you stand. Unfortunately, close to 100 percent of dissatisfied customers will go elsewhere without saying a word. Worse, every unhappy customer will tell ten people about the problem, and, in most cases, you will not be among those ten.

Within Asian immigrant communities, this difficulty is exacerbated by two factors. First, the Asian customer generally considers it inappropriate to say anything negative. Like the worker who quits because of loss of face rather than confront you with a difficulty, the Asian customer will disappear, and do so more quietly than his or her dissatisfied native-born counterpart. Add to this the problem of softened negatives mentioned above, and you really have no way of knowing if these customers are satisfied. If, for example, you ask an Asian a question like, "Is everything all right?" and he or she answers with, "It's OK," you really cannot tell if you should take that response literally or if it is a vague answer designed to cover up real dissatisfaction.

How can you as customer-service professionals and frontline employees, encourage complaints from immigrant and ethnic customers who might otherwise be reluctant to let you know of problems? The following will help:

1. Learn to recognize the softened complaint.
2. Invite anonymous complaints (complaint forms, suggestion box).
3. Make it easy for customers to complain in private thus minimizing embarrassment to all parties.
4. Make certain that your customers understand how to complain (to whom and by what mechanism).
5. Let customers know that you want and need their complaints and advice in order to run a more successful business.
6. Make certain that your customers know that their suggestions will be listened to and that they will make a real difference.

One of America's favorite proverbs is, "The squeaky wheel gets the grease." Contrast this to the Japanese saying, "The nail that sticks out gets hammered down," and it becomes clear how different our views are on this issue.

6. *Do not be put off by silence or pauses.* Silences and pauses do not necessarily mean that your prospect or client is upset, angry, or disapproving. A pause in the conversation can be an indication of respect for what you have just said, a sign that your proposal is being thought about, an indication that the listener is trying to figure out a way to give you what you want without losing face, or, simply, an indication that the prospect is taking time to translate what you have said and formulate a comment or question.

Remember not to succumb to the temptation to say something just because you are uncomfortable with the silence. Do not make concessions just to keep the conversation going. Follow the guidelines presented in Chapter 5 and remember that if you break the silence, it could be interpreted as weakness and place you at a disadvantage.

7. *Contracts have varying meaning in different cultures.* In the United States, we have a passion for putting everything in "black and white," for "getting it in writing," and "putting pen to paper." In corporate America, writing something down means that it has real importance. We respect a handshake, but a written contract is what really matters.

In other parts of the world, contracts have very different meanings. In the Middle East, for example, insisting on a contract can be taken as an insulting implication that he or she is not trustworthy. Asians generally think of contracts as merely symbols of good faith, not something to force a party to submit later. Contracts are flexible in Asia to allow for changes in circumstances. A similar attitude prevails in many Hispanic countries.

This does not mean that the contracts you sign with immigrant or ethnic businesspersons will not be honored. It just means that a request for a contract should be approached with greater diplomacy and awareness. Not all parties are as anxious as you to get to the contract stage.

Summary

Selling and delivering customer service to people from other backgrounds requires you to use the most sophisticated of your cross-cultural communication and negotiation skills. Many of the people you will be dealing with are worldly negotiators and consumers who have built successful new lives in a strange land. This chapter, along with the more detailed exploration of some of these issues in the rest of the book, will help you cultivate mutually profitable intercultural relationships. Remember to:

- Identify the decision makers (do not make any assumptions).
- Learn about and respect the immigrant's decision-making process.
- Identify culturally specific needs, tastes and desires.
- Take the time to build trusting relationships.
- Refine your presentation techniques.
- Recognize and understand culturally different responses and negotiation styles.
- Persuade, do not push.

Solidifying Your Learning

What are the three most important things you learned from this chapter and how you might apply them in your work?

1.

2.

3.

The Multicultural Work Force

How to Manage across Cultural Boundaries

It is immigrants who brought to this land the skills of their hands and brains to make of it a beacon of opportunity and of hope for all men.
—*Herbert Hohenman*

Louis has three employees: a Californian, fond of jogging; a New Yorker, very assertive and fast-paced; and a Southerner, elegant and soft-spoken. You might argue that Louis has a work force of mainstream Americans, whose individual needs and values are largely the same. That's what Louis thought until the day he learned that the Californian was unhappy with the conventional dress code that was required on the job, the New Yorker was bored with the slow pace of the business, and the Southerner was uncomfortable with the aggressive manner of her supervisor.

Skill at managing a diversity of individual personalities, backgrounds, and styles is needed in any workplace. The only thing that is different when managing employees who were born and raised in other cultures or who adhere to the values of other cultures, is that the variations are more obvious, the similarities more obscured, and the specific information that you need to learn more important.

Interviewing and Assessing the Culturally Different Worker

Interviewing and assessing culturally different employees and applicants, whether initially or during a performance appraisal, can be difficult. Language barriers and varying presentation styles can create confusion, misunderstanding, and frustration for both parties. The following will help minimize these difficulties and improve your chances of formulating an accurate and fair assessment of the worker's abilities.

Some General Tips on Interviewing

Be cautious not to stereotype the applicant or employee on the basis of his or her ethnic background, name, or accent. If you find an image coming into your head as soon as you see an Hispanic surname or an Asian face, shove it aside. Think back to what happened to our friend Nancy in Chapter 1 and you'll know how dangerous this practice can be. Evaluate each individual for who he or she is; do not allow stereotypes to block your view.

Do not draw rash conclusions from a gentle handshake, direct or indirect eye contact, or any other behavior related to cultural style. These are just the trappings of culture, the cloak that conceals the person beneath. You cannot make any assumptions about what a person is feeling or what his or her personality is like on the basis of external, culturally dictated behaviors. The Hispanic woman, for example, who drops her eyes as she speaks to you is probably not hiding something about her previous employment, but, instead, is simply being polite.

Conduct the interview in private. The applicant will feel more at ease, more open about himself or herself, and more comfortable speaking English.

How to Interview the Modest Applicant

We have already seen that Asian and Hispanic applicants and employees are often reluctant to praise themselves, an attitude that grows out of the value placed on personal anonymity and respect for authority. As gracious as this is, the interviewer still has the problem of finding out what the worker's qualifications really are. Without the worker's testimony there is the temptation to conclude that he or she does not have any qualifications. The following will help you discover the applicant's strengths and weaknesses even in the face of extreme modesty:

1. **Look at objective proof of past performance.** Ask to see reports that applicants have written or samples of products they have produced in previous or current positions. You might also examine hard data of the employee's product rejection rate and ability to meet quotas.

2. **Supply workers with job-related problems to solve.** In short, test them on their ability to do what is required. Whether this is testing a social skill (such as supervision) or a manual task, it is a quick and accurate way to check for qualifications.

3. **Check references.** Unfortunately, this can be a difficult, time-consuming, and even impossible if the applicant has just arrived in this country. It should be no problem, however, for those who have previously worked in the United States.

4. **Allow workers to praise themselves in writing.** Writing down one's qualifications and personal attributes can be less threatening and embarrassing than stating them out loud. Also, this exercise serves a secondary function of checking for English-language writing skills.

5. **Ask applicants or employees what coworkers would say about their performance.** This technique makes applicants more comfortable by creating the illusion that someone else is doing the praising. Workers might, for example, report that fellow employees would probably say they are easy to get along with, conscientious, and hard working. Whatever it is, you will know more than you did before.

6. **Have someone else report on the applicant's qualifications.** This is not the same as checking references because this person is not apt to be a former boss, but, more likely, a former or current coworker. I am not saying here that this testimonial would be completely reliable but, combined with other data, it can be very helpful.

7. **Ask a series of specific questions in order to learn of past accomplishments.** Gathering together many small details will give you more information than asking a few general questions. An all-encompassing question puts workers in a position of having to praise themselves, but a series of smaller queries allows them to answer objectively:

General Question:
I understand you were a supervisor on your last job, were you good at it?
More Specific Questions:
1. How well did the workers under you get along with each other?
2. Did your workers generally understand and follow your instructions or did they often make mistakes?
3. Would you want to be a supervisor again or would you rather not work in a supervisory position? If not, why not?

You will notice that these are not "yes" or "no" questions, but require somewhat lengthy responses. In this way, you avoid the possibility of eliciting nothing more than terse "yes" or "no" answers.

Assessing English Language Ability

Depending on the position, there are times when you must assess how much English foreign-born applicants understand, speak, read, and write. If you have never had to judge a person's English-language facility, you may think this a simple task. Those of you who have hired employees, only to discover that they have great difficulty speaking to customers or understanding instructions, realize that this is not so easy. The following will help you make this assessment as efficiently and compassionately as possible:

1. **Ask workers to complete the job application in your office and to do so alone.** This negates the possibility of workers getting help from family members or friends and allows you to assess how well they read the instructions and filled out the form.
2. **Have some of the instructions on the application be more complex than just "name," "address," and "education."** The applicant may be familiar with those words from previous experience; lengthier instructions are a better test of the ability to read English.
3. **Include a request for a short essay somewhere on the application so that the worker will be forced to demonstrate English writing skills.** This might be the essay that was mentioned above in which the applicant writes down his or her personal qualifications for the job.
4. **Engage the applicant in extensive conversation in order to tell how much English is spoken and understood.** The techniques found in Chapter 2 are useful for encouraging this exchange.

Although not all positions require English language facility and it is not always appropriate or legal to test for this skill, these four simple steps can facilitate the process when it is necessary.

Cross-Cultural Motivation: Achieving Employee Behavior Change

Effective motivation strategies are based on the ability to assess an employee's needs and match them to those of the organization. The challenge comes when we realize that the needs of employees, even within one company and from one culture, are diverse. One worker might need more money; another might prefer more authority; a third might be satisfied by something as simple as a better parking spot.

This challenge is amplified in the multicultural workplace. Something that motivates a worker from one ethnic or immigrant group might easily be meaningless to another. The six steps listed below and discussed throughout this section, will help you design motivation strategies for a harmonious and productive multicultural workplace. These six steps are:

1. Interpret the behavior correctly.
2. Explain your expectations and the expectations of American management.
3. Compromise.
4. Speak the worker's "cultural language."
5. Honor culturally specific felt needs.
6. Positively reinforce the desired behavior.

Each of these steps can be used as part of an overall strategy or taken individually depending on the situation.

Throughout the previous chapters, we have looked at a number of core behaviors commonly found in the multicultural workplace. Among these are:

- Hesitance to take independent initiative on tasks
- Reluctance to complain or make negative statements
- Failure to admit lack of understanding
- Reluctance to seek or accept promotions
- Reluctance to praise self
- Speaking of foreign languages in the workplace

These behaviors will be used to illustrate the six steps. Of course, each technique can be applied to any behavior—not just those discussed here. You will find that these approaches are particularly effective for behaviors that are most deeply rooted in differing values and expectations.

Overcoming Resistance to Change

Any thinking human being, including your ethnic and foreign-born workers, will, of course, resist being changed by someone else. Before managers can effectively use any motivation techniques, they must understand the reasons for this resistance and learn how to overcome it.

Much reluctance to change arises from the workers mistaken impression that employers and managers are trying to change their basic values. Although you are concerned only with modifying a specific behavior, workers might assume that you are trying to eradicate their entire culture.

Understandably, and rightly, many immigrants are committed to maintaining their cultural identity. When they perceive a threat—real or imagined—these workers naturally feel considerable anxiety. For most of us, our culture is a part of our essential identity. When our culture is compromised, we are too.

Behavioral scientists know that in order for change to occur, the subject—in this case, the culturally diverse worker—must feel psychologically secure enough to make that adjustment. Anxiety about losing one's cultural identity, can only interfere with receptivity to new ideas and behaviors. A defensive reaction is even more likely when the employee is already in a state of culture shock—disoriented and threatened by being immersed in a strange culture.

Exercise 7–1 will help you understand these feelings. Each question assumes that you have been suddenly transported to an unfamiliar culture and are being asked to do something that does not fit with your most basic principles.

To the first question, you probably responded with "diminished," "trapped," "insulted," and "dominated." Similarly, you might have felt, in response to the second question, that the boss was not accepting his or her responsibility, that you were being asked to be dishonest, and, certainly, that the boss was not very good at his or her job.

If told to pretend to understand everything that is said, most of us would feel as if we were being asked to be dishonest. We also might conclude that the supervisor does not care whether we learn the material.

Being forbidden to strive for promotions would instantly call up feelings of bondage, frustration, and insult. Similarly, if we are not allowed to mention our achievements in appropriate settings, we tend to feel that they do not matter, that we might as well not strive anymore, and that we are less accomplished than we previously thought.

The specifics of your responses are not what is important here. The point is that when you are asked to behave in ways that counter the values of your up-bringing—in the case of this exercise, straight forwardness, ambition, and pride—your emotional reactions can be very strong. Among those emotions are likely to be confusion, resentment, possibly anger, and certainly, resistance.

A second reason for resistance to behavior change is the worker's

Exercise 7–1. Culturally Challenging Requests

1. If my boss told me that I was never to take the initiative on tasks but wait to be told to make every move, I would feel . . .

2. If someone tried to convince me that I should keep everything that goes wrong from the boss and never complain, I would feel . . .

3. If my supervisor told me that I should always pretend to understand what has been said and never ask any questions, I would feel . . .

4. If a manager told me to stay in my place and never seek promotions, I would feel . . .

5. If someone told me that I was never to say anything about my accomplishments or skills, I would feel . . .

belief that the manager, in requesting a different way of doing things, is implying that the worker's old method was somehow deficient and wrong. (We will see in a moment how to overcome this problem.)

Finally, foreign-born and ethnic workers might be reluctant to adapt new behaviors for the simple reason that some of the things they are being asked to do seem very strange. Realize that to ask an Asian to praise him- or herself in front of a group, for example, is like asking you to walk into a party and immediately begin bragging to the first stranger who comes along. For Hispanics to seek promotions over countrymen older than themselves would be like asking the mainstream American to sabotage the professional progress of a dear friend just to advance within the company—to do so would be a source of shame, not pride.

As far as taking the initiative on tasks, it would be like expecting you to stride into the boss's office and begin cleaning his or her desk without having been asked to do so. To expect an Asian worker to complain about something is like demanding that you inform the boss of every insignificant negative event that happens on the job—it just does not feel right.

This should give you and your managers some idea of what the culturally different worker feels when asked to meet the expectations of American employers. These generalities do not, of course, apply to every immigrant or ethnic worker, but they do make the point.

Now that we understand the roots of resistance, it is time to look at how this defensiveness can be overcome. Obviously each of the following six steps to cross-cultural motivation is designed in some way to diminish resistance. There are, however, two other techniques that must be mentioned: the use of reassurance and the bestowing of power.

The truth is, or ought to be, that you are concerned only with maintaining a properly functioning workplace, not with altering any personally held beliefs or cultural values. By reassuring the worker that you are merely asking him or her to change an isolated behavior, that you have no interest in modifying his or her entire culture, a great deal of resistance can be overcome. Reassurance should also be provided that you are not implying that his or her previous way of doing things was wrong but merely that it does not function well in the American workplace.

A second way to overcome resistance is to give the worker as much power as possible. People do not resist changing; they resist being changed. By including employees in the decision to change, they are more likely to make the behavior their own.

Do not just tell workers what to do; ask them how far they are prepared to go in modifying their usual way of doing things. By giving them the power to participate in the decision and in the specific details of the change, you will decrease anxiety and defensiveness and increase the chance of compliance. Even if you find that your workers do not wish to contribute to this decision because of discomfort with participative management, you will still have asked for their comments, a gesture that is empowering unto itself.

Interpret the Behavior Correctly

The first of the six steps to successful cross-cultural motivation is to understand why a worker behaves a particular way. This is important for two reasons. First, it communicates to workers that you respect them enough to learn what might be very culturally specific reasons for particular attitudes and behaviors. This respect enables the worker to feel less defensive and, therefore, to be far more willing to cooperate.

Second, correctly interpreting behavior has to do with the development of appropriate and successful motivation strategies. Only if we understand why a person behaves a particular way can we design the correct approach to modify that behavior. Assessing why workers do what they do can be difficult enough when you all share the same background; it is even more difficult when a given worker's values and expectations are different from your own.

The following case study addresses the issue of speaking a foreign language in the workplace. Although, as of this writing, it is inappropriate and illegal to insist that workers speak only English in the workplace unless such a prohibition is a legitimate business necessity, there are still times when it is proper to suggest that English be spoken especially around customers, clients, or other workers. The resolution to the case study will give you some idea of how such suggestions can be made.

Shea is a supervising nurse on the night shift of a large metropolitan hospital. Her staff consists of many nurses who were born and trained overseas. One of her nurses, Cecilia, is from the Philippines and is a wonderful caregiver except that she speaks Tagalog within earshot of her patients. Shea assumes that Cecilia is doing this so that she can gossip with her friends and talk about the patients without being understood.

Although they originally liked Cecilia, some of her patients have begun to complain, and it is obvious that they have lost faith in her. Shea finally got fed up with the situation and became angry with Cecilia in front of the other nurses. Because Shea knew that Cecilia has a great deal of respect for authority, she was surprised to find that she has continued to speak her own language around the patients.

What might Shea have done wrong? Why didn't Cecilia respond to her supervisor's obvious dissatisfaction with the situation? The answer is that Shea failed to understand the causes of Cecilia's behavior. If Shea had tried to put herself in Cecilia's place and if she had more knowledge of immigrant workers, she might have resolved the problem successfully.

Shea might have tried to imagine what it would be like if she were working in a stressful job in a foreign country where most of the workers speak a language that Shea understands but has trouble speaking. She might have imagined having few English-speaking coworkers and how tempting it would be to speak English with them when she is in need of relaxed companionship.

Had Shea attempted to understand Cecilia's emotions and culture, she would have realized that Cecilia was probably not speaking Tagalog in order to gossip behind the backs of colleagues and patients. She more likely was using her own language in an effort to function more efficiently in the often stressful health-care setting. Possibly she did not realize what she was doing and simply slipped into her language when she was rushed or fatigued. She might also have been lonely and felt the need to communicate with someone who would readily understand her.

If Shea understood these possible motivations—had interpreted Cecilia's behavior correctly—she would have been in a better position to approach the matter more effectively and with more sensitivity. Perhaps what Cecilia needed was a refresher course in the English vocabulary most often used in her job, some ideas of how to relieve the stress that caused her to forget English terminology in times of crises, or some other English-language training that would benefit her by allowing her to move up within the organization.

Throughout the last few chapters, a lot of discussion has been directed toward the proper interpretation of various behaviors. Because of the importance of this material, table 7–1 has been compiled to serve as a quick review.

Even if you have difficulty remembering all the specifics in table 7–1, the key point is that if we fail to understand the reason behind a behavior, it is nearly impossible to know how best to motivate the desired change.

Explain Your Expectations

This may seem like an obvious step but you would be surprised how often employers and managers fail to explain what they want and why they want it. Immigrant workers are rarely formally instructed in the values of U.S. culture and even less often in the desires of American management. They are never told, for example, that it is appropriate and

TABLE 7–1
Correctly Interpreting Employee Behavior

Behavior	Correct Interpretation
1. Hesitance to take independent initiative on tasks	Respect for authority, fear of loss of face, desire for anonymity, fear of job loss
2. Reluctance to complain or make negative statements	Desire for harmony in relationships, respect for authority, compassion for the other person, fear of a negative reflection on the group, fear of job loss
3. Failure to admit lack of understanding	Fear of loss of face, fear of embarrassment for the speaker, fear of not understanding the material if it is repeated
4. Reluctance to seek or accept promotions	Desire for anonymity, belief in leaving things to fate, desire not to be elevated above the group, respect for informal group hierarchy, desire to fulfill one's present role, fear of loss of face, varying personal needs, wishes of family members
5. Reluctance to praise self	Desire for anonymity, desire not to be set apart from the group
6. Speaking of foreign languages in the workplace	Fatigue, loneliness, forgetfulness, response to stress and crises, desire for efficiency

expected to take the initiative on tasks, seek promotions, or keep the employer or manager informed of problems in the workplace.

Explaining what we want from others is not easy. Often it is the most

---

Exercise 7–2. Explaining Your Expectations

1. Taking the initiative on tasks

2. Voicing complaints and problems

3. Admitting lack of understanding

4. Seeking and accepting promotions

5. Praising oneself

6. Speaking English in the workplace

---

familiar procedures, policies, and expectations that are the most difficult to articulate. Exercise 7–2 will give you an opportunity to practice figuring out what you really want and explaining those desires to employees. In a few sentences, write what you expect from workers with respect to each of the behaviors listed in the exercise.

Probably you will discover that it is not so easy to explain clearly that which is so obvious to you. Let us move through each of these and see what might be said to the worker.

1. **Taking the initiative on tasks.** "In the United States, taking the initiative reflects well on workers. To do so helps the manager and enables the workplace to run more efficiently. Also, managers feel that it is good to take chances. As we say, 'Nothing ventured, nothing gained,' and 'We learn from our mistakes.' If you take the initiative on tasks after having been given instructions, you will most likely be thought of as enthusiastic, courageous, creative, committed, and ambitious. You will also be helping your fellow workers by getting the job done more quickly and easily."

2. **Voicing complaints and problems.** "In the United States, managers like to know what is going on in the workplace, even if it is bad. A good employee keeps the manager aware of problems. Reasonable complaints are a sign of a cooperative, aware, and involved employee."

3. **Admitting lack of understanding.** "The employee who admits that he or she doesn't understand something is thought to be more concerned with getting it right, more enthusiastic, and more committed. You are not helping the manager by pretending; you are only creating problems that will show up later. If you pretend to understand, you might be thought of as dishonest and are risking making an error later that will create problems for everyone."

4. **Seeking and accepting promotions.** "When you seek promotions, you are thought of as more confident and committed to the corporation. It shows that you are involved with the job and is a signal to us that you have the ability to do it well. It is not considered in poor taste or disruptive of harmony."

5. **Praising oneself.** "Praising oneself shows confidence and ability.

It aids the manager in that he or she can then make more informed decisions about hiring and promotions. This, in turn, helps the manager to do a better job and makes the entire company run better."

6. **Speaking English in the workplace.** "Speaking a foreign language around those who do not understand can make others feel left out and uncomfortable. I'm sure you understand, just think about what it feels like to you when you do not understand what is being said around you."

These suggestions are not, by the way, to be used word-for-word; they are intended just to get you started. For one thing, they are constructed on the assumption that the worker understands English and do not reflect the tips on how to bridge language barriers suggested in Chapter 2. Your remarks should reflect your own personality, the specifics of the situation, the personality of the worker, and the degree of English language skill that he or she possesses. In addition: think out carefully what you want to say; conduct the conversation on neutral territory rather than in your office (this will be less intimidating); and, use the written word to lend your message importance and give the worker an opportunity to discuss its contents with colleagues and countrymen.

If you become frustrated, remember that your efforts are perhaps the first that anyone has made to familiarize immigrant workers with the expectations of American management. Be patient, follow the guidelines on how to bridge language barriers presented in Chapter 2, and you will be amazed at the progress you and your workers will make.

Compromising with the Employee's Culture

Compromise is always possible even in the face of the most diverse cultural values and behaviors. Being willing to compromise is one of the primary ways in which respect can be shown and is also an effective means of encouraging cooperation and change.

This third step builds directly on the first in that it is impossible to devise successful compromises if you do not interpret the worker's motivations correctly. Exercise 7–3 gives you a chance to jot down your ideas about what compromises might be made around our core behaviors. Use the information gained thus far along with your own common sense, experience, and instinct.

Exercise 7–3. Finding a Way to Compromise

1. Hesitance to take independent initiative on tasks

2. Reluctance to complain or voice problems

3. Failure to admit lack of understanding

4. Reluctance to seek or accept promotions

5. Reluctance to praise self

6. Speaking of foreign languages in the workplace

Let us examine each of these behaviors and propose some compromises that might augment your own lists.

1. **Hesitance to take independent initiative on tasks:** One way to deal with this issue is for you to recognize that some workers are not comfortable with taking the initiative and to compensate for this discomfort by telling the employee which specific tasks can be done without further orders. Another compromise might be to go further than you ordinarily would in giving specific instructions. By doing this, you will relieve the employee's anxiety about possibly making an error. Following up to make certain that everything is going smoothly and posting reminders on the bulletin board can also be helpful.

2. **Reluctance to complain and voice problems:** A compromise here would be to say that complaints and negative statements may be presented by the group as a whole, thus taking the responsibility off any one worker while honoring the value that is placed on the group over the individual. You might also mention that complaints and problems could be represented to management by the informal group leader. This approach, too, will preserve the anonymity of the specific worker.

Another compromise is to use the age-old device of a suggestion box. In this way, workers can share their problems without fear of appearing disrespectful. The suggestion box will not, of course, work if the worker's identity must be known in order to solve the problem. Inviting complaints in private and reassuring workers that their anonymity will be honored are also helpful techniques.

3. **Failure to admit lack of understanding:** A similar compromise can be entered into when you want to encourage the admission that something has not been understood. Giving the worker the opportunity to voice confusion in private can relieve the worker's concern that he or she will look foolish in front of others. When conducting group training, you might allow questions to be submitted anonymously in writing; this will also help minimize embarrassment.

4. **Reluctance to seek or accept promotions:** Finding ways to compromise on this behavior can be a little more difficult. As we have seen throughout the book, there are many reasons why advancement may not be actively sought, and most of these reasons spring from deeply rooted values.

A compromise that might help would be to allow the process to take place through a third party—that is, encourage the worker to send a representative when asking for a promotion. Although this seems strange

TIP: If you find it necessary to promote a worker who is not the informal leader of the group, you can avoid any tension by simply telling the leader what is going to happen. It is not that you are asking his or her permission but merely that you are compromising with the values of the group by acknowledging the leader's importance and position. To take it one step further, you might also invite that leader to announce the promotion to the group.

to the American manager, it is standard practice in many other countries. Also, being discrete about the fact that an employee is being considered for a promotion will spare the candidate loss of face should his or her application be turned down.

5. **Reluctance to praise self:** We saw some suggestions for how to compromise on this issue at the outset of this chapter. Among the techniques mentioned were conducting interviews in private, allowing the worker to record his or her achievements and strong points in writing, or to look at concrete evidence of the worker's performance.

6. **Speaking of foreign languages in the workplace:** If, in your particular business, it is necessary, legal, and appropriate to restrict the speaking of foreign languages on the job, you can compromise with workers by allowing them to speak their language in certain areas of the workplace and/or at certain times. Allowing foreign languages to be spoken on breaks, for example, is one way of compromising on this very delicate issue.

TIP: Because of the legal and social delicacy of this issue, I strongly suggest that all business owners, managers, and human-resource professionals become thoroughly familiar with all aspects of the laws pertaining to the speaking of foreign languages in the workplace.

Another compromise is to encourage foreign-language speakers to translate what they are saying for those around them. This is a common courtesy that few immigrant workers would resist.

Finally, it can be very helpful for managers and colleagues to learn a few words of the worker's language. If we are able to say such commonplace expressions as, "Good morning," "Have a nice weekend," or "Happy birthday," we are communicating both respect and a willingness to meet the worker halfway. You will be surprised how effective this effort is in encouraging workers to attempt English. The appendix contains several foreign-language phrases just to get you started.

A form of compromise that can apply to many behaviors is to place the worker in a position where his or her strengths will best be shown. An example of this type of adjustment was seen at a mid-size Washington State hotel. This property employed several Asian-born workers who were extremely gracious and hard working, but who were not comfortable with approaching hotel guests in the restaurant to ask if they needed anything. By simply stationing these workers at the concierge desk where they were not required to approach guests—the guests took the initiative and came to them—their gracious attitude and courteous demeanor was utilized to the fullest.

With any behavior that you wish to change, the best way to establish an effective and permanent compromise is to ask the workers themselves. Inquire if they have any ideas about how they and the employer or manager can meet halfway to make the workplace more efficient while still preserving the integrity of the employee's culture.

Speak the Worker's "Cultural Language"

Speaking the worker's "cultural language" is another way of communicating respect and thus increasing the chances of successful motivation. This means that you voice your request and the reasons for it in terms that can readily be understood in the context of the workers' cultural values and priorities. Cynics, for example, often say that members of mainstream American culture always understand the "bottom line"—that is, always respond favorably when a proposal is couched in terms of how much money it will make. In most cultures, it is the dual values of saving face and honoring the group as a whole that are most well understood.

SAVING FACE. As we have seen, saving face is central to Asian, Middle Eastern, and Hispanic cultures and clearly constitutes an important piece of vocabulary in the "cultural language" of many immigrant and ethnic workers. As such it can be used as a way of communicating your position in a fashion that will most likely be listened to and readily understood.

Point out to workers that one of the reasons that the failure to take initiative, complain, or admit lack of understanding creates problems in the workplace is that each of these practices can cause loss of face for the managers and employers. When the initiative is not taken on tasks, the job does not get done—a situation that reflects adversely on the manager's ability to supervise effectively and on the employer's talent at running an efficient operation. Similarly, you might mention that if you are left ignorant of problems in the workplace, you are incapable of fixing them and end up looking bad in the eyes of your superiors and colleagues. Also, if you are unaware that instructions have not been understood, mistakes will be made and you, as well as the worker, will suffer loss of face and embarrassment.

Reference to saving face can also be made as part of your efforts to encourage workers to seek promotions and praise themselves. You might point out that if they do not let you know of their qualifications, you will be unable to make correct staffing decisions and will lose face in the eyes of your superiors. Loss of face also affects the issue of speaking a foreign language in the workplace. Explain that when a foreign language is spoken to the exclusion of other people—be they superiors, colleagues, clients, or customers—those who do not understand the language may feel left out, uncomfortable, and anxious, all of which result in loss of face and embarrassment.

Each of these cases involves a loss of face for someone. Since this value is so common to the multicultural workplace, why not use it when motivating behavior change? Not only will your request be quickly understood, but you will also be demonstrating that you care enough to use a concept that the worker can relate to.

RESPECT FOR THE GROUP AS A WHOLE. Respect for the group as a whole is another bit of "cultural language" that can be used as a means of encouraging cooperation. Some workers are hesitant to seek promotions or praise themselves because they consider it inappropriate to call attention to the individual at the expense of the group.

One way to modify these behaviors is to point out that promotions and achievements also reflect well on the group as a whole. The same argument might be made for the worker who does not want to take the initiative on tasks because he or she is concerned about standing out above the group. If that person does well at the task, his or her accomplishment will make the entire group look better.

Acknowledge Culturally Specific Needs

Becoming aware of and catering to culturally specific needs is the fifth step toward successful cross-cultural motivation. The thing to watch out for here is that we all tend to project our own desires and needs onto others and assume that everyone responds to similar rewards.

Exercise 7–4. Employee Motivators

	Universal?	Importance to You
Recognition/respect	_____	_____
Responsibility	_____	_____
Financial gain	_____	_____
Social needs	_____	_____
Professional and personal growth	_____	_____
Advancement	_____	_____
The work itself	_____	_____
Power	_____	_____
Chance to contribute ideas	_____	_____
Chance to see concrete results	_____	_____
Job security	_____	_____
Autonomy	_____	_____
Structure	_____	_____
Chance to compete	_____	_____

Exercise 7–4 demonstrates this problem. Take a moment to examine the list of motivators. Which ones do you think are desired throughout the world and which are specific to just a few cultures? Check the ones you feel are universal. Then rank the items according to their importance and value to you. In other words, how strong a motivator is each of them in your professional life?

As you can see, most of these motivators are what have been termed "soft currencies." Only financial gain and job security fall into the category of concrete external motivators.

This exercise serves two functions. First, by deciding which motivators are universal, you become aware of how few really are. Probably the only one of these motivators that is universal is social needs—the desire for human contact, comfort, and companionship. In Thai and Vietnamese cultures, for example, maintaining a positive relationship with others is the most powerful motivator of productive behavior. The rest of the list is specific only to certain cultures and, particularly, to Western industrialized societies.

Second, the exercise helps us to learn what motivates us so we can avoid projecting our own needs and wants onto others. You may have discovered that recognition, the chance to contribute ideas, and advancement are particularly important to you. This would not be surprising because American culture values any forms of reward that single out the individual for attention. Praise, the prospect of a premium parking spot, a picture in the company newsletter, a prestigious promotion, or the title of "employee of the month" are widely sought by workers raised in mainstream American society. Indeed, Japanese managers marvel at how soon after being hired American workers seek promotions.

Competition, too, is valued in the West but considered disruptive of harmony and counter to productivity in many other countries. Even a monetary bonus, so highly valued in the United States, would bring humiliation to the Chinese, Japanese, or Eastern European worker, who would feel that such a reward is in poor taste. We tend to forget that Western culture is almost unique in its emphasis on the material. When deciding how to motivate workers, look closely at what the individual employee really values and take care not to assume that all workers, from all cultures, value the same thing.

THE FAMILY AND THE GROUP. As we have seen, the family and the group are of paramount importance within most immigrant and ethnic communities.

> TIP: When deciding on incentives, employers should not neglect the offering of education and training as an effective motivator. Education in the specifics of mainstream American culture, English-as-a-second-language training, and accent-reduction programs are valued by many workers as an opportunity to become qualified for higher and more lucrative positions.

This statement is, of course, a generality, but it serves as a guideline when trying to assess the needs and desires that are of greatest concern to your workers. It might, for example, be appropriate to motivate some Hispanic or Asian workers by offering them time off to return home for family events and holidays. The prospect of gala family gatherings and picnics can also constitute strong motivation, and one that shows that you care enough about the worker and his or her values to seek out ways to satisfy those needs.

Related to the value placed on family is the wish to work overtime so as to be able to send money home, or to accumulate funds with which to bring family members to the United States. Allowing for the celebration of customary national holidays is another way of providing for family time while showing respect for the traditions of the group.

JOB SECURITY. Because many ethnic and immigrant workers share a precarious socioeconomic status, job security often takes on great importance for them. The loss of a job can be a tragedy for the individual and his or her family. Reassure workers that as long as their work is good, they are in little danger of losing their jobs. Mention, in particular, that the behaviors that you wish to encourage—initiative, negative statements, complaints, admitting lack of understanding—will not result in job loss even if the errors are made or they do not always say what you want to hear.

VERBAL ACKNOWLEDGMENT OF NEEDS. It is not always necessary or possible to meet every need you encounter in the multicultural work force. Sometimes it is enough to acknowledge that you know the need exists and that you respect a worker's right to feel that need. Acknowledging, for example, a worker's need for relaxation, companionship, and identity can diminish his or her desire to speak a foreign language while on the job. Sometimes just knowing our needs are understood can encourage cooperation and motivate behavior change.

Positively Reinforce the Desired Behavior

Providing positive reinforcement for the desired behavior is an important final step in any motivation process. Unlike negative reinforcement—criticism—which often leaves a worker feeling inordinately nervous and self-conscious and which produces short-term benefits at best, positive reinforcement, especially if provided in the early stages of a new behavior, can be very effective.

Most of the time, positively reinforcing behavior is simple: just notice when the worker is doing what you want and praise him or her for it. When it comes to motivating across cultural boundaries, however, this step is a bit trickier. There are four problems to watch out for:

1. **Not all ethnic and immigrant workers are comfortable with praise.** This point has been emphasized throughout the discussion. Many workers dislike being praised because they want to avoid having attention drawn to them as individuals and want to maintain the harmony and balance of their group. Another reason your praise might not get the desired reaction is that compliments sometimes imply surprise that the worker has done well. This is rather like the situation in which a colleague comes to work dressed particularly nicely and you react by exclaiming, "My goodness, you look good today!" leaving the impression that you are shocked and surprised that he or she looks so attractive.

The resistance to praise can be minimized by being discrete, using a third party or word of mouth, praising the group as a whole, putting a complimentary note in the worker's file, and being certain not to overpraise. Remember that fewer words are more effective, easier to understand, and less embarrassing.

2. **It is difficult to praise if an error has been made.** Mistakes will inevitably be made when employees take independent initiative on tasks. These errors present a great challenge to the cross-cultural manager or employer who must correct the error while preserving the pride of the employee and continuing to encourage the taking of independent action. If pride and face are lost through an error, the chances of that employee's being willing to take the initiative again are slim.

The solution in this case is to treat the error as a separate issue from the initiative. You must point out the mistake, but at the same time you can put greater emphasis on how pleased you are that the worker had the courage to go ahead and act independently.

3. **It is difficult to praise when bad news is brought to you.** It is a natural human response for managers to find it difficult to bring themselves to praise the worker who arrives bearing news of a missed deadline or a broken piece of equipment. It isn't easy, but try to distance yourself from your distress long enough to praise the worker for keeping you informed and to encourage him or her to continue to do so.

4. **There is always the danger of taking certain behaviors for granted.** American managers are, for example, so accustomed to seeing workers take the initiative on tasks or seek promotions or praise themselves during an assessment interview that it is difficult to remember that these behaviors must be reinforced and encouraged with ethnic and foreign-born workers. The same applies to the speaking of English in the workplace. To speak English constantly can be a great effort, and yet it is a behavior you are likely to take for granted. Try to stay aware of behaviors such as these. What seems commonplace to you may be quite an accomplishment for the immigrant or ethnic employee.

Performance Evaluations, Criticism, and Coaching

There are many euphemisms today for criticizing, reprimanding, or disciplining a worker. Among them are "coaching," "counseling," "evaluating," and providing "developmental feedback." Each of these reflects the belief that behavior change is more likely to come about if the employee does not feel personally threatened or attacked. I am not saying that you cannot say what you want or that there are not times when a more direct and forceful approach is necessary and appropriate. However, people are more likely to hear and understand what you are saying and to consider it if they are not simultaneously having to defend themselves.

This applies, of course, to all employees, but can be particularly important when working with those who fall into one or more of the following categories:

1. Those who are from a culture in which loss of face is a major concern. Being criticized by a superior is, of course, a situation that can cause humiliation to anyone.

2. Those who feel that their self-esteem is closely connected to their performance on the job. This is the case, as we have seen, among many who were born and raised in other countries.

3. Those immigrant and ethnic workers who are concerned that you are attempting to change, not just one behavior, but their entire culture.

4. Those employees who may already feel inadequate and disoriented because of the challenges of adjusting to a new culture.

Exercise 7–5 gives you a chance to examine some good and bad elements of cross-cultural criticism. Look at Michael's situation and see if you can figure out what he did right and what he did wrong.

Exercise 7–5. Better Late Than Never?

Ever since she was hired some months ago, Dia, a forty-year-old Hispanic woman, has been late to work at least once every two weeks. Besides this one flaw, Dia is a very hard worker who is well liked by everyone. One day, Michael, Dia's manager, happened to be by the door when she arrived, once more, a half-hour late. Michael had let the behavior pass on previous occasions, but this time was really angry. As there were other people around, he asked Dia into his office to discuss the matter. Once there, Michael offered her a seat and, while leaning against his desk, told Dia that he liked her work, but if she did not start coming on time, she would have to be let go. He then began to speak for ten minutes about each worker's obligation to carry his or her share of the load.

When Dia tried to say something, Michael raised his voice and said that there was nothing more to be said. He then made a sarcastic joke about how he had made her even later to work by calling her into his office. As they were walking out, Michael tried to smooth things over by putting his arm around Dia's shoulders and inquiring after her husband and children.

What did Michael do right and what did he do wrong?

The answers to the exercise will show up in this discussion of the basic rules of cross-cultural criticism:

1. *If there is a problem in performance, comment on it as soon as possible.* Do not let the behavior become habitual or cause other difficulties. This is one of the mistakes that Michael made in our scenario. Why did he wait so long to comment on Dia's lateness? Because he did not say anything earlier, she began to feel that it really did not matter that much. Meanwhile, Michael became angrier and angrier until the entire issue was blown out of proportion.

2. *Conduct criticisms and evaluations in private.* Loss of face and feelings of shame are worse for everyone when experienced in front of others. You probably recall how upset you were in grade school when the teacher criticized you in front of your friends. Middle Eastern and Asian workers are particularly uncomfortable with this treatment. Michael was right in inviting Dia into his office in order not to conduct the conversation in front of other employees.

3. *Allow the worker plenty of physical space, do not stand above him or her, and be careful of inappropriate touching.* All of these can make a person feel trapped and threatened. Although it was gracious for Michael to offer Dia a seat, he shouldn't have stood over her while he spoke. Probably his intentions were good in that he was trying to be casual and friendly by not sitting behind the "boss's desk." He should not have put his arm around Dia as they were leaving—a gesture which could be considered patronizing at best.

4. *Do not lose your temper or shout.* Although Michael did not actually shout, he did get visibly upset and raised his voice. Venting anger in a management situation is rarely productive, and even less so when the anger is directed at an immigrant worker who, although probably accustomed to an authoritarian boss, expects to be treated with fairness and paternalism. Also, remember that Asian cultures regard excessive displays of emotion as improper and diminishing of respect and that Hispanic workers are quick to lose respect for a boss who loses his or her temper. Another problem with getting upset is that it

is apt to cause you to talk so fast that the immigrant worker will have difficulty understanding you.

5. *Do not talk too much.* You may have noticed that people talk more when they are uncomfortable or nervous. This is why employers and managers will sometimes begin to jabber when they are speaking to an employee about a problem. The difficulty with this is twofold: first, the nonnative speaker may have trouble understanding you and, second, he or she may stop listening because there is just too much to listen to. I would wager the Dia stopped listening to Michael about halfway through his speech about the virtues of teamwork.

6. *Mention, as Michael did, the things that the worker has done right.* Remember, though, not to overdo it with the Asian employee who might become embarrassed by your enthusiasm and even question its sincerity.

7. *Listen carefully to the worker's perspective and try to reach an agreement as to what the difficulty might be.* Do not assume that you understand how he or she feels or what the circumstances surrounding a particular behavior might be. Because of difficulties with the language and a reluctance to speak candidly with authority figures, it may take a bit of patience to get the worker to open up, but your effort will be rewarded with a better relationship. One of the worst things that Michael did was not to listen to what Dia has to say. Possibly she was trying to apologize or maybe she needed to inform him of transportation problems that he could have helped solve. By refusing to listen, Michael showed disrespect for Dia while missing out on information that might have made his job easier.

8. *Try to criticize an action, not a person.* This is often nothing more than a matter of how you phrase the problem. It is hard to tell from our scenario if this is what Michael did, but his general tone probably means that Dia experienced the meeting, not just as a criticism of something she did, but as an attack on herself as an individual.

9. *Be concrete and specific in what you expect.* Vague statements will only lead to misunderstandings. This is especially true if there is a language barrier that requires you to

speak in simple terms. In Dia's case, the desired behavior, punctuality, is a simple idea that would be difficult to misconstrue.

10. *Discuss the positive and negative outcomes of the worker's behaviors.* Concrete examples of how his or her actions affect the workplace are far more valuable than vague statements about the "right" or "wrong" way to do things. Although, as rule number 5 says, it is important not to talk too much, Michael might have taken just a few moments to point out the good and bad consequences of Dia's behavior. About all he did was to threaten her with the loss of her job and, on top of that, he used an English idiom, "let go" which she easily might not have understood.

11. *Consider criticizing the group as a whole rather than an individual.* Of course it depends on the situation (it would not work in Dia's case unless a large percentage of workers were also being late), but one way to soften the blow of a problem is to comment on it, at least initially, to a larger group without singling out an individual.

12. *Be courteous and, if appropriate, formal.* Michael's offering Dia a seat was a step in the right direction. Mainstream Americans believe that an uncomfortable situation is made less stressful by behaving as informally as possible. For many immigrants, the opposite is true. In a formal encounter, the worker will know where he or she stands and have a much better idea of how to behave. Remember that, formality is not coldness—but merely restraint.

13. *Use humor sparingly.* Another thing we do when uncomfortable is make jokes in an effort to lighten the situation. Some workers might misinterpret your behavior to mean that you are not taking them or their work seriously. Michael's effort at sarcasm showed poor judgment.

14. *If appropriate, inquire about any cultural background that might be a factor in the worker's behavior.* By doing this you will communicate an interest in who this person is and what he or she values while possibly uncovering some information that will help you interpret the worker's action more accurately. It would have been premature and possibly patronizing for Michael to take this approach with Dia. However, if the

behavior had continued over a very long period of time or if it were exhibited among large numbers of other Hispanic workers, inquiring into cultural background could be helpful.

15. *If the purpose of your interview is to conduct a periodic performance evaluation that is routine for everyone, make certain that the employee knows this and that he or she is not being singled out for individual scrutiny.* Make it clear that the interview itself is not an indication that you feel his or her performance has been poor.

16. *Throughout the interview never lose sight of the importance of communicating respect for both the worker and for his or her culture.*

Summary

Managing a multicultural work force requires finding ways to attract and retain quality workers, learning new techniques that allow you to utilize workers' diverse skills and personalities, and gathering new ideas about how to motivate in the face of culturally different needs and desires. The material in this chapter will help you reach these goals. It will also enable you to help immigrant and ethnic employees adapt to the needs of American business while maintaining the integrity of their own cultural attitudes and values. To recap briefly:

- Be aware of cultural and language differences that can affect the accuracy of assessment interviews.
- When seeking behavior change, provide reassurance that you are not trying to alter the worker's culture.
- Understand the worker's perspective.
- Involve workers in decisions concerning the desired behavior change.
- Ask employees for ideas regarding compromises and inquire how much they are willing to adjust.
- Help workers to feel psychologically safe and secure even in the face of change.
- Communicate respect for workers and their culture.
- Interpret behaviors correctly.
- Explain what you expect and why it is important.
- Compromise when possible.

- Speak your employees' "cultural language."
- Meet workers' culturally specific needs.
- Remember that positive reinforcement is essential to successful motivation.
- Be familiar with the art of cross-cultural criticism.

Solidifying Your Learning

What are the three most important things you learned from this chapter and how might you apply them to your work?:

1.

2.

3.

A Recap of What You've Learned

The following is a review of the most important information covered in this book. To keep this list from becoming too cumbersome, it was necessary to exclude detailed examples and solutions. Also, because each point is provided without elaboration and can, therefore, be easily misunderstood, I caution you not to rely on this list as a substitute for reading the material in context. For additional solutions to the problems listed and for more detailed information, utilize the index and table of contents to locate the in-depth discussion of each topic.

General Information about Culture

Culture consists of a shared set of rules concerning style, etiquette, values, language, tastes, preferences, traditions, customs, belief systems, and world views. There are many kinds of cultures: regional, occupational, corporate, and recreational. One way to distinguish culturally specific behavior from individual personality is to establish if large numbers of people from the same group exhibit the behavior in question.

Culture Shock

Culture shock can strike anyone who lives and works around people from other cultures. Culture shock happens because:

- Someone behaves in an unexpected way.
- The response you get to your behavior is not what you anticipated.
- You do not get the credit for your actions that you expected.

Culture shock can make you feel irritable, aggressive, frustrated, inadequate, sensitive, and fatigued. Culture shock can be cured by:

- Exposing yourself to cultural diversity
- Learning about other cultures
- Bringing the "ailment" out into the open

Acknowledging Cultural Differences

It is all right to notice the cultural differences among peoples. The reasons we are hesitant to notice differences are:

- Fear of appearing racist
- Fear of not noticing the commonalities
- Fear of perpetuating stereotypes
- Fear of making relationships, and business, too complicated
- Fear of having to question one's own culture

The advantages in acknowledging differences are:

- Fear is reduced through knowledge.
- To do so communicates respect for other cultures.
- It allows us to function successfully in the multicultural business world.

Stereotypes

Stereotypes are inflexible statements about a category of people. They can be about positive or negative characteristics and function to relieve anxiety and uncertainty. Stereotypes do not apply to everyone within one culture because of differences in:

- Socioeconomic status
- Geographic origins
- Age and gender
- Degree of assimilation
- Historical experiences
- Individual psychology
- Variations over time and circumstance

Moreover, stereotypes are dangerous and destructive because they have the following effects:

- They limit how we see and define the other person.
- They negate the individuality of the other person.
- They can be self-fulfilling (we see what we expect to see).

An effective way to eliminate stereotypes is to (1) identify the ones you hold; (2) learn about other cultures; and (3) spend time with diverse people.

Ethnocentrism

Ethnocentrism is the belief that the behaviors of others can be interpreted according to the rules and values of one's own culture. People from other cultures are as likely to project their own cultural interpretations onto mainstream American culture as we are onto them. Ethnocentrism can be overcome by learning about other cultures and about our own. Mainstream American culture values materialism; quantification; experiential proof; linear, cause and effect thinking; youth; independence of the individual; control of the future; productivity; efficient use of time; social and physical mobility; action; assertiveness; perseverance; creativity; change; the future; focus on the end product.

The Importance of Being Yourself

It is best to "be yourself" when interacting with other cultures because to do otherwise can cause:

- Others to feel patronized
- Misunderstandings to occur
- You to feel resentment
- Other groups to feel resentment
- The opportunity to teach the ways of American culture to be missed
- Embarrassing mistakes to be made

Language and Accent Barriers

Some General Information

- When people do not speak the dominant language, it can make them feel lonely, frightened, passive, and inadequate.
- A foreign accent tells us very little about the abilities of the speaker.
- It is far easier to understand a new language than to speak it.
- There is far more to understanding a language than just knowing the vocabulary and grammar.
- Sometimes the intonation of the speaker's native language along with a lack of softening phrases can make the immigrant sound inadvertently rude.

- Immigrants speak their native language usually as a means of relieving feelings of isolation and/or in response to a crisis.
- Pretending to understand usually reflects a desire to avoid embarrassment for all concerned.

How to Make Yourself Understood

- When communicating to those whose English-language facility is undeveloped: do not shout; speak slowly and distinctly; emphasize key words; allow pauses; let the listener read your lips; use visual aids; organize your thoughts; keep your sentences short and simple; use the written word; be aware of your tone of voice; repeat and recap frequently; check for understanding frequently; do not cover too much information at one time; do not mix topics in a sentence; use bilingual group leaders as liaisons with foreign-born workers.
- When speaking with those whose English-language facility is undeveloped, choose your words according to the following rules: use words familiar to the foreign-born listener; avoid pidgin English; avoid jargon, slang, and idioms; be concrete and specific in your choice of words; avoid vague modifiers; choose simple, but not patronizing, words; employ the active voice; use positive phrasing.

How to Tell If You Have Been Understood

- Watch for body language (see "Body Language" section).
- A lack of interruptions, efforts to change the subject, and the absence of questions all can indicate that you have not been understood.
- Inappropriate laughter can indicate that the person is embarrassed about not understanding and wants to conceal that embarrassment.
- Invite questions in private and allow plenty of time for the foreign-language speaker to formulate questions.
- Be alert to cultural and grammatical differences in the meaning of a positive response to a question (see the discussion in Chapter 2).
- Have the listener repeat back what you have said.
- Inspect a worker's job performance.

Translating the Written Word

- A translator should be a native-born speaker of the foreign language; as familiar with English as he or she is with the other language; familiar with both cultures.
- Make certain you have the correct language or dialect.
- Be certain that the idioms and level of language that you use is appropriate to your target audience.
- Have one person translate the message into the foreign language and someone else translate it back into English.
- Test your materials prior to mass distribution.

How to Use an Interpreter

- Note the rules for translating (especially those for how to choose a translator); they also apply to using an interpreter.
- Plan what you are going to say.
- Brief the interpreter on what it is you are going to discuss.
- If possible, provide a written document.
- Introduce the interpreter and allow time for the foreign-language speaker to feel comfortable with him or her.
- Look at the foreign-language speaker during the entire conversation, *not* at the interpreter.
- Keep your language simple.
- Do not raise your voice.
- Speak in short units.
- Limit the amount of "private" conversation that the interpreter has with the foreign-language speaker.
- Do not have "private" chats with the interpreter in the middle of the meeting.
- Allow plenty of time.

How to Understand the Nonnative English Speaker

- Share the responsibility for good communication.
- Invite the immigrant to speak more slowly.
- Repeat what you believe the immigrant has said.
- Encourage the nonnative speaker to use the written word and/or spell out what he or she is saying.

- Read the speaker's lips.
- Give the speaker plenty of time in which to communicate.
- Listen to all the speaker has to say before concluding that you do not understand.
- Observe body language.
- Remember to listen and expect that you will understand.

How to Encourage the Speaking of English

- Learn a few words of the immigrant's language.
- Smile, look enthusiastic, and be patient.
- Ask open-ended questions.
- Ask a series of short questions to keep the conversation going.
- Do not laugh at a speaker's English, even if he or she does.
- Positively reinforce good communication.

Body Language

Why Body Language Is Important

- Body language constitutes as much as 50 percent of the entire communication process.
- Body language is more important to people from other cultures than it is to most mainstream Americans.
- The less English a person understands, the more likely he or she is to rely on body language.
- Immigrants are likely to become more sensitive to body language as they become fatigued and disoriented.
- Body language often contradicts the words that are being said.
- Body language presents emotions; words present facts.
- We are often consciously unaware of body language.
- Body language gives us clues to cultural style.

How You Should Respond to Differences in Body Language

In general, if the immigrant's body language is more outgoing and expressive than yours, do not attempt to match it; if, however, the person is more restrained, it is a good idea to tone down any tendency to gesture, touch, and stand close during conversation.

Physical Distance and Touch

- Those cultures which stand the closest and tend to touch the most are Middle Eastern cultures (between people of the same sex); eastern and southern Mediterranean cultures; some Hispanic cultures.
- Those cultures which have a moderate attitude toward physical distance and touch are mainstream American culture and western European cultures.
- Those cultures which stand the furthest away and touch the least are Asian and some African cultures, Middle Eastern cultures when the contact is between men and women, and northern Europeans.

Eye Contact

- Those cultures which maintain very direct eye contact are Middle Eastern culture (especially men), some Hispanic groups, and southern Europeans.
- Moderate eye contact is maintained by mainstream Americans, northern Europeans, and the British.
- Indirect eye contact is characteristic of Asian cultures, East Indians, and native Americans.

Facial Expressions

- Hispanics and southern Europeans tend to have more animated facial expressions than most other cultures.
- Asians tend not to express emotions on their faces. This does not mean, however, that they are being deliberately manipulative or dishonest.

The Meaning of a Smile

Although a smile is generally an indication of good will, it can have varying functions among different cultures. Asians, for example, might cover up embarrassment or anger by means of a smile and Soviets tend to feel that it is inappropriate for someone in authority to smile too much.

Handshakes

- Mainstream Americans and Germans tend to have firm handshakes, whereas Asians, the British, the French, Hispanics, and Middle Easterners maintain a gentler grasp.
- With Germans, the French, Hispanics, and Middle Easterners, shake hands on both arrival and departure.
- It is a good idea to match the intensity of the immigrant's handshake.
- Follow the lead of those around you.
- Remember to shake hands with the children.

Hand Gestures

- Hand gestures function to demonstrate the style of a culture, to communicate specific information, and to express positive and negative emotions.
- Southern Europeans and Hispanics tend to gesture the most and northern Europeans and Asians the least.
- In most cultures, pointing is considered to be in poor taste.
- Do not beckon to immigrants or international visitors with upturned fingers, palm facing the body. It is better, as a general rule, to turn the hand so that the palm faces the ground and the fingers are moving.
- The "OK" sign, "V" for victory gesture, and "thumbing-a-ride" motion are obscene in most cultures.
- Avoid gesturing with or using the left hand around Muslims.

The Legs and Feet

Do not cross your legs or stretch your feet out in front of you when in the presence of Middle Easterners or Asians.

Posture

Maintain formal posture when around immigrants and international visitors.

Signaling "Yes" and "No"

- Mexicans and Middle Easterners signal "no" with a back-and-forth movement of the index finger.
- The Japanese indicate "no" by waving the entire hand in front of the face.
- In parts of the Middle East, India, and Pakistan, the head is shaken to indicate "yes" and nodded to signal "no."
- In the Philippines, the head is sometimes moved downward to indicate "no" and the head and eyebrows raised to indicate "yes."

The Functions of Values

- Values dictate "felt needs."
- Values dictate what is defined as a problem.
- Values dictate how problems are solved.
- Values dictate expectations of behavior.

The Value Placed on Avoiding Negative Confrontations

Asian, Hispanic, and Middle Eastern cultures place great value on avoiding direct and negative confrontations. The value of avoiding negative confrontations is manifested in a reluctance to

- State directly that a task cannot be completed by a specific time or in a particular way
- State directly that a favor or concession cannot be granted
- Complain directly about conditions or about a product or service
- Bring problems to superiors

The Value Placed on Saving Face

Saving face is a central value in Asian, Middle Eastern, and Hispanic cultures. Saving face involves a concern that *neither* party in an interaction suffer embarrassment and is manifested in:

- A reluctance to refuse the other party directly and a sensitivity to being refused
- A tendency not to admit lack of understanding nor to ask questions

- A sensitivity to being criticized, or criticizing, in the presence of others
- A hesitance to take the initiative on tasks or to perform tasks in a new way
- A reluctance to seek promotions or other boons that might be refused
- A discomfort with being given major concessions, granted large favors, or being complimented in front of others
- A reluctance to complain about a product or service

The Value Placed on Not Calling Attention to the Individual

Asian cultures and, to a lesser extent, Hispanic cultures are concerned with not calling attention to the individual at the expense of the group. The value of not calling attention to the individual is manifested in:

- A reluctance to complain of physical pain or other difficulties
- A reluctance to praise oneself or one's product
- A reluctance to voice innovative ideas in meetings or training rooms
- A reluctance to seek promotions that would elevate the individual above the group
- A discomfort with public or excessive praise

The Value Placed on the Group over the Individual

In Hispanic, Asian, and Middle Eastern cultures, the welfare and reputation of the group is considered of paramount importance. In these cultures:

- Distress over a mistake or a sin results from how it will reflect on the group as a whole, not on how it will affect the individual.
- A person's identity is determined, not by individual achievement, but by one's association with a family, community, region, company, or other affiliation.
- Purchasing and other decisions are often made by the group as a whole, not by the individual.
- The responsibility for achievements and failures rests with the group, not with the individual.

- Competition among members of a group is thought to be destructive to both creativity and harmony.
- The goals of the group and family come before those of the individual.
- It is considered irresponsible for adult children to live their lives completely independently from the extended family.

The Value Placed on the Whole Person

- In most other cultures, friendships are formed slowly and are based on a gradual development of mutual trust and knowledge.
- In many countries, hiring decisions are based on a thorough knowledge of the applicant's personal virtues, past associations, and peripheral talents.
- Many immigrant prospects and colleagues would prefer not to agree on a transaction until they have developed a well-rounded knowledge of and relationship with the salesperson or negotiator.
- Among many immigrants and international businesspersons, respect for a professional or superior is based, not only on fairness and skill, but also on social connections and talents not directly applicable to the job.
- Some immigrant and ethnic workers feel that to criticize an employee is also to criticize his or her entire being.

Attitudes toward Authority

Informal and Formal Group Leaders

It is important to get to know and cultivate the informal and formal leaders within the ethnic and immigrant community and workplace. Informal group leaders in the workplace can be utilized as liaisons between managers and workers and can be valuable in your efforts to do business within ethnic and immigrant communities. Informal group leaders can be identified by:

- Noticing who is the eldest
- Making note of those who held powerful positions in the past
- Their gender (most are male)

- Noticing those who currently hold a formal position of responsibility
- Observing relationships within the community or workplace
- Asking members of the group

Other Authority Figures

- In most immigrant cultures, age is an important factor in determining who should be in authority.
- Female authority figures are sometimes looked down upon by immigrants and international visitors.
- Many immigrants come from countries in which authority figures have the power to bend the rules of government and corporations to benefit individuals.
- Many immigrant workers feel that the boss should not consult workers with regard to decisions, should keep a formal, but friendly, distance, and should never work beside employees.
- Immigrant consumers and workers often feel that they have no right, or obligation, to question authority of any kind.
- Most foreign-born workers are not used to being motivated by persuasion; many are more accustomed to coercion.
- Many immigrants feel they have no right to judge the performance of employers or vendors.
- A large number of immigrants bring a distrust of government and public agencies with them from their native countries.

The Value Placed on Fatalism and Tradition

Controlling the Future

- Many immigrants do not agree with the American perspective that the future can and should be controlled.
- This fatalistic view is manifested in workers who do not actively seek promotions.
- This fatalistic attitude is also seen in consumers who are uninterested in buying products with which to control the future. (Sample Solution: Emphasize the other benefits of the product while deemphasizing its ability to control the future.)

Bringing about Change

- American culture is almost unique in its belief that change is always equated with growth, improvement, and progress.
- Many immigrant consumers and workers feel that change needs to be weighed against the virtues of tradition and continuity.
- Sales professionals and marketers need to know that immigrant consumers are not necessarily receptive to new and improved products, to new ways of doing things, to disposable goods, and to the constant acquisition of new possessions. (Sample Solution: Minimize the emphasis on the "newness" of the product and find other benefits which have a stronger appeal to the immigrant's cultural background.)
- Employers and managers must recognize that immigrant workers might be resistant to new ways of doing things and to wholesale changes within the organization. (Sample Solution: Explain why the change needs to be made and how it will make the worker's job easier and more productive.)

Etiquette

Some General Information

- Etiquette functions to (1) express the style of a culture; (2) let us know what to expect in the behaviors of others; (3) tell us how to make a good first impression on others; and (4) allow us to feel comfortable in unfamiliar settings within our own culture.
- It is the spirit of etiquette that matters, not the letter—that is, if your attitude is respectful, a lot of mistakes will be forgiven.
- It is all right to ask immigrants about cultural differences in etiquette.
- It is all right to learn about etiquette by observing the other person's actions.
- It is all right to apologize if you make a *faux pas*.
- By figuring out which culturally different behaviors bother you the most and learning more about them, you will find that your irritation will diminish.

The Importance of Formality

- Formality does not automatically indicate or communicate coldness and superiority.
- Formality can be particularly important when the parties are in a stressful situation.
- Do not project your idea of social comfort onto others.
- Be alert to the importance of "physical formality," such as maintaining good posture and keeping the hands out of your pockets.
- Build relationships slowly; this means that you should maintain a more formal and less intimate relationship longer than you might ordinarily choose to.
- Do not ask intrusive questions prematurely.
- Avoid the use of jokes and sarcasm.
- Use and be receptive to last names and title.
- When speaking with Asians, especially in the presence of others, be restrained with compliments.
- Respect and observe the small rituals of relationships.
- Respect the older members of a group.

The Etiquette of Language

- When appropriate, match the communication style of the other person.
- The Asian-born speaker is restrained when it comes to interruptions whereas the Middle Easterner and southern European is comfortable with several people talking at once.
- Pauses in the middle of conversation—especially with Asian immigrants—do not necessarily indicate that something has gone wrong; try to redefine the meaning of pauses and learn to utilize them to your advantage. (Sample Solution: Use them to show self-confidence or to formulate a reply.)
- Southern Europeans and Hispanics tend to be spontaneous in their speech whereas Asians are more deliberate; do not draw any conclusions about the speaker's energy or enthusiasm from these differing conversational styles.

- Do not form any rash conclusions about the personality of an immigrant speaker according to how loudly (southern Europeans, some Hispanics, Middle Easterners) or softly (Asians) he or she speaks.
- Be patient with those who "talk around" a subject before getting to it (the French, Japanese, Germans); it is just a different style of conversation.
- Do not overreact to the embellishments and repetition that is characteristic of Middle Eastern conversation.
- It is sometimes appropriate to match the Middle Eastern tendency to repeat answers in order to make it clear that you are sincere in your response.
- Be alert to the fact that some English expressions that are meant as ritualistic courtesies can be taken literally by the immigrant; for example, "Come to dinner sometime."

Time and Punctuality

- The cultures that are the most relaxed about time and punctuality are the Hispanic cultures, Middle Eastern cultures (with the exception of the Iraqis), the Caribbean cultures, and some Filipinos.
- Among the most punctual and concerned with deadlines are the northern Europeans, Iraqis, Asians (with the exception of Koreans), and the Americans.

Sales and Customer Service

Some General Information

In order to sell, negotiate, and deliver service successfully, you must

- Build trust.
- Be at least somewhat liked.
- Be able to communicate.
- Know and satisfy the prospect's needs and expectations.
- Be able to make the prospect feel comfortable.
- Know how to make it easy for the client or customer to buy.

Identifying the Decision Makers

- Observe group dynamics as a way of establishing who the decision makers are.
- It is often the elder immigrants who have the most power.
- Even though it may not appear so in public, women often have considerable decision-making power in Hispanic, Chinese, Japanese, Korean, Filipino, East Indian, and Middle Eastern cultures.

How the Decisions Are Made

- On the corporate level, the Japanese generally make decisions based on group consensus.
- When decisions are being made for the family or small business, many immigrant groups, Middle Easterners and Hispanics for example, will make the decision as a group; be patient with this process as it can be quite lengthy.
- Some groups, on the other hand, will designate one individual to make the decision after listening to the needs and preferences of other members of the group.

Assessing the Prospect's Needs and Desires

- Utilize marketing surveys to assess the needs of particular groups, but do not overlook the uniqueness of each individual within those groups.
- Take cultural variations in values and world views into consideration when designing marketing, sales, and customer service approaches (for example, the importance of the family and attitudes toward change).

How to Approach the Culturally Diverse Prospect

- Take time to build relationships by being formal, taking an interest in the other person, sharing of yourself, and using your connections.
- When presenting your product or service, do so in person if possible.

- Do not make your presentation too soon.
- Do not present too much detail at one time.
- Consider using emotional and personal appeals.
- Praise the competition or at least refrain from criticizing it.
- Refrain from bragging about your importance or your influence.
- Persuade, do not push.
- Refrain from getting upset or at least from showing your emotions.
- Question prospects cautiously and respectfully by (1) explaining why you need the information; (2) reassuring them that it will be used for that purpose alone; and (3) questioning the prospect in private.

Concessions and Bargaining

- Bargaining is considered a sign of good business acumen among Koreans, Southeast Asians, the Chinese, Mexicans, and Middle Easterners.
- Even a small concession on your part will fulfill the symbolic function of saving face for the other party.
- Do not make concessions too soon.

What to Expect from the Immigrant and International Prospect

- Lateness to appointments and interruptions during meetings do not mean that the prospect is uninterested in your product, service, or business transaction. (Sample Solution: Double check meeting times shortly before the appointment.)
- When an Asian client is self-deprecating, it does not mean that he or she is lacking in confidence.
- Do not overreact to the assertive style of the Korean, German, Middle Eastern, and Chinese customer or client.
- Be alert to the softened rebuff and cushioned complaint that is so common among Asian, Middle Eastern, and Hispanic clients and customers.
- When you hear a "qualified yes" that you think means "no," back off; do not continue to hammer away at the client.
- If you are unsure of the meaning of a client's response (for

example, does he or she mean "yes" or "no"?) ask someone from the same cultural background or someone who has worked with the client before.
- Consider softening your own negative responses as a way of saving face for foreign-born colleagues.

How to Encourage Customer Complaints

- Learn to recognize the softened complaint.
- Invite anonymous complaints by using complaint forms and a suggestion box.
- Make it easy for customers to complain in private thus minimizing embarrassment.
- Make certain that your customers understand how to complain (to whom and by what mechanism).
- Let customers know that you want and need their complaints and advice in order to run a more successful business.
- Make certain that your customers know that their suggestions will be listened to and that they will make a real difference.

Managing Immigrant and Ethnic Workers

Interviewing and Assessing Culturally Diverse Employees and Applicants

1. Do not prejudge the worker or applicant on the basis of his or her surname, ethnic background, or accent.

2. Do not draw rash conclusions from any behavior which is related to cultural style.

3. Conduct the interview in private so the applicant or employee will feel more comfortable, more likely to speak English, and more willing to speak of his or her qualifications.

4. Uncover the qualifications of modest applicants and employees by:

- Asking to see products or reports that the worker has produced in the past
- Asking workers to solve job-related problems
- Checking references
- Allowing workers to praise themselves in writing

• Asking applicants what coworkers would say about their past performance
   • Having someone else report on the applicant's qualifications
   • Asking a series of specific questions in order to learn of past accomplishments

5. Assess English language ability by:

• Asking the worker to complete the job application in your office and to do so alone
   • Having some of the instructions on the application be a bit more complex than just "name," "address," and "education"
   • Including a request for a short essay somewhere on the application so that the worker will be forced to demonstrate English writing skills
   • Engaging the applicant in extensive conversation in order to tell how much English is spoken and understood

Motivating the Multicultural Work Force

Effective motivation strategies are based on the ability to assess an employee's needs and to match those needs to those of the organization. Overcome resistance to behavior change by:

- Reassuring workers that you are not trying to change their culture
- Reassuring workers that their previous way of doing things was not wrong or deficient but merely that it did not function well in the American workplace
- Including workers in the decision to change

The six steps to successful cross-cultural motivation are (see detailed discussion in Chapter 7):

- Interpret the behavior correctly. (Example: reluctance to take the initiative can come from a respect for authority, not from laziness.)
- Explain your perspective.
- Compromise with the employee's culture (Example: allow worker's to voice complaints anonymously.)
- Speak the employee's "cultural language" by referring to values

that they can relate to. (Example: point out that you will lose face if you do not know of problems in the workplace.)
- Acknowledge culturally specific felt needs and do not project your own needs onto others.
- Communicate respect for the worker's culture.
- Positively reinforce the desired behvior.

It can sometimes be difficult to reinforce behavior because:

- Some workers, especially Asians, are uncomfortable with elaborate praise. (Sample Solution: Place a note in the worker's file and quietly let them know that it is there.)
- It is difficult to praise if an error has been made.
- It is difficult to praise when bad news has been brought to you. (Example: When you have finally persuaded a worker to admit that they do not understand an instruction.)
- There is always the danger of taking certain behaviors for granted. (Example: The speaking of English in the workplace.)

Cross-Cultural Criticism

- If there is a problem in performance, comment on it as soon as possible.
- Conduct criticisms and evaluations in private.
- Allow the worker plenty of physical space, do not stand above him or her, and be careful of inappropriate touching.
- Do not lose your temper or shout.
- Do not talk too much.
- Mention the things that the worker has done right.
- Listen carefully to the worker's perspective and try to reach an agreement as to what the difficulty might be.
- Try to criticize an action, not a person.
- Be concrete and specific in what you expect.
- Discuss the positive and negative outcomes of the worker's behaviors.
- Consider criticizing the group as a whole rather than an individual.
- Be courteous and, if appropriate, formal.
- Use humor sparingly.

- If appropriate, inquire about any cultural background that might be a factor in the worker's behavior.
- If the purpose of your interview is to conduct a periodic performance evaluation, make certain that the employee knows that this is routine and that he or she is not being singled out for individual scrutiny.
- Throughout the interview, never lose sight of the importance of communicating respect for both the worker and for his or her culture.

Epilogue
The Finishing Touches

If I were to ask you to tell me one thing you learned from this book, what would it be? Pause a moment to think about it. You might answer by citing a bit of information ("It is inappropriate to pat a Korean on the back") or you might be thinking of a more general principle ("It is important to know your own culture so as not to project it onto others").

If you can come up with even one idea that will help you in your work, I consider this book a success. This may seem like a rather low standard of achievement but, as the Japanese proverb tells us, "You can know ten things by learning one." Even the smallest piece of information about cultural diversity will give you a clue to understanding a great deal more.

The seed of knowledge you have retained may seem insignificant, such as the awareness that many Asian customers will not complain openly; but that one fact will remind you that they also are sensitive to direct confrontations, will issue polite, understated rebuffs to your proposals, and, in the workplace, will be inclined not to complain to employers of difficulties or conflicts. On the other hand, the one thing that sticks in your mind might be a broad concept such as the importance of acknowledging differences between cultures—an insight that will help you remember to approach immigrant and ethnic consumers according to their specific needs, to design culturally aware motivation strategies for the workplace, and to resist the temptation to project your own culture onto others.

From the most general of principles to the tiniest morsel of knowledge, this book has provided information that will help overcome some of the discomfort and confusion of working across cultural lines. I am not promising that there will never be times when you fall into a state of temporary culture shock and feel disoriented, confused, and completely ignorant of what to do next. I can see it now: All of a sudden, you find yourself in a situation to which your hard-earned knowledge of the nuances of cultural diversity does not apply; you feel like a novice who has never encountered anyone more different than a visitor from the next town, and, above everything else, you are irritated with this author for not having covered this one contingency.

What do you do when you feel completely lost? **Do not panic.** You have everything you need to cope with any intercultural situation right inside you. You have had what you needed ever since you first learned to stop fighting with your older brother or sister or figured out how to get along with the other kids in school.

Call on these skills and remember, a certain amount of discomfort is normal to any new relationship. More so if that relationship is between people very different from one another. Accept this discomfort and use it as a motivation to find solutions to your difficulties.

Next, be yourself. After all, it is what you do best. Do not try to imitate other cultures. You probably will not do a very good job of it anyway; and, besides, if everyone pretended to be like someone else, it would be profoundly confusing. **Feel and show compassion.** If this gets difficult, take a moment to stop and think how you would feel were you trying to do business or work in a strange culture, and I predict any judgmental attitude will soften very quickly.

Communicate respect for other people's right to be who they are. This does not mean that you have to like or agree with everything they do, but merely that you recognize and honor their uniqueness.

Look for the simple answers. Will Shakespeare said it well, "All difficulties are easy if measure for measure they are known." Cultural diversity *is* complex, but if broken down into finite units, easy solutions usually appear. You do not need to be a philosopher or anthropologist to figure out that the written word can aid communication, that the use of a last name will demonstrate respect, or that a more formal attitude seems to be appreciated.

Finally, do not become so wound up in the subject of cultural diversity that you forget that underneath the cloak of culture, underneath the variations in cultural style, etiquette, and ways of doing business, is a human being whose most basic agenda is just like yours. We are all in this thing together, each of us, despite our differences, doing our best to work together and create profitable and harmonious relationships. Perhaps Whitney Young, Jr., put it best when he said, "We may have come over on different ships, but we're all in the same boat now."

Appendix
Foreign-Language Phrases

The following phrases can be used as a courtesy when conversing with immigrant and international customers, clients, and workers. Each phrase has been rendered in informal English phonetics to help you with the correct pronunciation. You cannot get the exact pronunciation from a book, but do the best you can; it is the effort that counts. Your gesture will be appreciated. The key provided here will help you decipher some of the less obvious sounds.

Although every effort has been made to compile an accurate list, the complexities of language and the subtleties of pronunciation make some errors likely. This is particularly true of the tonal languages: Thai, Vietnamese, and Mandarin Chinese. In these cases, the meaning of the words can change according to the tone with which the syllable is pronounced. Should you discover that you are making errors, ask for assistance from native speakers of the language; they will be glad to help refine your pronunciation and usage.

You will notice that not all of the English phrases have been assigned a foreign equivalent. This is because some of our greetings are not used in other languages and would, therefore, be inappropriate. In the Philippines, for example, one person does not wish another "a good weekend" because the weekend is not clearly distinguished from the rest of the week.

In some cases, alternative formal and informal ways of saying the same thing are provided. The choice of which to use depends on the nature of the relationship; the more intimate the friendship, the more informal the greeting. **If you have any doubt about which to use, begin with the more formal.** The person to whom you are speaking will correct you if he or she would prefer the more casual phrasing.

Key to Pronunciation

a = "ah," as in *sock*.

à = the sound "uh," a staccato sound as if it were cut off in the throat.

aw = the "aw" sound in *saw*.

e = the "e" in *egg*.

ee = the "ee" sound in *see*.

eye = the "ear" sound in *bear*.

i = the "i" in *it*.

I = a sound like the pronoun *I* or the "ie" in *pie*.

kh = a very exaggerated "h." The closest thing would be almost like clearing your throat.

o = "oh."

oo = the "oo" in *boot*.

ow = the "ou" sound in *ouch* or the "ow" in *how*.

oy = the "oy" sound in *boy*.

rr = the trilled or rolled "r" used in Spanish.

r* = a guttural (French) "r."

u = the "u" in *pun*.

uh = the "u" sound in *cup*. You will find this sound at the end of a syllable or word.

' = Place the accent on the syllable or word indicated.

(⁓) = Parentheses surround any sound that is formed but is barely audible. This is a difficult concept for the English speaker to grasp. Do the best you can.

‿ = a slurring connection between the two sounds.

Spanish

Good morning   bwenos dee'as

Good evening (when leaving work at the end of the day)   bwenas noches

Hello   o' la

Goodbye   a deeo's

Have a good weekend   kay pa'say oon felees feen day sema'na

Please   por favo'r

Thank you   gra'seeas

Happy Birthday   felees koomplayanyos

That's all I know [of the language]   no say mas—es todo lo kay say

French

Good morning   bo(n) jou'r

Good evening (when leaving work at the end of a day)   bo(n) swa'

Hello   bo(n) jou'r

Goodbye   or* vwa

Have a good weekend   bo(n) weeke'nd

Please   seal vou pla'y

Thank you   mer*se'e

Happy Birthday   bo(n) aniver*sair*e

That's all I know [of the language]   say toos kuh juh say

German

Good morning   goo'ten mo'rgun

Good evening (when leaving work at the end of a day)   goo'ten a'bent

Hello   halo

Goodbye   owf ve'eder zayne

Have a good weekend shu'hrus vo'khun e'nduh

Please bi'ttuh

Thank you da'nka

Happy Birthday Say it in English; this phrase is commonly used and understood.

That's all I know [of the language] dus ist allis vas ikh kahn

Tagalog

Tagalog is the primary language of the Philippines.

Good morning maganda'ng ooma'ga

Good evening (when leaving work at the end of a day) pá a'h lam

Hello koomoosta' ka

Goodbye pá a'h lam (poetic and provincial); ba bye (informal, most often used)

Have a good weekend This is not a phrase normally used in Filipino culture.

Please pweday ba *or* pa kee (*Paki-* is actually a prefix added to verbs to distinguish them from commands. On occasion, it will stand alone.)

Thank you sala'mat

Happy Birthday Use the English, it is widely used and understood.

That's all I know [of the language] yan lang ang ala'm kong ta ga log

Vietnamese

Good morning chao boo'ee san(g)

Good evening (when leaving work at the end of a day) chao tam be(t)

Hello chao ko (when speaking to a female); chao anh (when speaking to a male)

Have a good weekend chook koo'ee toong voo'ee ve

Please mooy moy

Thank you   kamon

Happy Birthday   sinh ny(o)(t) voo'ee ve

That's all I know [of the language]   toy chee b(e)(t) choo i(t) chay b(i)(t)

Khmer (Cambodian)

On the borders of Cambodia, Thai, Vietnamese, and Laotian are also spoken.

Good morning   arro'on sooe(r) sday

Good evening (when leaving work at the end of a day)   leeyehhI

Hello   choomrreeapso'or

Goodbye   leeyehhI

Have a good weekend   ban so(k) sabI' naopel cho'(b) somra(k)

Please   sowmmeta'

Thank you   awko'on

Happy Birthday   rre'e rreeay tnI bon koob komna(d)

That's all I know [of the language]   knyom man dan(g) tyeta'y *or* knyom che neeyay tI boneh ta'y

Laotian

Good morning   sabI dee

Good evening (when leaving work at the end of a day)   pI dee uh or nuh

Hello   chang dI

Goodbye   la kon *or* pI duh

Have a good weekend   sooksoon vanpak

Please   karoona (followed by the request in English or perhaps a nonverbal signal) *or* state the request first and follow it with: deh

Thank you   hob chI

Happy Birthday   sooksan van k(u)(t)

That's all I know [of the language]   hoy hoo pak pasa lao dI to nan *or* hoy hoo pak pasa lao dI to nee

Thai

Good morning   svat dee krap

Good evening (when leaving work at the end of a day)   pI dee krap *or* sok dee krap

Hello   yang ngI (informal)

Goodbye   la kon krap

Have a good weekend   sooksan vanpak

Please   karoona (fill in the request in English or use a nonverbal signal) krap

Thank you   kob koon krap

Happy Birthday   sooksan vank(u)(t)

That's all I know [of the language]   pom (chan, if you are a female) rroo puut pa'satI dI thao nee krap

Korean

Good morning   anyo'n(g) ha say yo

Good evening (when leaving work at the end of a day)   anyo'n(g) (You might add, if you wish: ha say yo.)

Hello   anyo'n(g)

Goodbye   anyo'n(g)

Have a good weekend   jo' en juma'l bo nay say yo (This is more closely "Have a good day off." The weekend is not significantly different from the other days.)

Please   This is impossible to translate because there are numerous different phrases used for the concept of "please," depending on the context.

Thank you   kam sa' ham ne da'

Happy Birthday   sang e'el chuka ha'm ne da'

That's all I know [of the language] ee go she′ naga′ a nun hangu′(g)mal ooee zanboo imnida′

Japanese

Good morning ohio (like the state)

Good evening (when leaving work at the end of a day) sIyonara

Hello ko nee chee wa

Goodbye sIyonara

Have a good weekend yo ee shoo ma tsoo o

Please dood zo

Thank you areegato

Happy Birthday o tan joobee, o me de too o

That's all I know [of the language] wa ta shee ga sheete eeroo no wa, ko re da ke de soo

Arabic

Although there are several principle Arabic dialects, this is the one most widely understood.

Good morning sabah al khe′yr

Hello sabah al khe′yr

Goodbye The person leaving says: alI sala′ynic. The person being left says: ma sala′yma (A very informal goodbye would be: ma alsalama. This amounts to "so long.")

Have a good weekend Not applicable

Please mn fa′dluk

Thank you shookra′n

Happy Birthday To a woman: kul es se′na wintuh tIe′ebuh. To a man: kul es se′na wintee tIe′ebuh

That's all I know [of the language] manara′fsh a′rabee a′ktar men hethuh

Farsi

Farsi is spoken in Iran.

Good morning   sobhbekhe'yr

Good evening (when leaving work at the end of a day)   shabbekhe'yr

Hello   salo'm

Goodbye   ho'da hafe'z

Have a good weekend   veekende shoma' hosh (formal); veekende shoma' bekheyr (informal)

Please   lotfan (formal); hawhesh mikoha'm (informal)

Thank you   me'rsee

Happy Birthday   tavalo' det mobora'k (informal); tavalode shoma' mobora'k (formal)

That's all I know [of the language]   man far*at hamin r*adr fa'rsee midoonam

Mandarin

This is the most widely spoken of the Chinese dialects.

Good morning   zow shang ha

Good evening (as when leaving work at the end of a day)   wan shang ha

How are you?   neen ha ma?

Goodbye   sigh geeyen

Have a good weekend   joe mor you quI

Please   chin(g)

Thank you   s(h)eee s(h)eee

Happy Birthday   sung er quI la

That's all I know [of the language]   je sure wha jer dah dee soy yo jung we(n)

(Compiled by Elizabeth Mariscal and Krystyna Srutwa of SpeechCraft, and by Susan Montepio, Paco Sevilla, and Elizabeth Estes.)

Notes

Preface and Acknowledgments

1. Paraphrased from R. M. Smith, *Emigration and Immigration* (New York: Charles Scribner's Sons, 1890).

What This Book Can Do for You

1. The format for this exercise is based on one found in George F. Simons, *Working Together* (Los Altos, Calif.: Crisp Publications, 1989).

Chapter 1. Making Diversity Work

1. Ruth Benedict, *Patterns of Culture* (Boston: Houghton Mifflin, 1934).
2. Ruth Benedict, *The Chrysanthemum and the Sword: Patterns of Japanese Culture* (Boston: Houghton Mifflin, 1946).

Chapter 2. Language and Accent Differences

1. Verbal Communication, *The Ken and Bob Company,* KABC Radio, Los Angeles, California.

Chapter 6. Cross-Cultural Customer Service and Sales

1. Germaine W. Shames and W. Gerald Glover, *World-Class Service* (Yarmouth, Maine: Intercultural Press, 1989).
2. Wayland D. Hand, Anna Casetta, and Sondra Thiederman, *Popular Beliefs and Superstitions: A Compendium of American Folklore* (Boston: G. K. Hall, 1981).

Index

Accents: meaning of, 38, 223; pronunciation problems, 38-39

Action: in order to bring about change, 140-41; in order to control the future, 139-40

African-Americans: eye contact and, 89-90; stereotypes of, 12

African cultures, physical distance in, 84

Age: authority and, 131-33; cultural diversity and, 14-15; leadership and, 129

Aggressive behavior, 185

American culture: action in order to bring about change in, 140-41; action in order to control the future in, 139-40; approval signs in, 95; assigning responsibility in, 119; authority and gender in, 133; authority and governmental agencies in, 132, 138-39; authority in, 131, 132; avoiding confrontations in, 104-7, 108; bargaining in, 183; beckoning in, 94; body language in, 82; contracts in, 187; cultivating relationships in, 123, 125, 149; decision making in, 119; degree of directness in, 160; degree of embellishment in, 160-61; employee decision making in, 132, 135; etiquette and giving of gifts in, 152; etiquette in use of last names and titles in, 150; etiquette in, 146; eye contact in, 88, 89-90; giving of gifts in, 152; goal setting in, 121; hand gestures in, 93; handshaking in, 3, 92; head movements in, 97; independence from family in, 121-22; indicating yes or no in, 97; individual identity in, 118; interruptions in, 154; leadership role in, 128; making mistakes in, 117; manager-employee relationships in, 132, 135-36, 137-38; meaning of competition in, 120; persuasion in, 132, 137; physical distance in, 84; pointing in, 94; position of legs and feet in, 96; proverbs and idioms in, 27-28; punctuality in, 162; questioning authority in, 132, 136-37; revealing personal information in, 181-82; ritualistic phrases in, 161; role of individual in, 123; rules in business and government in, 132, 134; saving face in, 109, 112-13; silence/pauses in conversation in, 155-57; smiling in, 90; spontaneity of speech in, 158; stereotyping thinking in, 12-13; tone of voice in, 82; touching in, 85; use of last names and titles in, 150; views of others regarding, 26; volume of speech in, 158-59

American Indian. *See* Native American culture

Amor propio, 113

Anonymity, 113-16

Anxiety: body language and, 82; stereotyping thinking and, 12

Apologies, 145

Approval, signs of, 95

Arab culture: cultivating relationships in, 123, 175; English language and, 38; etiquette and intrusive questions in, 149; fatalism in, 140; geographic differences and, 14; interruptions in, 154-55; loyalty in, 116; will of God in, 1-2. *See also* Middle Eastern cultures

Arabic, sample phrases in, 251

Asian cultures: asking of personal questions in, 177; authority versus persuasion in, 137; avoiding confrontations in, 106, 107-8; bargaining in, 183; beckoning in, 94-95; complaining in, 186; contracts in, 187-88; cultivating relationships in, 149; decision making in, 119, 167; degree of directness in, 159; emotional and personal appeals in sales in, 180; English language and, 38; etiquette and use of business cards in, 153; etiquette and use of compliments in, 151; etiquette and use of

About the
Author

Dr. Sondra Thiederman is president of Cross-Cultural Communications, a San Diego based training firm that offers programs on managing the multicultural work force, selling to immigrant and ethnic consumers, and delivering customer service across cultural and language barriers.

Since receiving her doctorate from U.C.L.A., her client list has ranged from such Fortune 500 companies as Marriott Corporation, Bank of America, and Rockwell International to notable organizations including the American Management Association, the Society of Consumer Affairs Professionals in Business, and American Medical International. In the course of her fifteen-year career, Thiederman has also served as consultant to the Affirmative Action Department of the University of California, the American Cancer Society, and The Center for Indo-Chinese Health Education.

A highly respected speaker, trainer, and consultant, she has been widely featured in the media, and published in such journals as *Real Estate Today, Personnel Journal,* and *Training and Development Journal.* In addition to *Profiting in America's Multicultural Marketplace,* she is the author of a second book on the topic of cultural diversity entitled *Bridging Cultural Barriers for Corporate Success: How to Manage the Multicultural Work Force* (Lexington Books, 1991).